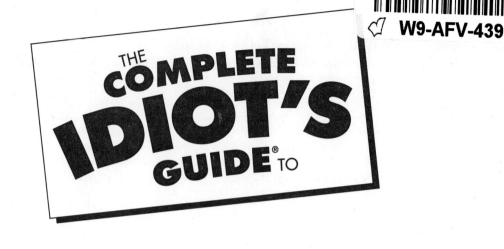

# THE COMPLETE IDIOT'S GUIDE® TO

# Genealogy

## Second Edition

*by Christine Rose, CG, CGL, FASG*
*and Kay Germain Ingalls, CG*

## ALPHA

A member of Penguin Group (USA) Inc.

International Standard Book Number: 1-59257-430-0
Library of Congress Catalog Card Number: 2005932755

10   09                8   7   6

Interpretation of the printing code: The rightmost number of the first series of numbers is the year of the book's printing; the rightmost number of the second series of numbers is the number of the book's printing. For example, a printing code of 05-1 shows that the first printing occurred in 2005.

*Printed in the United States of America*

**Note:** This publication contains the opinions and ideas of its authors. It is intended to provide helpful and informative material on the subject matter covered. It is sold with the understanding that the authors and publisher are not engaged in rendering professional services in the book. If the reader requires personal assistance or advice, a competent professional should be consulted.

Most Alpha books are available at special quantity discounts for bulk purchases for sales promotions, premiums, fund-raising, or educational use. Special books, or book excerpts, can also be created to fit specific needs.

For details, write: Special Markets, Alpha Books, 375 Hudson Street, New York, NY 10014.

**Publisher:** *Marie Butler-Knight*
**Editorial Director:** *Mike Sanders*
**Senior Managing Editor:** *Jennifer Bowles*
**Senior Acquisitions Editor:** *Randy Ladenheim-Gil*
**Development Editor:** *Ginny Bess Munroe*
**Production Editor:** *Megan Douglass*
**Copy Editor:** *Jan Zoya*
**Cartoonist:** *Richard King*
**Book Designer:** *Trina Wurst*
**Cover Designer:** *Bill Thomas*
**Indexer:** *Julie Bess*
**Layout:** *Ayanna Lacey*
**Proofreading:** *Mary Hunt*

# Contents at a Glance

**Appendixes**

# Contents

## Appendixes

# Foreword

You've been curious for quite a while. You've asked some questions of other members of your family, maybe poked around in the family papers, or even searched for others of your name on the Internet. But now you're serious about tracing your ancestors. However, just because you're serious doesn't mean you know how to tackle what seems like an unusual research project. That's why this book was written, to provide the background knowledge and skills necessary for successful genealogical digging.

Christine Rose and Kay Ingalls are both experienced genealogical researchers and teachers. They have done successfully for many years what they are teaching you to do—they interviewed relatives, pored through volume after volume in libraries, poked through old or abandoned cemeteries looking for elusive tombstones, wrote letter after letter, searched in courthouses and archives across the country. Throughout this book they identify pitfalls to avoid and tips to assist your research—the fruits of their accumulated research wisdom.

Genealogical research is challenging, but it is not necessarily difficult. Like any acquired skill, it takes learning and practice. Every genealogical researcher, no matter how skilled or experienced, started out like you; with a little knowledge about the family, a few records, and a consuming curiosity. Don't feel that you have to know everything at the beginning. Read through the book once to start, but come back to it again as you progress in your research. It will be there for you as you tackle new record sources or new steps in your search.

As your research progresses, you will likely discover what many genealogists eventually realize—the searching is almost as much fun as the finding! You will find yourself making time to "do genealogy." Supper can wait so you can have just another half hour in the library; you give up watching television to stare at computer screens; or you realize that since your family vacation plans take you so close anyway, maybe you can fit in a half day at a distant courthouse. And don't forget to share what you've found with your family. One find shared may stimulate further clues to investigate.

You will make discoveries along the way—and not just genealogical discoveries. You will learn more about yourself and the members of your immediate family. You will find ancestors that led quiet, ordinary lives. You may find scandals and secrets, or things our ancestors thought were scandalous but today hardly raise an eyebrow. You may find medical history details or hereditary factors that affect you and your family today. And you will find history much more interesting. Your view of the Battle of Gettysburg, the immigrant experience at Ellis Island or its predecessors, or the Salem witch trials is enhanced by the knowledge that your ancestors were participants.

Your ancestors are patient. However much time you put into searching for them, a couple of days vacation, one weekend a month, a few minutes whenever you can spare them, there will always be more you can do—another letter or e-mail to write, another microfilm to scan, another website to investigate, another book to check, another courthouse or archive to scour for clues. And when you do identify your fifth great-grandparents on your father's mother's side, each person in that distant generation had two parents waiting patiently for you to find them. You'll never run out.

James L. Hansen, FASG

*Since 1974, James L. Hansen, FASG, has been the reference librarian and genealogical specialist at the Library of the Wisconsin Historical Society, where he assists thousands of researchers a year. He has taught genealogical research courses since 1975. Among his publications are articles on a variety of genealogical topics, a bibliography of territorial Wisconsin newspapers, and a guide to the library in which he works. He is a nationally known speaker, having lectured at numerous conferences and seminars in the United States and Canada. He was the 1994–1995 president of the Association of Professional Genealogists, and is a Fellow of the American Society of Genealogists.*

# Introduction

We hope you will be swept along with us in our fascination with family history. As a little girl, one of us spent many weekends at the home of grandparents. Creeping out of bed, perched at the top of the stairs, she spent hours listening to the elders recount the family stories. "But why didn't Dad, who had grown up in the same tiny town, ever discuss his *own* mother and her family?" she wondered. Her curiosity was aroused and simmered for years. During these same years, the other one of us, sparked by family memorabilia, was consumed with a desire to know the people who shared bits of their lives in their diaries. Who played with the marbles in the old-fashioned box, and who told stories of the bear whose tooth is still preserved? Who *were* these people? What were they really like?

Driven by our individual interests, we each picked up the same guidebook to genealogy and set upon a path that changed us forever. We didn't know each other then. In fact, we lived in different states. But we shared this passion for poking around courthouses, for solving the many puzzles we encountered, and for walking the ground our families walked before us.

During the years of research, we each made mistakes and learned from them. We read books, listened to countless lectures, and worked in the field. Then each of us, never losing the thrill of working with the dusty old records, obtained our certification from the Board for Certification of Genealogists and worked on the families of others, too. We still didn't know each other, but a move by one eventually brought us together in neighboring cities, and we began working as colleagues and enjoying a special friendship.

Several years ago we had a rare opportunity to introduce you to the adventure and challenge of genealogy, and to share with you some of the knowledge we acquired. Soon, we think, every minute you can spare will be spent delving through the treasure troves of records left by your family long before you were born. You will enjoy the exhilaration of discovering that first document mentioning your ancestors, and then eagerly looking for the next, and then the next. You will be hooked.

Though you can't do all your genealogy on the Internet, it is one more valuable tool to use while on the trail of your ancestors. For this updated edition of our book, we devoted a chapter to the Internet, and throughout the entire book we added tips and explanations to jump-start your use of the resources on the Web.

With the guidance on these pages, you'll learn to use the Internet to enhance your family history. At the same time, we show you how to go beyond the Internet to find and experience the thrill of holding a fragile and aged document—a document that not only tells something about your ancestors, but may be the same piece of paper actually held by one of them. Your family tree will take shape as you uncover stories that surprise, inspire, and enthrall you. History comes alive. Your ancestors become real. Records that include height, weight, complexion, eye and hair color, all enable you to visualize them. You'll learn if they were shoemakers or lawyers or farmers. You'll follow their moves as the frontier opened, and marvel at their initiative (and their anxiety) as they trekked west with their large families. These pages give you all the basics to launch your own adventure, and include advanced ideas to apply as you develop expertise and a lifelong interest.

# How This Book Is Organized

In this book, we take you step by step through the process of genealogical research. You'll master the techniques and learn about resources to track down the information on your family's unique history.

**Part 1, "Who Are You?"** gives you a glimpse of the excitement that awaits you in genealogy. We tell you how to begin gathering the information you need to start your search and how to keep track of what you've found.

Your ancestors left a trail, and in **Part 2, "Finding the Trail,"** we teach you how to pick up that trail. You'll learn to track the correct surnames and to connect with distant relatives. You'll start looking for evidence of your ancestors' existence in their hometowns and in libraries, and, yes, also on the Internet.

**Part 3, "Following the Trail,"** guides you in the use of one of the most basic tools for finding your ancestors, the census. You'll learn to research effectively from home via the Internet and by corresponding with individuals. You'll also get detailed instructions of using those records whether online or at repositories.

**Part 4, "In Your Ancestors' Footsteps,"** takes you on the road to the exact places where your ancestors made their own history. We practically tell you how to pack your suitcase! (But if you can't travel now, don't skip this—the information here helps you even if you rely on searching from home.) We'll introduce you to the wonders to be discovered in courthouses and the enlightenment to be found from digging in cemeteries. Thought you knew how to read a newspaper? We'll show you new ways. And some surprises are in store: you'll learn how wartime service provides peacetime data.

The "paper mountain" that grows from your research will be tamed in **Part 5, "Making Sense of It All."** This includes the sound practice of citing your sources and some techniques for writing your family history. You don't want just the dry dates of your ancestors' existence. You want to wrap them in the history of their times, so that they come alive to you and others. And we'll help you over, under, around, or through the brick walls that every researcher hits.

**Part 6, "Expanding Your Horizon,"** offers tips on getting the most for your money, and opens the door a crack to some advanced research opportunities, concluding with some advice to keep in mind as you follow the crooked paths to knowledge of the past. New to this edition is a chapter on the dynamic new tool for genealogists, DNA testing. We explain what it's all about and how you can use it effectively.

The appendixes include suggested books, computer programs, and contacts for instruction to use as you pursue your family history. Books and programs mentioned throughout the chapters are fully cited in the appendixes. There are worksheets to keep you on track and census forms so you can readily see the questions asked of the population every ten years from 1800 through 1930.

# Extras

Within each chapter are some special boxed notes to call attention to things that will help you:

You have an interest in your family's past. Our interest is shepherding you through the excitement and challenge in your pursuit of your own personal history. We'll see you at the courthouse!

**Pedigree Pitfalls**

These sidebars offer cautions to help you avoid common mistakes.

**Genie Jargon**

Here are definitions of common terms as used in genealogy.

**Tree Tips**

These boxes contain genealogy gems to help your research.

**Lineage Lessons**

Here you'll find notes covering extra information to enhance your study of genealogy.

## Acknowledgments

Many thanks to the staff of Penguin (listed at the beginning of this book) who assisted us in so many ways—to Randy Ladenheim-Gil, senior acquisitions editor who was responsible for our updating this book, and to Ginny Bess Munroe, our development editor who constantly gave good advice. We also thank Megan Douglass, the production editor and Jan Zoya, the copy editor for their help. We couldn't have brought this edition to you without their assistance. To all the others, the illustrators and the production team, our thanks, too. Though we didn't work with them directly, each had a hand in producing this book. You would not be reading it without this dedicated staff.

Our thanks, too, to David Brown, project administrator of one of the largest family DNA projects in the United States, who graciously provided time and knowledge in the preparation of Chapter 23 on DNA. To James L. Hansen, FASG, our thanks for writing the foreword. His expertise in the field makes him sought after in many capacities. And, to our colleagues who helped with and are named in the first edition, our continuing appreciation for their prior assistance.

And, we again thank our husbands, Seymour Rose and Don Ingalls, for their enthusiasm in embracing the first edition, and now this second.

## Trademarks

PAF™, FamilySearch®, Ancestral File™, International Genealogical Index™™, and the Family History Catalog™ are trademarks of the Church of Jesus Christ of Latter-day Saints.

Outlook™ is a trademark of Microsoft Corporation.

TreePad™ is a trademark of Freebyte.com.

Clooz® is a trademark of Ancestor Detective.

DeedMapper™ is a trademark of Direct Line Software.

Reunion™ is a trademark of Leister Productions.

The Master Genealogist™ is a trademark of Wholly Genes, Inc.

Family TreeMaker™ is a trademark of MyFamily.com, Inc.

Certified Genealogist℠, Certified Genealogical Records Specialist℠, Certified Lineage Specialist℠, Certified Genealogical Lecturer℠, Certified Genealogical Instructor℠, CG℠, CGRS℠, CLS℠, CGL℠, and CGI℠ are service marks of the Board for Certification of Genealogists.

AG® and ICAPGen® are registered marks of the International Commission for Accreditation of Professional Genealogists.

# Part 1

# Who Are You?

What's the fascination? A curiosity as to why Grandpa never spoke about his family? A yearning to know your ethnic roots? Whatever it is, Part 1 will get you going. Starting the search with your own family, you'll learn how to spot the significance of all the papers and memorabilia you are sure to find. If you've already started with the Internet, we'll show you how to build on that.

You'll also get the basics of recording what you find and an introduction into some of the charts, forms, and logs that will help you keep on track. You are laying the groundwork for a wonderful adventure.

# Chapter 1

# Why Genealogy?

## In This Chapter

- ◆ Why you might be interested in tracing your history
- ◆ The benefits of making the effort
- ◆ Not knowing if you'll get what you expect

Your friend is excited about the family reunion and the chart showing his descent from Pocahontas. You've just listened *again* to your mother's oft-recited tale of her grandmother's nomad existence with her itinerant preacher father. And this morning, when filling in your child's baby book, you realized how little you know of your family. Perhaps it was Alex Haley's *Roots* or a PBS series on ancestors that made you regret that you didn't quiz Aunt Mabel before she died about your French-Canadian antecedents. Or someone may have told you she found a website devoted to your surname. Whatever the reason, you now long to know about the people whose bloodlines you share. Is it possible, you wonder, to find your roots?

## What's the Fuss About?

*Genealogy* is said to be the third (some say the second) largest hobby in the country. Just ask the librarians. They will tell you that their shelves are bursting with genealogy books. The available computers are in continual use with those seeking clues on their lineages. The fascination is hard to describe. Some enjoy "putting the pieces of the puzzle together." Some love history. If your great-grandfather served in the Battle of Gettysburg, instantly you connect to that historical battle site. If Great-Aunt Peggy was the first white child born in Monroe, Indiana, then there is a bond to that town. Some are curious about a family story. Was Grandfather really expelled from college because he and some others hoisted a cow to the top of the belfry?

**Genie Jargon**

**Genealogy,** Webster tells us, is the account or history of a descent of a person, or a study of a person's family. Genealogy, the hobbyist will tell you, is a madness, an addiction, which will forever change how you spend your every spare moment!

Some embark upon the journey because of the need for a medical history. A disease or congenital condition may encourage a descendant to document the condition as it was passed down in the family. Another may be interested in a lineage society, and want to join the Society of the Colonial Dames or the Sons of the American Revolution. Whatever the reason, all who begin the journey of tracing their ancestry share a common opinion. It is addictive. All your extra time is spent writing relatives, searching documents, and going online the minute you arrive home. This addiction does have many rewards: new-found relatives, friends in every part of the country, and fascinating bits of history and folklore to enrich your life.

All states have a major genealogy *repository*, and some have several. It could be within the state library or the state archives, or there may even be a special state library specifically for genealogy.

**Genie Jargon**

A **repository** is a physical location where things are placed for safekeeping. This could be a museum, library, archives, courthouse, or another similar place.

If you are a newcomer to genealogy, you will be amazed at the variety of information in a multitude of sources. Your first trip to a genealogy library will be overwhelming, as will a trip to a National Archives branch. "I can't believe there is really a book written about my family," you will exclaim when you find a genealogy published in 1875. As you begin to realize all the information you can find online, too, you'll spend more time at a computer. You will feel excitement when you find your grandmother and grandfather in the 1930 census, and your mother listed as a small child in their home. With them, to your surprise, is an uncle you never heard about. What joy! You may even acquire an obituary of your relative or a biography with a photo, either in a published book or online.

## Why the Effort?

With all the entertainment available, why would you want to spend your time writing letters, talking to relatives, visiting libraries and cemeteries, and pounding a computer keyboard? A definitive answer defies all who attempt to explain. A sense of identity is foremost for many. Those who believe that their family was too ordinary or too poor to be interesting are amazed to realize the sense of value

> **Lineage Lessons**
>
> There are 13 branches of the National Archives spread through several states, in addition to the main Archives I in downtown Washington, D.C., and Archives II in College Park, Maryland.

they place on their family and heritage after delving into the family background. The tales of hardship, of endurance, will instill within you an understanding of the conditions under which they lived. My husband's grandfather would tell with pride how they were too poor to buy fruit, but his mother grew tomatoes and learned to make a wonderful sweetened green tomato pie. The courage and resourcefulness of your ancestors will bond you with them no matter what their station in life. You will feel their pain when they lost the little babies, and when the older children had to drop out of school because they had no shoes to wear.

Among reasons for interest are these:

- To determine ethnic origin
- To explain why your dad wouldn't talk about his family
- To find out if you are *really* descended from Paul Revere
- A passion for history
- To note traits in the family such as temperament and talent
- The need for a sense of identity
- Congenital health problems
- A desire to join a hereditary society
- To track down a family tradition
- An interest in migratory patterns
- To identify the owner of artifacts in the family
- To determine ancestors in a particular occupation
- To reclaim the family cemetery

## Will It Really Grab Your Attention?

You have your own reasons for your interest. However, though the spark is there, you still wonder whether it is going to be worth the effort. "Why bother?" you think. "My ancestors are all gone. What difference does it make?"

**Tree Tips**

Ask your family members if there is a genealogy book or chart within the family. Someone may have already worked on the family tree, and it will give you a wonderful start.

It is hard to recognize, this early in your quest, that your search will affect positively not only your immediate family, but others as well. Within a short time you will experience the enjoyment it provides. When I developed my own interest in genealogy, my husband's grandmother was grateful that someone was interested enough not only to listen to all the stories, but to make sure the family mementos were not discarded: the locks of hair, the mother's pin worn during the war, the old postcards that were exchanged, and the very old letters that were written by family members. It brought her considerable peace to know that these would be treasured and preserved. On another branch, our interest generated a family reunion, and relatives who had not seen each other for years were able to once again connect. An interest in family history touches many lives.

# Starting down the Road

My own adventure started about 1960. A small act was destined to shape the years that followed. My husband's maternal grandfather visited and brought with him some family papers. He thought we might like to look at them. That look changed the whole course for this family! I decided to write down the names of the grandparents and their parents, "just in case the children will ever be interested." My curiosity was immediately piqued when I noted that some of the spouses were unknown. "Who were *they?*" I wondered. Interest began to heighten.

## The Path to Addiction

I went to the local library and borrowed a little book, *Searching for Your Ancestors*. I read it cover to cover. Our children were still young, and a hobby away from home was impractical. However, here was something I could do in my spare time, from home, and with no timetable. I could do as little or as much as I pleased, and whenever I pleased. No deadlines to meet—just write letters when I could, go to a library when I wanted—it was ideal. My interest in history also was appeased. While researching our ancestors' migrations from the East to the pioneer West, their service in various wars, their encounters with Indians and dry prairies, history came alive for me. I could (and did) spend hours going through family memorabilia and documents, becoming acquainted with each ancestor. The daily mail was the highlight, as I eagerly sought answers from county clerks, National Archives, fellow researchers, and relatives. Computers were in the future, when I started, but I used all the traditional methods to search and wore out many typewriter ribbons writing to repositories, potential relatives, newspapers, and anyplace else I could think of.

## Who Is an Ancestor?

Perhaps by now you are wondering which of your many relatives are "ancestors." Whose bloodlines do you share? Your ancestors are those from whom you are directly descended. The term is usually used for someone earlier than your grandparent. Your aunts, uncles, and cousins are relatives, but they are not your ancestors.

Your great-grandfather is an ancestor; his brother is related to you but is not your ancestor. You have two parents, four grandparents, eight great-grandparents, sixteen great-great-grandparents, and so on. By 10 generations (approximately 300–350 years), you have 1,024 ancestors. An impressive figure that will be more than enough to keep any searcher busy for a lifetime.

The following ancestor diagram starts with "You" at the left, and moves backward for three generations. The father's line moves at the top of the chart, with the mother's line at the bottom. See Chapter 4, for another example of a pedigree chart.

> **Lineage Lessons**
>
> A **maternal** ancestor is an ancestor on the mother's side of the family; a **paternal** ancestor is from the father's side of the family. Your father's mother was your paternal grandmother, while your mother's mother was your maternal grandmother.

## What Family to Trace?

You will, as you progress, need to make some decisions about which lines are of the most interest. Otherwise, you will be overwhelmed. Decide whether you will be content to trace those lines to the immigrant who arrived in America, or whether you will want to pursue some of them in their countries of origin.

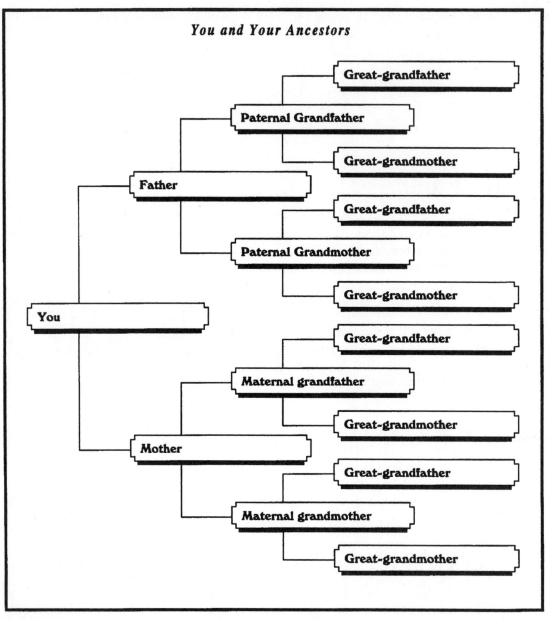

*You and Your Ancestors*

*Ancestor diagram.*

The generations closest to you are the family names that first appeal to you. The name you bore at birth (your father's line), your mother's family, your paternal and maternal grandparents' families—these are familiar names and will influence your choice. As your search continues, other names will capture your attention. Perhaps the line that produced artists will fascinate you, especially if your child has some talent in that direction. The family that left their comfortable surroundings in Philadelphia and moved to the "wilderness" of Ohio bringing only meager possessions might stimulate your imagination.

## What Will You Get from This?

Ask 10 people what they get from genealogy, and the answers will vary widely. A distraught mother is sure to respond: "A messy house! Files overflowing." The young father may say, "the poor house" as extra funds go for books and purchasing documents. A wife will sigh as her husband dashes to the computer every evening. But what are the rewards? Meeting relatives you never knew. Making friends all over the country. A sense of completeness. Identifying with your ethnic background and someday visiting that country. Satisfying a passion for history. The list is endless. The rewards come not only to you as the researcher, but to all those you touch. Relatives will be forever grateful for your efforts and will embrace you eagerly when you meet.

Your interest will spark contacts beyond your own. Your children will become acquainted with relatives they never knew existed and visit towns and areas they would not otherwise have seen.

# Embarking on the Adventure

When starting our own search, I found that my husband's paternal southern line was a real challenge. His great-grandfather had crossed the plains to California in 1856. My husband's grandfather was the youngest of his children, and he was only four when his father died in the Sierra Mountains in 1879, still searching for gold. The tooth that was saved from the bear he killed in the Sierra Mountains, shown in the following figure, is a reminder to his descendants of the frontier dangers he faced.

My husband's mother did recount a few stories, but she had not known her husband's family. Grandfather knew only that his father was from Alabama. The search seemed insurmountable. Then a family Bible turned up, and there was listed the county of his birth. I wrote some letters and located the family. What excitement to finally find these relatives!

*Bear tooth from bear killed in the Sierra Mountains.*

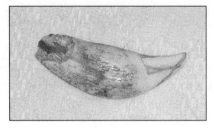

### Tree Tips

When meeting a large group of your family for the first time, ask each to sign a "Trip Memories" book for you. This would include their full names and addresses, and, if they have one, their e-mail addresses. You then have a way to get in touch with them later. If they add the names of their parents, it will also help you in identifying their branches as you become familiar with the family.

Later we packed up four small children in a tiny trailer and undertook a trip with a great deal of trepidation. We knew not what to expect. It had been 112 years with no personal contact between the families. However, what a warm and loving reception we received. Amid a huge family reunion, we met hundreds of relatives. We will always remember the ones in their 80s (first cousins of Grandfather) telling the stories they had heard about the final good-byes when their uncle left, never to be seen again, and the tears in their eyes when they met my husband, their first link to our branch. Everyone was wonderful.

### Pedigree Pitfalls

One common problem you will encounter in family stories is that many assumed the family was related to others of the same surname. If the name was Adams, they assumed a relationship to the two presidents carrying that name. If they carried the name Lincoln, they assumed there was only one Lincoln family.

While we visited at an old farmhouse with its big front porch, large yard, and cornfields across the road, our relatives told us the stories we yearned to hear. They took us to the cemeteries, to other relatives, and treated us as their own. Others had us in their homes, too. This was only the first of many visits. Going back to Alabama, walking the ground on which the ancestors lived, visiting their final resting places, we felt a part of their history and their lives. Until then, we had been isolated. Why genealogy? Because the joys are there.

# You Won't Find Perfect People

The results of your search may surprise you. I had been told many times that one of our relatives was famous in the Revolutionary War. And indeed he was, on the other side! The supposed tie to a president may prove unfounded when you accumulate the facts. Grandpa's uncle perhaps never died young, as the family said, but instead was jailed and branded for stealing a horse, and the humiliated family never spoke of him again.

Be prepared. Know from the beginning that you will not find all you expected. Be charitable, not judgmental. They made mistakes; they had weaknesses and strengths; they were human. Realize that you are not embarking on the research path to find perfect people. You are seeking knowledge of their way of life and what made up the fabric of their character. The remarkable musical skill of your youngest child may be explained when you learn that three of the family were fiddling in the Blue Ridge Mountains at the age of four. There will be disappointments. Your hopes of joining the Daughters of the American Revolution may disappear when you cannot find any ancestors who participated in that war effort. However, whatever disappointments the search may hold, they will be replaced hundredfold by understanding their lives and enjoying the friendships you make while on your search.

> **Lineage Lessons**
>
> Many middle and secondary schools now offer school projects involving genealogy to trace a physical trait (biology), to improve letter-writing skills (English), and to enhance various other study courses. Even using a computer for research can be a skill honed by a genealogy project.

# Genealogy with Success

There are no guarantees that you will be able to trace your lines successfully. But certainly, out of the 1,024 direct ancestors in 10 generations, there are some whom you can trace to their entry into America. Be patient and follow all clues. Those who achieve the most success are those who constantly follow all leads: church records, obituaries, vital records, military files, census—everything that could have a record created about their ancestor. They constantly restudy the material as new data is found, to glean clues they may have missed previously. If you are systematic and use sound research techniques, you will be rewarded. No one is pushing. If you need to take two years off from the search to complete your college education, no one is demanding that you write genealogy letters. When you are ready, genealogy is there for you to pursue.

## No Two the Same

Remember that every life is different. Each is important. Each had its joys and its sorrows. The stories of courtship, of moves by teams of oxen and early rail, will enthrall you. When I learned that one great-grandfather left New York as a small boy and sailed the Great Lakes to Wisconsin, it led to a study of the great sailing era when hundreds of boats dotted the lakes. Finding that a great-great-grandfather was a "forty-niner" to California and had sailed around the Horn was almost as much fun to study as learning that within a couple of years his young daughter followed from the East, by way of the treacherous Isthmus of Panama crossing.

**Tree Tips**

Periodically reexamine the material you have accumulated. Today the name of "Elias Jenkins" in an old letter may mean nothing, but three months from now you may realize that had to be the son-in-law's name.

## The Past Has a Personality

You will find opportunities along every step of the search to bring history alive for you and your family. The search is not about collecting names. It is about identifying, with certainty, each of your ancestors and learning enough about their lives to forge a connection. When you read a will written in 1715 and realize what few possessions they had and how they parceled them out, you will understand their lives of bare necessities. When you find the 1850 inventory of an estate that lists shoemaker's tools, you will realize that your shoemaker grandfather was following in the family trade. The 1906 letter written from San Francisco will give a jolt when you realize that was the year of the big earthquake and fire. Opportunities to know your ancestors are endless. Enjoy them at every step of the search.

## The Least You Need to Know

- ◆ Genealogy makes no demands; you are free to invest as little or as much time as you want.

- ◆ Reasons to trace the family are numerous.

- ◆ You can follow their trails in various ways.

- ◆ Your ancestors are those from whom you descend, the ones whose bloodlines you share.

- ◆ The only guarantee is that you will become totally absorbed in this fascinating pursuit.

# Chapter 2

# Start with Mom and Dad

## In This Chapter

- ◆ What you need to get started
- ◆ Interviewing the relatives
- ◆ What you can find among the family mementos

A notebook and pencil get you started. That is one of the major appeals of genealogy—it requires only the basics, plus an inquiring mind and a sense of adventure. A tape recorder, though not essential, helps immeasurably to preserve the stories you hear. Someday those family members will be gone, and you will treasure the sound of their voices telling the tales of their past.

Later (in Chapter 4) you will learn about genealogy charts. It is best, however, not to be confined by charts. You do not want to be restricted by a form that doesn't have adequate space for your notes. Use them only as a means of summarizing the information after you obtain it.

## Getting It Down on Paper

When you take notes, date the first page. Write the name of the person you are interviewing, your name as the person conducting the interview,

and where the interview was conducted. You may think that you will never forget, but after 10 such interviews you will. Years later, when your grandchildren find the notes, they will want to know these details.

Keep your interview notes in a loose-leaf notebook. You will refer back to this often. Section it by family, so that you can instantly find them. If you have a computer, then immediately after the interview transfer the notes to your word processor, entering them by family name for easy retrieval or in the appropriate place in your genealogical software.

While you are querying your relatives for dates and locations of family events, also ask about the personalities and physical appearances of your ancestors. You want to know whether your ancestors were kindhearted, quiet or boisterous, or big-framed with a flowing beard—not just when and where they were born.

When talking about women, always ask, "Was that the maiden name?" Uncle John told you his grandmother was Martha Jackson when she married his grandfather. Later you find her obituary and puzzle for weeks over why it shows she was born Martha Smith. You finally visit Uncle John again and ask him. "But of course," he says, "She was born a Smith but married first to Joseph Jackson." Ask the right questions!

Questions trigger recollections of incidents and people that older relatives haven't thought about for years. Give them time for those memories to return. Don't rush

through your questions; encourage them slowly. You won't get all your answers in one day. If you sense that the memory is confused, and your relative is getting flustered trying to remember, go to another subject. Later, on another visit, come back to it.

If you traveled a long distance to visit elderly relatives, you may need to get as much information as you can on one visit. Proceed gently. If they are confused, turn to other questions. Later in the interview you can return to the previous subject.

# Don't Be Too Pushy

Watch for signs that Grandma is reluctant to give details. Don't press. If she says, "I don't want to talk about it," let it go for now. There may be a "secret" and pushing too hard can silence her for good. Be patient. The "secret" may be nothing more than her grandfather's divorce, which was scandalous indeed in 1850. Don't ridicule or discount a family member's reluctance to discuss it further. Some family rifts have existed for years; feelings run deep.

Remember that times have changed. Behavior that is tolerated today was shameful then. Deep hurts could have resulted when Great-Grandma married two months after she was widowed, to a man half her age, or because Great-Uncle Al enjoyed playing cards on the riverboat. And heaven forbid if there was a shooting or jail term.

**Tree Tips**

Be sensitive. Let your family know you are not being "nosy." Assure them you just want to know about your family because it is interesting to know your roots.

These obstacles can slow a search, but getting the information is often crucial to continued success. If you don't know that there was a second marriage, you may not know under what name your grandmother was buried when you try to find her tombstone. Be patient. Ask the same questions of a number of relatives; you are likely to get the needed information in time, although you may never get the full details from the family.

If you suspect a notorious scandal, check the local newspaper instead of pressing the family too hard for details.

# Don't Believe Every Story You Hear

As a child it was fun to play the game of gossip. Two lines were formed, a story was whispered into the ear of the first person in line and traveled by whispering to the end of the line. The end person in each line recounted what he or she had been told, and the one closest to the beginning story was the "winner." How often was it even close to the same tale? Even with only five or six people in each line, the original story was often unrecognizable. How can we then expect a story, or *family tradition*, to be accurate after five or six generations?

**Genie Jargon**

**Family traditions** are those stories handed down from generation to generation, usually by word of mouth.

> **Lineage Lessons**
>
> Don't be confrontational if you know the information being told is incorrect. Memories can be faulty and age might be a factor. You will be taking steps to verify all you learn.

Be cautious of the tradition that the immigrant came disguised as a little girl to hide him from kidnappers, as an extraordinary number of families have similar stories. Another common tradition is that "three" immigrants came: "one went north; one went south; and one went west." All family traditions should be carefully noted, but effort must be made to document them before you, as the genealogist, can accept them. Don't ridicule the family traditions, even when you suspect that they are false. Respect the feelings of those who believe them. You can tactfully correct them as you accumulate evidence.

As you learn the techniques of tracing your family, you can examine various documents to assist in determining if a family tradition is correct. The tradition that your family was related to President Adams or to Jesse James can be confirmed or discarded after a step-by-step process to prove the family's lineage.

# Questions to Ask Your Family

The best way to start is with your own family. Ask lots of questions. Not just of Mom and Dad, but of everyone: aunts, uncles, cousins, and especially all the older relatives. Write down all their answers fully. The purpose of the questions is to give you a beginning point for the search. You need to know the names of those you are seeking, some idea of dates so you will know which records to search, and very important, the various locations in which they lived. Make a list of questions. These might include the following:

- What was Grandpa's full name? Nickname?

- When and where was he born?

- What was his father's name?

- What was his mother's maiden name?

- Did Grandpa have brothers and sisters? What were their names? When were they born? Where were they born?

- Where did they live? Did they always live there? Where else might they have lived?

- What were the names of Grandpa's aunts and uncles?

- ◆ What did Grandpa look like?

- ◆ Does anyone have any photos of him?

- ◆ What did Grandpa do to earn a living?

- ◆ Where is he buried? Is there a tombstone?

- ◆ Did Grandpa ever serve in one of the wars?

- ◆ What church did he attend?

- ◆ Did he have a trade? A hobby?

- ◆ Did he own land?

- ◆ What was his nationality?

These basic questions will get you started. Ask the same questions about your grand-mother. The answers will lead you to more questions and to the records your ancestors left. Until you know approximate dates and locations, there is no track to follow.

# Roamin' the Attics and the Basements

Remember those old trunks and boxes you saw when playing around the attic and basement as a child? When you asked, Mom said they were just "family things." Ask Mom to go through the attic with you. Make sure you have plenty of time. Don't hurry her. She hasn't seen these things for a long time, and as they are lovingly removed from boxes, memories will come flooding back. Have a pencil and paper to make notes. Get the stories behind the items.

Have a tape recorder handy as you go through the boxes and trunks. Record descriptions and ask questions regarding the objects. Be sure to announce on the tape the date, location of the interview, your name, and whom you are interviewing. Leave it running; you don't want distractions caused by turning the recorder on and off.

The little doll—who owned it? It was wrapped with such care—it had to be very important to a little girl at one time. The little toy soldiers at the bottom of the trunk; they are sure to stir memories of the little boys who played with them end-lessly. Who were they?

*A little china doll like this one, packed with loving care, can stir up a lot of memories with your interview subject.*

## The Objects with Tales to Tell

What about the objects that are going to help tell you about your grandpa, and those before him? How can you find them in that old trunk? But, look. There is a batch of old letters, with a ribbon carefully tied around them. They are still in good condition after all this time. You open them, and read in amazement. There is a letter from Great-Great-Grandpa, written in 1889, when he went to Texas to look for a piece of land. He wrote back that he was getting discouraged, that he missed the family, and was about to come home. But then, three weeks later, another letter. He finally found what he wanted. He described the land, and the little farmhouse on it. He promised to be back home soon to bring the family to Texas. Uncle George found a place, too. They will be living nearby. George's wife Mary is already starting to fix up their home. Now you have some names and locations. These will prove important as you search.

**Tree Tips**

Many scraps of old paper provide clues of some kind. What appears unimportant to you today can later lead to the answer you seek.

Family members, when queried, will often say, "But I don't have anything that would help." It is not that they are reluctant to assist; they just don't realize the significance of what is stored in the old boxes.

Among the family mementos to look for are these:

- Photographs
- Bibles
- Documents such as deeds
- Letters
- Applications for lineage societies
- Scrapbooks and news clippings
- Funeral cards
- Account books
- Diaries and journals
- Baby books
- Christmas lists and address books
- Greeting cards
- Needlepoint samplers
- Report cards and school diplomas

These are but a few of the *memorabilia* that hold some clues. Perhaps there is a yearbook, a letter from an alumni association, or an invitation to a school reunion. Be alert to anything that will give you an idea of where you might find further information.

## Picturing the Past

Likenesses of your ancestors are treasures. They may be faded *daguerreotypes* or hardly recognizable *tintypes*. But hopefully someone has included a note as to who they were. (A good photo shop can restore them with amazing results, as can some photo software programs such as Adobe's Photoshop). Many of the old black-and-white photographs are remarkably preserved, especially if they have not been subjected to light. Examine each for names and

**Genie Jargon**

Within a family, **memorabilia** are those items with significance to the family. This may be the first baby shoe, the wedding announcement, or any other items that evoke memories of the family.

**Genie Jargon**

**Daguerreotypes** and **tintypes** are early photographic processes with the image made on a light-sensitive, silver-coated metallic plate or made directly on an iron plate varnished with a thin sensitized film.

dates. Note, too, the city of the photography studio where the photo was taken; it can provide a location for the family.

When you visit relatives, take some photographs with you. It will bring back memories. If you have a scanner attached to your computer, scan some photographs and take copies to leave, or make photocopies. The family will be thrilled. And they may be able to identify some of the people in old photographs for you.

Sometimes it is possible to connect two branches of your family by the photographs they own. Your Ohio branch and the Missouri branch may have lost touch 75 years ago. If both have the same photo of the original family home in Ohio, the photo in common can assure you they are of the same family. The photos belonging to your relatives can also assist you if they have the same photograph, which was unidentified on your family's copy, but identified on theirs. Your photograph of an unidentified Civil War soldier may be the same photo in another branch, with identification.

## The Old Family Bible

Have you ever really looked at the old family Bible? Take a good look now. Surprised to find that there is a section of family records? This was not only common, but often is the only written record of the births and marriages in a family. Examine it carefully. Some of the old style script can be difficult to read. The flourishes render the capital letters especially hard to decipher, and numbers can be a problem, too. However, as you improve your *transcribing* skills, you will be able to read many styles of handwriting. Some websites have very good examples of the old writing. In fact, www.Cyndislist.com, the granddaddy (or grandmommy!) of all genealogical websites, has a special category for the subject. At that website scroll down to "Handwriting & Script." You'll even find oldstyle abbreviations for names and locations listed with links to the websites.

**Genie Jargon**

**Transcribing** is to faithfully duplicate the exact wording, spelling, and punctuation of the original.

Get a photocopy of the Bible pages (or a photograph if it is too fragile to copy), and be sure to include the title page to show when and where the Bible was published. "Why would I want to know that?" you wonder. It is important to establish when the entries were written. If the Bible was printed in 1850, but the first entry is 1775, then you know the entries were either copied from an older record or are based on some other source. They are subject to errors from copying or transcribing the older record.

Knowing the publication date may help you resolve discrepancies when comparing the Bible with other documents. If the Bible was printed in 1850 and the first entry is the marriage in 1852, followed by births of the children in the order they were born, the entries were probably made at the time of the event and are therefore more apt to be correct. Pay particular attention to the handwriting. Were all the entries in the same hand? Were some of the dates added with a ball-point pen in a later, more modern hand? These observations will help you to evaluate the accuracy. Try to find out not only the name of the present owner, but all the previous owners of the Bible.

**Tree Tips** _____

www.cyndislist.com is an absolute "must" for anyone doing any genealogical research on the Internet. This site has over 200,000 links.

---

**Lineage Lessons**

Entries in the Bible made sometime after the event are more apt to have errors. Entries copied into a newer Bible from an older Bible are subject to error, too, because of a possible misreading of a name or date, or the omission of an entry.

## "This Deed Dated the ..."

Scattered among those family papers you may find old *deeds, mortgages,* and perhaps even an Army discharge. The names and locations they mention can reveal many clues. Other documents of value might be a will that was never discarded after a new will was made, or a life-insurance policy with family background. Take careful notes. List the documents so that you can refer to them in the future as you learn new search techniques.

**Genie Jargon** _____

A **deed** is a legal document used to transfer title; a **mortgage** is a pledge to repay money borrowed.

## Letters: Speaking from the Grave

Faded and hard to read, those old letters can capture a bit of your family's life once they are deciphered. A letter written to a sister in 1855, "My wife Mary died and I have no one to help with the little ones ... Can you come and help for a while? ..." or

---

**Lineage Lessons**

When you transcribe the old letters, follow them word by word in the exact spelling and punctuation. Do not be concerned with the errors they made in writing. The fact that they could even write, when schooling was so scarce, was an accomplishment. It is important to retain the original exactly as is in your transcription.

"We just arrived at the mines in Placerville, where the people are fighting for a spot to camp …," written from California in 1850, points you to events, locations, and individuals to find. It will be frustrating when the letter is written to "Dear Sister" or "Dear Son" with no further identification of the recipient. However, as the search progresses, the identity may emerge. The names within the letter then become valuable new leads.

Also take note of the envelope that accompanied the letters: to whom it was addressed, the manner in which it was addressed, and the dates.

**Pedigree Pitfalls**

Beware of salutations such as "Cousin" Joe and "Aunt" Hattie. Relationships were often stated loosely. "Cousin" could really mean second-cousin or another relationship; "aunt" may be a great-aunt or step-aunt. Rarely did anyone include the "great" in a relationship when speaking of another. Also watch for "Sr." and "Jr." for they were not necessarily father and son. They were often used in letters and in legal documents only to distinguish between two people with the same name, living in the same town. They might be related, as uncle and nephew or in some other manner, or not related at all. If they were related, when Sr. died, Jr. often became Sr. If the latter also had a son by the same name, the son (probably previously known as III) would have become Jr. Watch for this switch.

## "Ancient and Honorable …": Lineage Societies

Joining lineage societies was very popular in the first half of the twentieth century and remains so. The societies are based on descent from veterans of various wars, from pioneers, from specific trades (such as tavern keepers), and many more. Watch for these applications. Information that the applicants provided about their ancestors can assist in the search. Though most lineage societies' documentation requirements were looser in earlier years than now, the application can provide valuable clues. Also note the names of the *sponsors*. They knew the applicant and might be leads to further records.

Membership in these organizations has grown and flourished; currently there are hundreds of such groups. Some have published their member-lineage records. Most have websites. Start with www.cyndislist.com and scroll down to "Societies & Groups." Alternately, if you know the name of the society, simply enter that name in your computer's Web browser. If you suspect that someone in your family joined such a group, obtain the society's address and write for the member's application.

In order to gain as many clues as possible from lineage papers, be sure to ask the organization for a copy of its membership requirements, or check their website. This can help you to understand the records connected with the application. Daughters of the American Revolution, for example, will admit descendants not only for Revolutionary service of the ancestor but also if the ancestor provided supplies for the war effort.

**Genie Jargon**

**Sponsors** were those people who vouched for the suitability of the applicant to be admitted to the society.

## Account Books: Not a Penny More

Account books, kept by the father (or head) of the family to record money transactions and other miscellaneous notes, often include the cash advances made to the children to purchase a farm, buy equipment, purchase household items, or for any other reason. And they were just that: advances recorded faithfully, to be settled at the time of death of the father if they were still due. When he made his will, he often meticulously listed the cash advances down to the penny. He made sure that those advances were accounted for against the child's portion of the estate when he died. The account books may contain various other transactions: money put out to interest; implements purchased; and perhaps even a family birth, death, or baptism. Scrutinize them carefully for clues on occupation, too.

**Lineage Lessons**

The sons in the family often were given more than the daughters. They inherited the land, farm implements, and most of the stock. The daughters usually received beds and bedding, perhaps a horse or cow, slaves (in the south), and personal items, unless the father had sufficient land to give to all.

## "Dear Diary"

Did a member of the family travel west or take a train trip through seven states? Travel back to "the old country"? The traveler may have left a journal. A careful reading might reward you with the names of relatives visited on the trip and perhaps some interesting sidelights.

It was especially popular to write diaries during the Gold Rush to California and during the several journeys west to Oregon, Wyoming, Colorado, and other points. The Civil War also produced numerous journals, though many did not survive. Those who were unable to write during the war period often put their recollections on paper after their return home.

Diaries can tell you much about the people and their daily lives. From the prairie, you hear about the heat, the dust, the deaths. And yes, the births, and the fun the little children had, and the fear when they were unexpectedly visited by Indians. Your ancestors' writings during the war tell you of the loneliness, the fear, the pain of losing comrades. But they also tell you of their hope for the future and of the pride in serving for a cause in which they believed. Your ancestors will come alive to you as you read their penned words.

Popular in the nineteenth century, charming autograph books contained poems, short writings, and eulogies. The following poem was inscribed at the bottom: "Selected for Belina Adams by her Grand Father in the 77th year of his age A Webster Lebanon Aug 30th 1828." Besides genealogical value, there is some historic interest, because her grandfather A. [Abram] Webster of Lebanon, New York, was a brother of Noah Webster, of dictionary fame. Look among your family's papers and you, too, are bound to find such treasures.

## Baby Books: A Mom and Pop's Joy

Baby books so lovingly written are wonderful to read. Mom's excitement when the first tooth poked out; Dad's pride when first steps were taken. Besides the list of gifts, which might name relatives, there could be notations: "He has deep blue eyes like Grandpa Smith." Or, "Everyone says she looks just like Aunt Margaret." Now you know there was an Aunt Margaret! Watch, too, for baptismal dates, new addresses, and other listings that point to more records.

**Tree Tips**

Look also for engraved silverware. The initials may give a clue to a husband's or wife's name.

## Address Lists, Samplers, and Other Treasures

Look for old address books, Christmas lists with addresses, and invitations to a fiftieth wedding anniversary. Old greeting cards also are helpful for names and addresses, and family news. You want to find anything that might give a lead to a relative or a town in which they lived.

How vain are all things here below
  How false and yet how fair
Each pleasure has its poison too
  And every sweet a snare
The brightest things below the sky
  Give but a flatt'ring light
We should suspect some danger nigh
  Where we possess delight
Our dearest joys and nearest friends
  The partners of our blood
How they divide our wavering minds
  And leave but half for God
The fondness of a creatures love
  How strong it strikes the sense
Thither the warm affections move
  Nor can we call them thence
Dear Saviour let thy beauties be
  My souls eternal food
And grace command my heart away
  From all created good

            Selected for Belina Adams
  by her Grand Father in the 77th Year of his age
Lebanon Aug 30th 1828          A Webster

*From an old autograph book of Belina Adams, daughter of Isaac Ward and Eunice (Webster) Adams.*

Don't overlook the cross-stitch sampler. A popular pastime was to create one with the names and birth dates of all the family members. Friendship quilts created by a bride's friends as a wedding present may feature embroidered names in each square.

# No Longer Junk

Those boxes and trunks have now taken on new meaning. No longer "junk," they are the means by which you are going to know your family, and the lives they led. It takes weeks to adequately search the memorabilia in your family, among the aunts and uncles and grandparents. Once you have, you are ready for the next steps in the path to your family's roots.

# Or Did You Start with the Internet?

You may be inwardly protesting, "But I started with the Internet. Not with the family." That's okay. Just set that Internet information aside for now and, using the ideas in this chapter, start collecting answers from your family. It won't take you long to realize that there are a whole lot of new clues now that you're tapping into the family's recollections and their precious memorabilia. Many new ideas will emerge, giving you a fresh start. You'll be excited at all the leads for exploring further on the World Wide Web.

## The Least You Need to Know

- Start your genealogical search with your own family members, not only your parents, but also aunts and uncles.

- Be sensitive; don't press when the family is reluctant to talk about an episode in the past.

- Thoroughly exhaust all the family mementos. Most will help in some way in your search.

- The old family Bible often is the only written record of a family.

- If you started your search on the Internet, now go back and do what's in this chapter to expand your knowledge of the family.

# Chapter 3

# You're Hooked—Now What?

## In This Chapter

- Getting the right information into your notes
- How to create logs to help keep track
- The importance of transcribing and abstracting
- Learning the language of old documents

As you gather the oddly shaped pieces of the puzzle of your family history, your excitement mounts. Eager to find the missing pieces and to fit them into the picture, you want to rush ahead. But before you plunge into the wonderful world of records and documents waiting to be discovered, pause for a few minutes and learn how to get the information you need from your research. This chapter and the next explain some tools and techniques to assist you.

## What Are You Looking For?

What are you trying to learn as you go through the family papers, interview family members, and research in libraries, archives, or on the Internet? For each ancestor and other relative, you want to know the following:

- ♦ A full name (and nickname if there was one)

- ♦ The date and place of birth

- ♦ The date and place of marriage

- ♦ The date and place of death

- ♦ The name of parents

**Genie Jargon**

A **collateral relative** is someone with whom you share a common ancestor but who is not in your direct line. Your mother's brother is a collateral. Your grandfather's uncle is a collateral, as are your cousins, because you and they share a common ancestor.

**Tree Tips**

Always use the same standard-size paper for all your notes. It facilitates filing the notes. Standard size paper (8.5" × 11" or 8.5" × 5.5") fits standard notebooks.

These dry facts don't give much insight into your ancestors' existence, their joys, hardships, or relationships. You need these basics, however, to know where to look for the records that will help you to visualize them as individuals.

You read in Chapter 1 that your ancestor is one from whom you are descended. The siblings of your ancestors are related to you, but they are not your ancestors. Your ancestors' cousins are related to you, but they are not your ancestors. Nonetheless, it is important to learn as much as you can about these *collateral relatives* because they may lead you to information on your ancestors.

It is important to collect the same information for your collateral relatives that you collect for your ancestors. It is especially important when you are at a brick wall. For example, I thought my great-great-grandfather, George Marvin, was the son of Sylvanus Marvin, but I could find no proof. There was no mention of George in Sylvanus's will, though several daughters (including Harriet Bush) were named. I started looking for the records of these collateral relatives, and eventually found Harriet's will. In it she named her brothers and sisters (including George), and willed to them her share of her father Sylvanus Marvin's estate. Because of the record she left, I could now connect another generation in my pedigree.

# What Should You Use to Take Your Notes?

When you become interested in genealogy, you quickly accumulate pieces of paper with family stories and details. Even if you use a computer to keep track, much of what you do involves note-taking with paper and pencil.

Avoid the temptation to take notes on any handy piece of paper: the backs of envelopes, credit-card receipts, and odd-size note pads. They will get lost. Take your notes on loose-leaf paper, or in tablets or spiral notebooks. Loose-leaf paper is particularly advantageous. There are no ragged edges, and the notes can be neatly filed under a variety of topics.

Develop a system of note-taking that works for you. I like to put this information in the top right corner of each sheet of paper:

♦ The surname of the family

♦ The location of note-taking (for instance, someone's home, a specific library, county courthouse, or the Internet)

♦ The date the notes were taken

With these headings, I can tell at a glance what family I worked on, and when and where.

Use separate sheets of paper for different surnames, even if the information is from the same person. If your mother recites family stories about her mother and father, put the information on two sheets of paper—one with the father's family and one with the mother's family. It is easy to get so involved in note-taking that information pertaining to several surnames ends up on the same sheet. This can create a confusing situation as you attempt to study each individual surname.

Whatever system you devise for yourself, keep it simple, and be consistent. However, be flexible enough to change your system if you read about or observe another that you think will work better for you.

**Tree Tips**

Use only one side of the sheet of paper for note-taking. If you want to refer to something in a group of clipped-together sheets of paper, it is much easier to shuffle through them.

Always try to take notes in a manner that minimizes recopying. Each time they are copied, the chance of error multiplies.

**Genie Jargon** _____

A **citation** is the authority or source from which the information was taken, added for support of the facts. In genealogy, every fact needs at least one citation.

After you label your notepaper, write a full *citation* for the source you are using. (For more on the correct format for citing sources, see Chapter 19.) You may get so excited about a "find" that you forget to write down where you found it. Undocumented information, that is, information with no source citation or an incomplete source citation, cannot be successfully used to prove your line.

Additionally, complete references to sources are needed for other reasons. In cases of conflict in information, you need to know the sources to properly evaluate which is most likely to be correct. Equally important, you may find that you neglected to get all the information the source offered and need to locate it again.

# Writing It Right

After you have labeled your paper and written the source citation, you are ready to take notes. Although your notes should be complete, you can use standard and recognizable abbreviations, arrows, and symbols. They should be clear to you or to anyone reading your notes. Don't be too brief. It is better to have too much information than not enough. Something that seems inconsequential now may be crucial as the search progresses.

**Genie Jargon** _____

A **given name** is the first name; the name given to a child at birth. It is sometimes referred to as the Christian name.

Write out the full names of individuals. If you know the middle name, include it. If there is a nickname, indicate that by putting the nickname in quotes after the *given name*. Do not use parentheses to show the nickname. Parentheses between a given name and surname are used to enclose the maiden name, and it will be confusing to use it for nicknames, too.

# What's in a Person's Name?

If someone is known by more than one name, put the alternate name or names in parentheses after the surname, preceded by "a.k.a." (also known as). As an example, John Smith (a.k.a. John Taylor). This situation might occur, for instance, when John Smith had been adopted by a Taylor and was known by both names.

Write down all the names by which a person was known. If he was known by his middle name, or known by initials only, note that, too. Laurence William Holmes has been known as Bill, Will, and Willie. It will be important one day for his descendants to know that, for he may be listed under any of those.

**Tree Tips** _____

A good rule to adopt is that if you find anything in the record that seems amiss or unusual, note it. It may be the evidence that proves or disproves a link you are trying to establish.

Always note the spelling variations you find. They can be insignificant, a reflection of times when names were spelled phonetically, or they can be important, suggesting that you have information on two different individuals rather than one. (See Chapter 7 for more on spelling variations.)

For names that can be either male or female (such as Gale-Gail, Gene-Jean, Marion-Marian, Frances-Francis, Leslie-Lesley) indicate whether the individual was a man or woman if you can determine that from the document. It eliminates confusion.

If you find an individual with a name usually given to someone of the opposite sex (remember the Johnny Cash song, "A Boy Named Sue"?), be sure to indicate that in your notes. A number of names once used for either sex have fallen into disuse for males: Eleanor, Mildred, Beverly, and Valentine. The Social Security Administration put together interesting databases of popular baby names by sex from 1880 to the present: www.ssa.gov/OACT/babynames. Look there to check the popularity of the names you're working on—or the popularity of your own name in the decade of your birth.

## Women and Their Changing Surnames

Women's names present a special problem. You may find women under their maiden (birth) or married name, or even the name of a prior husband. You want to establish a woman's birth name in order to identify her parents, for they are your ancestors, too. List her by that maiden name, and indicate the names of her husbands. In your notes, list Mary Jordan (her maiden name) and show that she was married first to John Jackson and then to Frank Swift. Her full name would properly be shown as Mary (Jordan) Jackson Swift, listing first her given name, followed by her maiden name in parenthesis, followed by the surnames of her subsequent husbands with the latest at the end.

When you are recording a female on charts, but do not have her maiden name, insert only her first (or given) name. In the preceding example, if you did not know that Jordan was her maiden name, then show her as Mary ( ). If you need to refer to her in your notes, show her as Mary ( ) Jackson Swift, indicating by the blank parenthesis that her maiden name is unknown. When her maiden name is established, you can fill in the blank.

Be careful with women's surnames. The name you find in documents can be a maiden name or a married name. If a woman is widowed (or divorced) and remarries, the surname in the marriage record may be that of the previous husband. Sometimes this is distinguished by the record: "Mrs. Margaret Smith married Richard Carter" indicates that she had a previous marriage to a Smith.

## Place Names Can Be Tricky, Too

Place names should be fully identified by writing down the town, county, and state (or the equivalent divisions for foreign countries). These geographic divisions are important in genealogy because many of the records you need are in the towns and counties where your ancestors lived. Because many states have towns and counties of the same name, be sure your notes always indicate the state, too.

If the records you find mention landmarks or geographic features such as creeks or hills or roads, include them in your notes. They may help to distinguish between two different families in the area with the same surname. Abbreviations of place names (except for states) can be confusing later, so write them out.

## Dating Problems

When you insert dates in your notes, use the format of day, month (spelled out), and four-digit year: 10 January 1988. If you write the date 10/1/88 or 1/10/88, later you or others will not be sure if the date was January tenth or October first, and whether the year was 1888 or 1988.

Sometimes the record is unclear as to the date, or the date is given in two places in the document and there is a discrepancy. Be sure to include these discrepancies in your notes. They may be important later in your research.

## Did You Miss Something?

A final word about your notes. Review them at the end of any research session or interview. Check to see if there is anything in your notes that is not clear. You may not have access to that source again; you want to be sure you have it right.

# Beyond Notes: The Other Papers You Need

You'll want to keep more than just your interview and research notes on paper. You'll also want to create some lists to keep track of the sources you check and the information you find when you do your research. You can create your own, use commercially printed forms, or download online forms from sites such as www.ancestry.com/trees/charts/researchcal.aspx or www.cs.williams.edu/~bailey/genealogy.

These lists, or logs, can help in organizing your finds, in deciding the next steps, and in eliminating duplication. Two kinds of logs are especially useful. One is the Research Calendar; the other is the Correspondence Log.

## The Research Calendar

The Research Calendar is labeled with the surname and problem you are researching and has at least four columns: the date of the research, the repository, a description of the record searched, and a brief summary of the findings. You can add other columns

**Genie Jargon**

**URL** is the acronym for uniform resource locator, the address of the page you view. Without that address you will have difficulty returning to that page. Because these addresses often change, it is important to note on your Research Calendar the date you viewed the page.

(time period, library call number, and more). The Research Calendar shows you at a glance what records (documents, films, or books) you have used. It is not, however, the place to record the more expansive notes taken during your research.

You'll need a variation of the Research Calendar to keep track of your Internet research. Instead of noting documents, films, or books, you'll list websites you visited with their *URLs*. If you follow links from the initial website, include them in your list.

_____

**Surname**

**RESEARCH CALENDAR**

| Search focus (brief statement of research problem) |
|---|
|  |

| Date | Repository/call no. | Source | Findings |
|---|---|---|---|
|  |  |  |  |
|  |  |  |  |
|  |  |  |  |
|  |  |  |  |

*Example of a Research Calendar.*

## Correspondence Log

The Correspondence Log is a record of the letters you've written and the replies received. The log should have a blank for the surname at the top and five columns with space for the date the letter was sent, the name of the person to whom the letter was addressed, a brief statement of the information desired, the date of the reply, and a brief note of the results. Some researchers also like to include a column to list any fees paid to get the information.

**CORRESPONDENCE LOG**

| Date Sent | To Whom | Request | Reply Date | Results (Positive, Negative, Burned) |
|---|---|---|---|---|
|  |  |  |  |  |
|  |  |  |  |  |
|  |  |  |  |  |
|  |  |  |  |  |

*Example of a Correspondence Log.*

# Word by Word: Transcribing and Summarizing Documents

The logs mentioned previously summarize your research activity. In addition, you will have your notes, analyses, and photocopies of what you found. Your notes contain all the details that do not appear on the logs. These notes include *transcripts* and *abstracts* of documents. Transcribing and abstracting are particular kinds of note-taking.

## Learning by Transcribing

Transcriptions are most useful when the document is very difficult to read (due to content or condition). It is also helpful when you are unfamiliar with the type of document, or when you have a particularly complicated or unusual document. You will be forced to transcribe if the fragile condition of the document restricts photocopying.

When you begin your research, it is helpful to transcribe all the documents you find relating to your family. The practice will assist you in becoming familiar with the old handwriting and will help you learn to recognize common phrases in similar documents. As your familiarity increases, you can switch to abstracting the documents except in selected cases.

**Genie Jargon**

A **transcript** is a word-for-word exact copy of the text in a document. Nothing is changed; everything is written just as it appears: errors, punctuation, misspellings, and all.

An **abstract** is a summary of the text of a document, retaining all its essential details.

You can hone your transcribing skills by visiting some online sites. Although the Board for Certification of Genealogists is aimed at individuals who want to become certified or for consumers wanting to hire a genealogist, the "test your skills" section is useful for all levels of researchers. You can print out two documents, transcribe and abstract them, and compare your results with the correct ones.

**Tree Tips**

Read a document several times before you begin to transcribe or abstract. Difficult words or handwriting may become clear after several readings, making it easier to take notes.

A particularly interesting site for learning to transcribe is www.dohistory.org/diary/index.html. Here you can transcribe right on your screen and compare your transcription with theirs. An interesting feature on this site is the "magic lens," which magnifies portions of the document as your mouse hovers over words. Practice reading the handwriting without the aid of the magnifier and then get instant feedback by checking your work with the magnifier.

## Abstracts: Summarizing the Document

For an abstract, you extract every detail that might shed light on your research problem. You are looking for *all* names, dates, places, and events. Examine documents carefully for unexpected information. A document may have a name that doesn't mean anything now, but may turn out to be a relative. Note any mention of a location; it may lead to other records.

Although an abstract is a summary and does not include every word and punctuation mark in the document, it does include names and places just as they appear. If you think there is an error in a name or place (or anything else significant), you can include your correction or explanatory remarks in square brackets after the word. The brackets enable others to easily distinguish what was actually in the abstract, and what you added. It is permissible to correct simple words in the abstract; "funrale" may be corrected to "funeral." It is important, however, to distinguish that some simple words can be corrected in the abstracts, but in the transcription the spellings are retained as they are in the original.

**Pedigree Pitfalls**

If the name appears as Jas., do not convert it to James. The abstract is not the place for the interpretation. After you have examined all the records, then you can determine if the person is actually James. What looked like an "a" might turn out to be an "o," and Jos. is the abbreviation for Joseph.

In the following figures you see a will from an actual probate file, followed by the transcript and abstract of the document. Compare the transcript and the abstract to the original document and then to each other. The transcript includes every word from the original; the abstract is a summary of the important information.

*Will of William A. Glass. Note the blotch and how it is treated in the transcription in the next figure.*

*The brief will of William A. Glass, filed in Decatur County, Indiana.*

La[st] Will & Testament of William A. Glass

Adams Ind. June 20th 1881.

I William A. Glass being of sound mind and memory do declare this to be my last Will

First: I Desire a desent Burial

Secondly: All of my just debts paid

Third All of my property both Real Estate and Personal property that I may own at the time of my death I will and Bequeath to my wife Mary Glass for ever for her to have the same in fee simple to have t[he?] wright to sell and convey the same in a[ny?] way that she may see proper

I also appoint my wife my Executor of my will and for her to settle the same in any way that she may see proper to save as much expense as possible


William A. Glass


Ezra L. Guthrie }

Joseph Dineger } Witnesseth

Did you think the name in the will was Glap? The last two letters are the "tailed s" and an example of how documents can be misread if there is not some familiarity with old handwriting. All spelling and punctuation are retained. When a word is not entirely legible or is partly gone (as are two words in this document), brackets are used.

*Abstract of the brief will of William A. Glass.*

[Abstract of will of William A. Glass, Will Bk 5 p. 182, Decatur County, Indiana.]

Adams Co., Ind. June 20, 1881, William A. Glass, all property real and person to wife Mary Glass in fee simple. Appoints wife Executor. Signed: William A. Glass. Witnesses: Ezra L. Guthrie and Joseph Dineger. [If the copy shows the date it is proved in court by the witnesses, that would also be included in the abstract.]

Although there are fill-in forms available for use in abstracting, they are constraining and not recommended. Trying to conform to the order on the form means rearranging the information from the document. In adapting the information to fit the form, omissions can occur or clues in the wording and order might be lost. I prefer to shorten the original while retaining the order of information in the document as closely as possible.

Learning the techniques for transcribing and abstracting is essential. Both are an integral part of genealogy research. Practice constantly, and examine various books of abstracts at the library when you are there. (See Chapter 14 for further discussion.)

**Tree Tips**

If ever in doubt as to whether something belongs in your abstract, include it. If it is something extra, it doesn't matter. If it is something you later need and don't have, it matters a great deal.

# It Says *What?*

Because you start your research with yourself and work backward, the first documents you are likely to research are more recent ones. These are usually not too difficult to read because they are in a more modern hand or typed. However, as you move back in time in your research, you will find many documents that are difficult because of terminology and handwriting.

**Tree Tips**

It can be helpful to enlarge the writing with a photocopier, especially if the quality of the original is poor.

## You Can Read It, But What Does It Mean?

The terminology that baffles you may be complex legal phrases or obsolete clauses. It could just be a peculiarity in the writing of the individual who created the record. Working with the official documents of a specific place and time, you will learn the terminology and recognize standardized words or sentences that aren't important to the interpretation of the document. But when you begin, if you transcribe the complete document as suggested, (including all words and punctuation), it won't take you long to recognize the common statements that you can ignore.

Until you become familiar with standard terminology or legal phrases in documents, read and copy everything in the document.

## "Strange" Old Words

As you do your genealogy research, you will encounter many unfamiliar words. Customs change, laws change, word meanings change. Occupations become obsolete, ethnic groups assimilate, and new inventions require new words. Language is constantly changing through usage.

> **Tree Tips**
>
> A common phrase may have variant meanings. "Meeting house" could refer to a New England town hall, or it could be a Quaker place of worship. The difference could affect your research.

Sometimes you can determine the meaning of a word through the context of the words around it. Or through the interpretation of other documents. Sometimes you'll find the words defined in your regular dictionary. (The Oxford English Dictionary is particularly useful because it includes many archaic terms.) You can also consult a genealogical dictionary. An excellent resource is *What Did They Mean by That? A Dictionary of Historical Terms for Genealogists*, by Paul Drake, J.D. In addition to definitions, this book includes documents that will help you become familiar with the kinds of things you'll encounter in your research. It reproduces two ledger sheets from the mid-1700s. You can practice your skills by reading the items in these documents and then looking at the compiler's lists to see if you interpreted them correctly.

Definitions for obscure or outdated terms or implements can be found at numerous online sites. One such site (www.cotswold.gov.uk/nqcontent. cfm?a_id=293&tt=cotswold) gives you a choice of categories (agriculture, costumes, and so on) from which to choose. The results provide pictures as well as definitions. Archaic medical terms can stymie your research. One comprehensive site to check for definitions and extensive explanations is www.kamous.com/translator/s.asp?l=503.

## Latin for Genealogists

Legal documents and court records are full of Latin terms that need defining. It is important for you to know that when an index lists a name followed by *et al.*, there are other names connected with this document in addition to the name that is indexed; or that *et uxor* or *et ux.* means "and wife." The best source for legal terms is a law dictionary. Consult *Black's Law Dictionary* whenever you encounter legal terms you do not understand.

> **Lineage Lessons**
>
> The term *et al.* is shortened from *et alii*, a frequently used legal term meaning "and others." When you encounter it in an index, pursue the full record to determine the names of the additional individuals. Often they are family members. Also seen frequently in an index is *et ux.*, shortened from *et uxor*, meaning "and wife." An examination of the document will probably disclose her name.

## Abbreviations

A number of abbreviations common in early documents are rare today. You will often see "inst" as an abbreviation for "instant." That will help to establish a correct date if you know that "instant" was the term used to indicate that the date referred to was in the same month as a mentioned date. Thus, in a response on December 28 to a letter dated December 4, the letter writer might say, "In responding to your letter of the 4th instant," which is to say, "I'm replying to your letter dated December 4."

"Ultimate," as a contrast to instant, refers to the previous month. An obituary in the newspaper of 25 July stating that the deceased died the 20 ult. would indicate he died June 20.

For help in deciphering many of the abbreviations you'll encounter, see Kip Sperry's compilation *Abbreviations and Acronyms*.

## Making Sense of Chicken Scratches

The handwriting in some documents may be nearly impossible to decipher at first glance. However, with practice and careful examination you will learn to read many styles. Even neat, clear handwriting will reflect the contemporary style or usage and can leave you wondering about some words. It helps to seek references with illustrations of letter combinations and writing styles. Consult *The Handwriting of American Records for a Period of 300 Years* by E. Kay Kirkham. In it are large illustrations of the manner in which letters of the alphabet were written through the years, as well as the abbreviations for selected names. The book also has some transcriptions. You can attempt to transcribe the same documents and then check your work against the published transcriptions.

The chapter "Reading Handwritten Records" by Raymond A. Winslow, Jr., pp. 97-105, in *North Carolina Research* has a good illustrated discussion of peculiar letter forms, symbols, and abbreviations that you may see in old documents.

Now that you've learned a little about how to extract information from your research, go on to the next chapter to learn how to manage that information.

## The Least You Need to Know

- You need to establish the name, and the approximate dates and places of birth, marriage, and death, to start searching.

- When making notes, add complete details of where you got the information.

- Carefully note full names, nicknames, and variations.

- Transcribing documents will help you learn to read the old writing and to understand the terminology.

# Chapter 4

# Keeping Track of What You Find

## In This Chapter

- ◆ Using charts to keep track
- ◆ Computer genealogy programs for record keeping
- ◆ Computer-generated reports

Genealogy research is a little like the connect-the-dots pictures you did as a child; if you did not connect the dots in the right order, the emerging picture wasn't quite right.

To help connect your genealogy dots in the right order, you will use genealogy charts and family group sheets to record the research data. You can use these basic structures with pencil and paper or with a computer.

The two general types of genealogy charts are *ascendant* and *descendant* charts. In addition to the charts, a family group sheet is used to keep track of individual families.

An *ascendant* chart starts with you and moves back through the generations of all your ancestors. A *descendant* chart starts with an individual and comes down through the generations listing that individual's descendants.

These charts are not your finished genealogy. They are research tools, reminders of where you are in your genealogy research.

# Pedigree or Family Tree Charts

The chart you begin with is a *pedigree chart*, an ascendant chart. On it you start with yourself and work back in time, generation by generation, filling in your parents, grandparents, great-grandparents, and so on, as far back as you can.

**Genie Jargon**

A **pedigree chart** starts with you and shows the line of your direct ancestors. It is some-times called a family tree, line-age, or ancestry chart.

Think of the pedigree chart as a shorthand master outline of your bloodline. A quick glance at it alerts you to the blank spots in the information you are gathering. This in turn helps you develop your research plan. When you notice that Great-Grandma Diana's maiden name is blank or that there is no marriage date or place for Grandpa Guy, you have a clear picture of the information you still need.

The format of a pedigree chart is always the same: your name (or the individual whose ancestry you are tracing) is on the first line, your father's name (or the subject's father's name) is on the upper line, your mother's on the lower line. The upper track in a pedigree chart is that of the father's (paternal) line. The lower track is the ancestral line for the mother's (maternal) line. You are number 1 on this chart. Your father is assigned number 2 and your mother number 3. On a pedigree chart the numbers for men are always even numbers, and the numbers for women are odd.

**Pedigree Pitfalls**

Pedigree charts have no space for source citation. Therefore, they should not be dis-seminated unless accompanied by an attached sheet with full citations keyed to the information on the chart, or a family group sheet, which does have citations.

As you can see, you quickly run out of space for all your ancestors on a four-generation chart. To list the additional generations, you must create additional charts.

In numbering the pedigree chart, you are number 1 on chart 1. One of your great-grandfathers is number 8 on chart 1. You will need to make a new chart to continue with his ancestors. That great-grandfather (who is number 8 on chart 1) will become number 1 on chart 2. Be sure to make a reference on chart 2 that he is also number 8 on chart 1, so you can easily follow the line in connected charts.

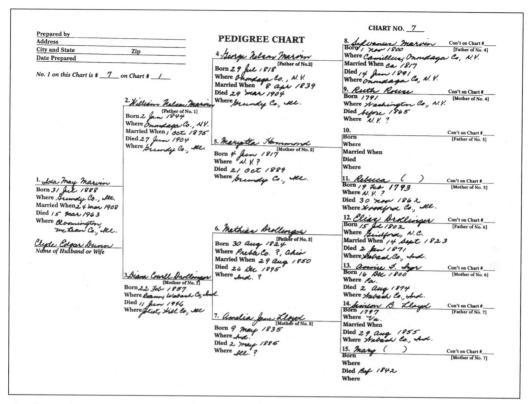

*A pedigree chart begins with a subject and works back through the generations.*

# Large or Small, They Chart Your Family

Blank pedigree charts accommodating 4 to 15 generations can be purchased. The four-generation pedigree chart is the most convenient to work with in your day-to-day research. The more generations on the chart, the less room there is for data about individuals.

Some decorative pedigree charts are suitable for framing. They can be fan shaped with the lines radiating out from you at the center. Some are in the form of a tree with limbs and branches representing family lines. Still others have spaces for photographs. Although attractive as wall art, these charts are too large to be useful as research aids.

## Filling in the Pedigree Chart

Completely fill in as many of the spaces on the pedigree chart as you can. If you know an individual's middle name, write it out rather than use the initial. Put nicknames in quotation marks after the given name. Use women's maiden names, and if they are not known, use a blank parenthesis, such as ( ). When known, geographic places should indicate the town or township, county, and state. Write the dates with the day first, the month written out next, and all four digits for the year.

Because the pedigree chart is an instant guide to your research, keep it up-to-date so that you can follow the clues. Add new information as you find it, and correct the information as you uncover errors.

Pedigree charts cannot stand alone as evidence of your ancestors. They are research tools, not the end result of your research. Consider the pedigree charts as notes to yourself that show at a glance where you are in your pursuit of your family history.

# Family Group Sheets

Each of your ancestors was a family member, first as a child and then as a mother or father. You collect information about the entire family to learn more about your ancestors. The information on the whole family is recorded on a *family group sheet.*

## They Keep You Organized

Family group sheets are the foundation for organizing everything you learn about your ancestors. The layouts of family group sheets may vary, but the categories of information are basically the same.

The top section of the record is for recording the names of the husband and wife and the following information about each:

**Genie Jargon**

The **family group sheet** is the form used to record information on a family unit. It is neither an ascendant chart, nor a descendant chart. It is merely a form on which all the members of one family can be listed (not just your ancestors).

- Birth dates and places
- Christening dates and places
- Marriage date and place for this couple
- Death dates and places
- Burial dates and places
- Occupation, military, religion
- Names of their parents
- Names of other spouses

# FAMILY GROUP SHEET

NO. ____

| **HUSBAND** [Full name] *William Nelson Marvin* | | SOURCES: Brief listing. |
|---|---|---|
| BORN 2 *Jan 1844* | AT *Warners, Onondaga Co., N.Y* | No.¹ *1900 census* |
| CHR. | AT | No.2. *Death Certificate* |
| MAR. *1 Oct 1875* | AT *Joliet, Will Co., Ill.* | No.3. *1880 census* |
| DIED *27 Jun 1904* | AT | No. 4. *Obituary* |
| BURIED AT *Braceville-Gardner Cemetery, Grundy Co., Ill.* | | No.5. *marriage license* |
| FATHER *George Nelson Marvin* | MOTHER [Maiden Name] *Maryetta Hammond* | (Complete source citations on reverse) |
| OTHER WIVES | | |
| RESIDENCES | RELIGION | |
| OCCUPATION *Farmer* | MILITARY | |

[Use separate forms for each marriage]

| **WIFE** [Full maiden name] *Diana Cowell Drollinger* | |
|---|---|
| BORN *22 Feb 1857* | AT *Roann,* |
| CHR. | AT |
| DIED *11 Jun 1946* | AT *Joliet, Will Co., Ill.* |
| BURIED AT *Braceville-Gardner Cemetery, Grundy Co., Ill.* | |
| FATHER *Mathias Drollinger* | MOTHER [Maiden Name] *Amelia Jane Lloyd* |
| OTHER HUSBANDS | |

| Sex | Children | Day-Month-Year | City/Town County State | REF. No. |
|---|---|---|---|---|
| F | 1. *Myrtle Olive Marvin* | b. *12 Oct 1879* | at *Grundy Co., Ill.* | Ref. *3,1* |
| | Spouse: *Jack Redmond* | m. | at | Ref. |
| | | d. *8 May 1941* | at *Evergreen Park, Cook Co., Ill.* | Ref. *2* |
| F | 2. *Emma Grace Marvin* | b. *21 Dec 1882* | at *Grundy Co., Ill.* | Ref. *1* |
| | Spouse: *Don C. Ritchie* | m. *4 Apr 1905* | at *Joliet, Will Co., Ill.* | Ref. *5* |
| | | d. *30 Dec 1943* | at *Detroit, Wayne Co., Ill.* | Ref. *2* |
| M | 3. *Sylvanus Jay Marvin* | b. *6 Apr 1885* | at *Grundy Co., Ill.* | Ref. *1* |
| | Spouse: | m. | at | Ref. |
| | | d. *25 May 1947* | at *Joliet, Will Co., Ill.* | Ref. *2, 4* |
| F | 4. *Ida May Marvin* | b. *31 Jul 1888* | at *Grundy Co., Ill.* | Ref. *1* |
| | Spouse: *Clyde Edgar Dunn* | m *24 May 1908* | at *Joliet, Will Co., Ill.* | Ref. *5* |
| | | d. *15 May 1963* | at *Bloomington, McLean Co., Ill.* | Ref. *2* |
| F | 5. *Etta Jane Marvin* | b. *20 Jun 1892* | at *Grundy Co., Ill.* | Ref. *6* |
| | Spouse: | m. | at | Ref. |
| | | d. *18 Oct 1893* | at *Grundy Co., Ill.* | Ref. *6* |
| F | 6. *Sarah Bernice Marvin* | b. *21 Jul 1895* | at *Grundy Co., Ill.* | Ref. *1* |
| | Spouse: *Rodney McKell* | m. *11 Apr 1911* | at *Salt Lake City, Salt Lake Co., Utah* | Ref. *5* |
| | | d. *28 Jun 1981* | at *San Dimas, Los Angeles Co., Calif.* | Ref. *2* |
| | 7. | b. | at | Ref. |
| | Spouse: | m. | at | Ref. |
| | | d. | at | Ref. |
| | 8. | b. | at | Ref. |
| | Spouse: | m. | at | Ref. |
| | | d. | at | Ref. |
| | 9. | b. | at | Ref. |
| | Spouse: | m. | at | Ref. |
| | | d. | at | Ref. |
| | 10. | b. | at | Ref. |
| | Spouse: | m. | at | Ref. |
| | | d. | at | Ref. |

| *PREPARED BY* | OTHER MAR. OF CHILDREN |
|---|---|
| Address | Use reverse for additional marriages |
| City and State | Zip |
| Date Prepared: | |

b.=born   m.=married   d.=death   ch.=christening   List references at top and use ref. numbers on items. Use reverse if necessary.

*Family group sheet. Form for recording information on a family unit.*

**Tree Tips** _____

Make a separate family group sheet for each marriage of an individual. If a woman is married three times, then you should have three family group sheets for her.

Following this information, the children of this marriage are recorded with their birth dates and places; marriage dates and places and spouses' names; death dates and places. If the family is a large one, the list of children should continue on a second page.

When you gather information, collect it on whole families, your ancestors and their siblings. Each person on your pedigree chart should be on two family group sheets: once as a child with parents and siblings, then as a mother or father with children.

## Family Group Sheets and Sources

Each fact on the family group sheet must be linked to a full source citation. If all the information came from the same source, the family group sheet notation might read as follows:

> All information on this family from 1860 U.S. Census, population schedule, Noble County, Indiana, Perry Township, Ligonier, page 105, dwelling 84, family 84.

As your research progresses, your information on the family will come from several sources. The same information may be in two or more documents. For example, the birth date of Mary Smith, 2 March 1846, might be based on both a family Bible and her tombstone. When you enter her birth on the family sheet, list those two sources, and key them to her birth date. (When you do enter the citation, be sure that you give sufficient information to properly identify it. See Chapter 19 for more on citations.)

Each fact on the family group sheet should be documented by a specific source citation. It is not enough to just add a list of sources to the group sheet with no indication as to which facts they document. Those using the information need to know where you obtained the information on each individual fact: every birth, every birthplace, every marriage, and so on. Use both sides of the paper if necessary.

# Descendant Charts

You will more often use descendant charts later in your research. These charts start with an individual and list that person's descendants. Because descendant charts begin with a *progenitor*, you must do some research to find the progenitors in your lines. Descendant charts include all the descendants of the progenitor, or as many as can be identified.

**Genie Jargon** _____

A **progenitor** is an ancestor in a direct line. When genealogists refer to a progenitor, they usually mean the earliest proven person in a line. If the earliest proven person in your paternal line is your grandfather, then he is the progenitor for that line. When you can go back one more generation and prove who your great-grandfather is, then he becomes the progenitor. Each of your lines has a progenitor.

## DESCENDANT CHART

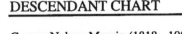

*A text-based descendant chart.*

```
George Nelson Marvin (1818 - 1904)
└─ Maryetta Hammond (1817 - 1889)
   ─George W. Marvin (1840 - 1889)
    └─Julia ( ) ( - dec.)
      ── Mary A. Marvin ( - dec.)
      ── Edward H. Marvin ( - dec.)
      ── Charles N. Marvin ( - dec.)
      ── Ada E. Marvin ( - dec.)
      ── Jesse D. Marvin ( - dec.)
      ── Dora M. Marvin ( - dec.)
      └─ Frank L. Marvin ( - BEF 1908)
   ─Emma Marvin (1842 - 1917)
    └─Augustus C. Van Horne (1844 - 1924)
      └─ Alfrieda Van Horne (1882 - 1924)
   ─William Nelson Marvin (1844 - 1904)
    └─Diana Courll Drollinger (1857 - 1946)
      ── Myrtle Olive Marvin (1879 - 1941)
      ── Emma Grace Marvin (1882 - 1943)
      ── Sylvanus Jay Marvin (1885 - 1947)
      ── Ida May Marvin (1888 - 1963)
      ── Etta Jane Marvin (1892 - 1893)
      ── Sarah Bernice Marvin (1895 - 1981)
      └─ William Manfred Marvin (1898 - 1909)
   └─Sylvanus Marvin (1845 - 1862)
```

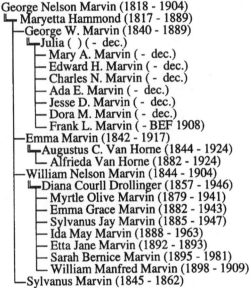

*Descendants of George Nelson Marvin*

| George Nelson Marvin 1818 - 1904 | Maryetta Hammond 1817 - 1889 |
| William Nelson Marvin 1844 - 1904 | Diana Courll Drollinger 1857 - 1946 |

| Emma Grace Marvin 1882 - 1943 | Sylvanus Jay Marvin 1885 - 1947 | Ida May Marvin 1888 - 1963 |

*This is also a descendant chart, but it is graphical rather than text-based.*

## Drop Chart

A variation of the descendant chart is the *drop chart*. Sometimes called a box chart, the drop chart is a clear representation of one line of descent.

*Direct descendant chart or drop chart.*

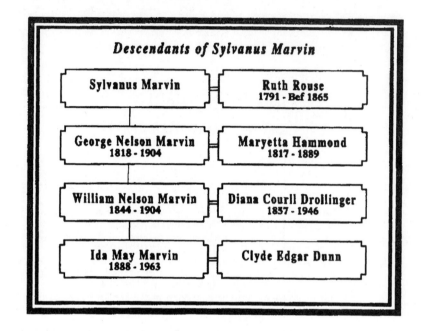

**Descendants of Sylvanus Marvin**

| Sylvanus Marvin | Ruth Rouse |
| --- | --- |
| | 1791 - Bef 1865 |

| George Nelson Marvin | Maryetta Hammond |
| --- | --- |
| 1818 - 1904 | 1817 - 1889 |

| William Nelson Marvin | Diana Courll Drollinger |
| --- | --- |
| 1844 - 1904 | 1857 - 1946 |

| Ida May Marvin | Clyde Edgar Dunn |
| --- | --- |
| 1888 - 1963 | |

**Genie Jargon**

A **drop chart** connects two people generation by generation through their direct line. Starting with the ancestor, the chart then lists one child of the ancestor, let's say a son; then it lists one of the son's children, the ancestor's grandchild, and so on down the line. It does not include all the progenitor's descendants, only those in one direct line.

Notice that the last three figures use individuals from the pedigree chart and the family group sheet (pictured earlier in this chapter) to illustrate the various ways to treat your genealogy information. The first is a descendant chart for individual number 4 on the pedigree chart. The next figure is a graphic descendant chart for this individual, one of his sons, and some of his grandchildren. The last figure in the group is a drop chart showing the direct line connection from individual number 8 on the pedigree chart to his great-granddaughter, number 1 on the pedigree chart.

# Using Computer Programs for Genealogy Record Keeping

Consider using a computer genealogy program to manage your genealogy information. These programs give you great flexibility in compiling and analyzing your research, as well as making it easier to share data.

After entering the data into the computer once, you can arrange it in many ways. All the programs use a family group sheet format to keep track of your information, and all print pedigree charts. The differences in genealogy programs lie in the amount of information they enable you to enter and what you can do with that information once it is entered.

The programs range from very simple ones, which are merely an organized collection of names with the capacity to print basic forms, to very sophisticated programs, which produce customized reports and allow for extensive research notes, footnotes, and bibliographies to help you produce complete family histories. Many programs incorporate multimedia and provide tools to connect you to the Internet and to put your genealogy on your own Web page.

**Pedigree Pitfalls**

Avoid computer genealogy programs that do not provide adequate space for source citations. Look for programs that advertise full documentation with complete sources for each piece of your information.

## Computer-Generated Reports

Computer genealogy programs are especially helpful for preparing charts, both ascendant and descendant. The program knows from the information you enter just what names and dates it needs to gather from your lineage-linked database to compose the chart you select. Using a computer program makes it easy to print new, correctly numbered charts as you add newly found information.

Putting together a complete descendant chart by hand is tedious work. You must scour your files for all descendants and group them by generations. This is a task well suited to computers. In moments the computer searches through all the material you entered and finds everyone connected to the person you designate as the starting individual. It then creates a descendant chart based on your preferences.

Having all your data in a computer program makes it easier to write research reports for yourself and to share information with others working on your lines. A good computer program enables you to enter everything you find. It provides space to write evaluations of your data and sources, and space for remarks to yourself or for recording research tasks, such as "Check the 1850 census of Indiana to find sibling's family."

## Computer Searching: What Do You Want to Know?

With a good computer program you can search your data for nearly anything. You can look for all individuals in your database born before 1900 in Grundy County, Illinois, get a list of every person in your database who had military service, or find the average age of marriage for all the females in your database. Just creating a list of all the marriages in your database can be helpful.

> **Lineage Lessons**
>
> Most commercial programs have a built-in conversion program, so that if you switch to another genealogy program, you do not have to reenter your data. Look for GEDCOM-compatible (Genealogical Data Communications) programs. However, these conversions are not fail-safe; you will have to carefully check your data for possible errors introduced during the conversion process.

Most programs let you view your materials in different ways, making the work of connecting people much easier. You can search for patterns or interesting statistics. How many men died of heart disease before age 60? Find all the women in your database for whom you need maiden names. How many relatives share your birthday? Remember, these searches depend on the data you have entered. If you have not entered information about military service, then the computer cannot give you statistics on how many men in your database served in some capacity.

You can determine your relationship to everyone in your database. How are you related to all the individuals you've researched so far? (If you collect records on several hundred people, you will have difficulty figuring this out without a computer.)

## Multimedia

Computer technology allows some sophisticated programs to store the photographs of your ancestors. All those charming photographs you have gathered, Aunt Lizzie on her first bicycle or Grandma tending her garden, can be stored on the computer and used to enhance your family histories.

Distant family members may not have seen the photos you can now incorporate into your genealogy. Pictures of the rude log cabin or the primitive sod house add immeasurably to descendants' understanding of what life was like in the early days of our country. Imagine the children's glee as they look at the very bushy eyebrows on third Great-Grandmother Harriet and discover the origin of their own eyebrows.

Some programs can incorporate audio clips with the material you gather. Grandpa recollecting his capture in the Battle of the Bulge or your cousins in Germany explaining the original pronunciation of your name add color to your family history.

Computer programs today are not usually bundled with CD-ROMs of resources, indexes, or family trees as they were at one time. However, those CD-ROMS are still used by some individuals working on their family history. Be cautious about accepting the information on them at face value. Many of the lineages on CD-ROMs that were bundled with computer programs have no source citations. Other materials in those bundled products, such as the Social Security Death Index, are now out-of-date and some resource materials were incomplete or had serious abstracting flaws. Though helpful as clues for further research, you'll need to research and document the information to be sure it is correct.

## Continuing Development

Technology advances continue to be integrated into genealogy. The proliferation of personal data assistants led to the development of genealogy programs for these mobile units. You can carry all your genealogy information in something the size of a cell phone. Utility programs (small software applications also called add-ons) work with major genealogy programs to enhance the products. They may facilitate printing fancy charts, prepare slide shows, or use artificial intelligence to analyze your data and deliver suggestions of specific resources to help you find the missing pieces.

## Finding a Computer Program

If you are interested in buying a computer genealogy program, find links to the programs' sites on Cyndi's List. Most programs have demonstration versions you can take for a "test drive" by downloading the demo from the site. Trying out the programs will make you more knowledgeable as you compare their features by reading reviews in the magazine *Genealogical Computing* or by reading the message boards devoted to computer software at RootsWeb.com. Many local genealogy societies have computer interest groups that meet regularly for demonstrations and discussions of various programs. Computer programs change constantly, so make your choice based on the latest information you can find.

## The Least You Need to Know

- ◆ You can use ascendant and descendant charts to assist you in record keeping.

- ◆ A valuable chart for recording the whole family is the family group sheet.

- ◆ Charts and forms are tools to use in your research; they are not your finished genealogy.

- ◆ Computer programs enable you to generate reports in many ways.

- ◆ Advancing technology continues to encourage development of exciting aids for genealogy research and information sharing.

# Part 2

## Finding the Trail

By this time, you are searching for the relatives you never knew. Part 2 will make a detective out of you, guiding you in techniques to find your kin.

You'll start with the Internet. You'll be so staggered by all the wonderful things there that you will think "everything is online." But, 'tisn't so, you'll discover as you read on. So that you won't be led astray, you'll be introduced to the variations in the names you will be searching. Then, you'll head for the library and find a whole world you didn't know existed.

You'll even take another look at your family's hometown, seeing it from a new perspective. Now the town is a hunting ground—a place where there are potential clues for you to follow. All you have to do is find them!

# Chapter 5

# The Internet: Online Any Time

## In This Chapter

- ◆ Research online 24/7
- ◆ Finding what you need
- ◆ Keeping track of where you've been
- ◆ Where to start searching
- ◆ The wide scope of information

Technology's impact on genealogy cannot be underestimated. New resources become available hourly and all of them can be perused on your schedule. You're not bound by staffing constraints or budget reductions that close libraries and archives the hours you are free. The Internet never sleeps—and if you're not careful, you won't either. That's the siren call of remote research.

# So Everything Is Now Online?

First, let's dispel the notion that "everything is online now and it's free." In spite of the whiz bang features that make the Internet so addictive, you cannot do all your genealogy online. Genealogy information and evidence is culled from many disciplines and countless repositories; not even Bill Gates has the wherewithal to digitize it all. However, you will experience exhilarating finds online whether it's the land patent for your fourth great-grandmother's purchase in Ohio or your seventh cousin who has pictures of your great-great-grandparents.

Although much genealogy information is free, some is available only by subscription or by paying fees to retrieve information or documents. There is no charge to search the Social Security Death Index, but if you want a copy of a complete Social Security application (Form SS-5), you will have to pay a fee to the Social Security Administration. Images of all available U.S. federal census records (1790-1930 population schedules) are online, but to search and view them, you must subscribe to a service.

> **Tree Tips**
>
> A few census images are accessible online without charge, but for the most part they are for single counties or partial counties.

# Traditional Methodology Still Applies

Even when you find online information, whether free or by fee, you still have to analyze and evaluate it before incorporating the data into your other family research.

The same basic research techniques you use to pursue family history in brick-and-mortar repositories must be applied to online investigation. Be systematic, working from the known to the unknown. Keep a record of where you've been and what you did. Cite sources completely. Evaluate your findings as you work.

> **Tree Tips**
>
> Online research does not substitute for traditional research. It complements it.

# Okay, How Do You Find All That Good Stuff Out There?

Accessing the wealth of genealogy data in the digital library can be as hard as finding gold in a stream. The information can be obscure and astounding or obvious and routine, but how do you find it? The chief methods for finding information on the

Internet are by using *directories* and *search engines*. Both are kinds of indexes to the Web. The links found in directories and by search engines provide entry to the knowledge you seek. You'll want to use both methods.

## Searching by Topic

To become familiar with the kinds of things pertaining to genealogy that are online is to sample several genealogy directories, such as Cyndi's List (www.cyndislist.com) or GeneaLinks (www.genealinks.com). These and other directories link to sites ranging from general "how to" topics to searchable databases. They cover diverse subjects: localities, ethnic groups, vital records, and military history to name a few. General subject directories such as www.yahoo.com may also be useful. Some directory sites are updated daily, while others not as often, but all change.

**Genie Jargon**

A **directory** is a list of categories, usually alphabetical, with links to websites within those categories. The topics and links are chosen by humans and placed on a website. A **search engine** is software that wanders the Web looking for specific Web pages as well as websites, placing them in a database.

**Tree Tips**

For extensive definitions and more information on the language of the Web, go to www.netlingo.com.

## Searching by Keyword

A directory search is conducted within a specific website. This gives you an overview of what online resources might help in your genealogy pursuits. Whereas directories provide you with links by searching for a subject, search engines allow for keyword searches. You can do a keyword search with an Internet browser, such as Internet Explorer or Netscape, but more sophisticated searches are done with specific search engines where you can zero in on one word or a phrase or a combination of words and phrases.

A search engine will also give you results for a general topic, but a directory is unlikely to return hits for a phrase or particular word on a Web page. If you were looking to see what might be online regarding Wyoming genealogy, you could go to cyndislist.com or the USGenWeb.com site, select Wyoming, and peruse the topics listed. However, to get more specific information about ranchers in Jackson Hole keeping the elk herd alive in the terrible winter of 1909-1910, you'd have more success using a search engine, such as www.google.com, where you might enter these keywords: winter 1909 Wyoming ranchers "elk herd." The quotation marks indicate the search engine should look for pages on which those two words occur next to each other.

Remember, there is no overall index to the Web and no one search engine covers everything. Additionally, the Web changes constantly. Because a search engine is software that collects websites and Web pages and places them in a huge database, you are searching that database, not the entire Internet. Search for the same thing on several search engines. They will likely give you different results. There are hundreds of search engines, so although it is wise to choose a couple to use regularly, it pays to occasionally check some out of your comfort zone.

Here are some search engines to try:

- www.altavista.com
- www.askjeeves.com
- www.excite.com
- www.google.com
- www.hotbot.com
- www.lycos.com

**CAUTION**

**Pedigree Pitfalls**

Some search engines are biased; they rank results not by their relevance to your search terms, but by fees paid for rankings. If a search returns a list with sponsored links, you know those rankings are fee based. That does not necessarily invalidate the results, but it should alert you to the fact that maybe the most relevant site for your query is not at the top of the list.

# A Simple Practice Exercise

Go to www.google.com, type your name in quotes into its search box, and look at the results. Chances are good that you'll find someone who shares your name. It may surprise you to know that many individuals have the same name you do and that some of their personal information is close to yours.

An incident years ago revealed that my husband was momentarily confused with someone who not only had the same name, but also the same last 4 digits of his Social

Security number. This has further implications for family historians than just getting the correct name in the search engine results. The search engine may find an individual in an online family tree that seems to fit with the information you have. But does it really? Carefully weigh all the evidence before you claim him or her as your own.

# Crafting a Search

Devising searches to yield the best results is a skill that develops with practice and experimentation. Search engines have help files and advanced search tips with examples. Getting acquainted with those tips and tools can reduce your frustration. You'll not only learn to search efficiently and cleverly, you'll be apprised of extra features such as calculators or translations.

The more you learn about search techniques, the more successful your Internet experience will be. By narrowing your searches, you are less likely to turn up thousands of irrelevant results. A section on cyndislist.com has links to articles and tutorials to help you understand how to build a search to return productive results.

# Lost in Space

Although randomly meandering in space, following links from one exciting site to another is fun, it isn't very productive—especially if you make no record of where you went or what you found. Intellectual curiosity is a plus, but with the temptation of a global library as close as your mouse, it is easy to spin out of control like an unbalanced washing machine, coming to a distinct thud as you become totally unbalanced.

Just as you learn to reduce the paper mountains that result from traditional research, you learn to curb the hyperactivity that results from the potential of visiting hundreds of websites in less time than it takes you to drive to a good research facility. The key is planning and organizing.

# GPS Won't Tell You Where You've Been

A Global Positioning System is not going to help you here and you may want to retrace your steps. Like walking on the beach, your footprints are soon washed away. Unlike the beach, you don't even have the coastline to guide you. Either on paper, or better yet on screen, keep a record of where you've been.

Whether you use a variation of the research logs mentioned in Chapter 3 or an electronic log, establish the habit of recording in them as a permanent part of your Internet experiences. You are more likely to record impulsive searches if there is a handy way to do it that requires little thought on your part.

Using an electronic log is expedient because you can select the URL displayed in the browser, click on "copy," and then paste the link in your log. Not only is it convenient, it also reduces errors made when writing down a particularly long URL.

**Tree Tips**

If you are familiar with your software's word processing, spreadsheet, or database programs, you can use any of them to create an electronic log.

Your log should include the date, the URL, name of the website, the search parameters, and the results. You can add columns for comments and surnames, but too many requirements can discourage you from keeping the record at all.

# Bookmarks or Favorites

Use your research log to keep tabs on all the sites you visit in every research session, and use *bookmarks* to list the places you expect to revisit. (Internet browsers all have a bookmark feature, but it may be called *favorites* rather than bookmarks.)

**Genie Jargon**

**Bookmarks**, or **favorites**, are a feature of your browser that enable you to create a shortcut list of websites you want to revisit. Because some of the URLs can be quite long, it is quicker and easier to click on the bookmark than to try remembering the URL or doing a search for it.

To keep your favorites list from becoming unwieldy, catalog your collection in folders, keying folder titles to your research, by states, counties, surnames, or other topics of your choosing. Arranging your bookmarks in a folder hierarchy results in more efficiency than scrolling through a list of 200 bookmarks to find the one you want.

Give each favorite a name that you'll recognize. Say you want to bookmark a site called Cotswold—The Collections, which contains a lot of useful definitions. If you add it to your bookmarks without changing its name, will you remember why it was important to you? If you label it something like "Definitions—Cotswold (implements, dress, etc.)," it's likely to be meaningful. And you might want to include it in your folder of bookmarks pertaining to historical perspective.

---

**Lineage Lessons**

If you access the Internet through some proprietary *portals* such as Compuserve or AOL, you may not have the option to create folders. You can overcome that by connecting through your Internet Service Provider (ISP) as usual, but instead of accessing the Internet through the *home page*, go online through Internet Explorer, Firefox (Mozilla), or Netscape. It is likely that your computer came with at least one of those browsers already installed. All of them have a folder option for organizing your bookmarks.

**Genie Jargon**

**Portals** are websites that serve as the gateway to other places on the Web. They can be general like Yahoo.com or Compuserve.com or specific like CNBC.com for investors. They provide services that can include e-mail, news, sports, stock quotes, weather, and other sites. **Home page** is the Web page set to open when you start your browser. Home page can also refer to the main page for a business, organization, or personal website. Usually, the home page serves as an index to the pages on the site.

# Setting Your Sights on These Sites

Many sites are important to every genealogical researcher. Some will be mentioned throughout this book, but here are a few you can go to right away to get a taste of what's out there in cyberspace. Start with these and you'll be engaged for hours.

The first two sites discussed in this section depend almost entirely on volunteers to run the sites and gather, *digitize*, or transcribe the materials. You may even find that you have information to contribute to one of the pages.

**Genie Jargon**

To **digitize** is to convert data to numerical form for use by a computer. Digital representations (documents, maps, photographs) can be stored and manipulated electronically and displayed seamlessly on your computer.

## Using USGenWeb and RootsWeb

At USGenWeb (www.usgenweb.com) the emphasis is on the county level with the ambitious objective of having an active website for every county in the United States.

Those sites vary from showcasing extensive records and links to those with merely a paragraph or two on the county.

Go to the USGenWeb site and select a state. Explore what's there, and then select a county to examine. You may find an index to early land records, cemetery transcriptions, or an Old Settlers list. There could be digitized maps and county directories. Often there will be a surname list and a query list.

Perhaps the most well-known resources on RootsWeb www.rootsweb.com are the RootsWeb Surname List (RSL) and the thousands of *mailing lists* and *message boards* on surnames, localities, ethnic groups, software, and hundreds of other topics of interest to family history researchers. The RSL is a surname registry for researchers looking for more information about the described families. The registry consists of well over a million names, each with a shorthand description of their locations, time periods, and an e-mail contact for the submitter.

**Genie Jargon** _____

A **mailing list** is composed of e-mail addresses of people with a common interest who subscribe to the list and receive e-mail of all messages posted to the list. A **message board** or forum is different from a mailing list in that messages on the common interest are not broadcast by e-mail, but are posted on the site where they can be read and responded to.

## FamilySearch

This site, www.familysearch.org, is sponsored by The Church of Jesus Christ Latter-day Saints. Headquartered in Salt Lake City, Utah, the church collects information to help members identify their ancestors so that they can perform religious ordinances for those ancestors. They have been microfilming records since the advent of that technology and readily share that information with the world through their Family History Library. No subscriptions or fees are assessed to use this site. See Chapter 8 for more about what you can find in their vast materials.

# Subscription Services

There are numerous websites on which some information is available only by subscription. Among them are Ancestry.com (www.ancestry.com), Genealogy.com (www.genealogy.com/), and Heritage Quest Online (www.heritagequestonline.com). Among the offerings of these three are images and indexes of the 1790-1930 U.S. population schedules. The rest of their content varies considerably, and the best way to learn about their resources is to visit the sites.

Ancestry.com and Genealogy.com sell subscriptions and products to individuals but also provide message boards and educational material free of charge.

Heritage Quest Online differs in that it is only available to libraries who then allow their patrons to access the information. Some public libraries require cardholders to go to the library for access; others allow patrons remote access from home. Many private libraries offer remote access to Heritage Quest Online as a membership benefit.

# Dipping Into the Layers

Have you ever gone to a party and encountered a layered dip? If you only scooped a taste from the top, you missed the delicious things below the surface. The same is true of some websites. The best genealogical information for you may be several levels deep on the website and the only way to find it is to explore more than the surface. Hover your mouse over the graphics. Does the cursor change to a pointing hand? Click on the graphic to see what lies beneath it. It may only be a paragraph explaining a photograph; then again, it may be a detailed recitation of an historical event with links to other material on this or other sites. You can't predict what you'll find on a website.

# Your Family Tree Is Online—You're Done!

Not so fast. Searching for genealogy information online will lead you to thousands of family trees. Examine them carefully. Lineages posted on the Internet are especially prone to error. It is an unfortunate fact that the compiled genealogies online are one of the least reliable of all the resources on the Internet. Similar names are often linked by conjecture instead of documentation. Never take posted compilations as the last word. Use them for clues and do your own search in the records to document the facts stated in them.

| Lineage Lessons |
| --- |
| Always verify the connections in online family trees with follow-up research. Anyone can post information on the Web. No gateway guard stands by checking for sources or the accuracy of evidence interpretations. No authority certifies that posted material is free of plagiarism or copyright violations, either. Be cautious about incorporating an online family tree into your own family history. |

One problem with the Internet age and genealogy is that errors take on lives of their own. The greater the exposure, the more chance of an error reaching epic proportions. And errors online are nearly impossible to eradicate completely. They will swirl around forever, replicated by well-meaning people who innocently send them on to others. The Internet excels in many ways, but not in its posted family compilations.

# What Else Is Online?

The resources for genealogy research defy itemizing. They range from digitized original documents to personal Web pages. There are maps, statistics, books, indexes, library catalogues, newspapers. There are downloadable computer programs and myriad forms. You'll find gazetteers, dictionaries, and photographic collections. Things as diverse as vital records and online classes are yours for the looking. Message boards and mailing lists can put you in touch with distant cousins and resources. Although online research cannot supplant traditional genealogy research, it does enhance it.

## The Least You Need to Know

- No family history is all online, nor is all that is online accurate.
- Carefully constructed searches yield more relevant information.
- Keep a record of every website you visit.
- Explore the links on Web pages.
- Trustworthy family histories are built on verifiable evidence.

# Chapter 6

# Kissin' Kin:
# How to Find Them

## In This Chapter

- The lost relatives
- How family associations and reunions can help
- Using the Social Security Death Index
- How you can use the Internet to find relatives

You learned in earlier chapters how to start your search with your own relatives. But what about those relatives with whom you have lost touch? Now you are going to get a chance to do some digging. To do so, you'll need to learn about a few records. If you have a bit of detective in you, get it working. Start with these, which we discuss more fully later in this chapter:

- Telephone and other directory listings
- Online forums and message boards
- Libraries
- Newspapers
- Queries (published inquiries about the family)

- Family associations
- Family reunions
- Social security

# Ma Bell Comes to the Rescue

Your local library's reference department may have a collection of current telephone directories covering the whole United States, or at least a few states. Better yet, use the various online directories such as www.argali.com, www.switchboard.com, and others. List the relatives who may still be living, and spend an evening at the library or on your computer. If you cannot find the specific person you're seeking, list all those by the surname in the area where you believe the person lived. If the list is not too long, you can easily do this at the online sites by specifying the surname and the town or city. For common names, such as Smith or Jones, you'll need to narrow the list the directory search returns by looking for familiar family-given names.

**Tree Tips**

If you do not have your own computer, your library may have one that is available for public use.

Prepare a letter giving some details of your family and your purpose. Send it to each person on your list. If the phone book does not provide the zip codes for the addresses, check the library while you are there for their zip code directory. You can also obtain the zip codes through the website www.usps.gov. Once there, click on "Find a Zip Code," enter the street address, and then "submit," and instantly get the complete nine-digit zip.

Several commercial companies used to issue CD-ROMs of residential and business telephone numbers. Their databases varied, but they were collected from a variety of sources such as utility companies, mail-order houses, voter registers, and telephone books. The margin of error was great; people move often and the lists were quickly outdated. Nonetheless, if you are looking for relatives, say, 10 to 20 years ago, you may find the family on those old CD-ROMs. Check your library for availability.

Your state or city library or historical society might have a collection of old telephone directories for selected areas. The series is rarely complete, but it will help. When the listing disappears from the directory, it could signify death or removal from the area, providing you with leads. In recent years the absence of the names cannot be easily interpreted, for the parties often choose to keep their numbers unlisted. Some of the online directories are not only from phone listings but also from a variety of other sources, and, therefore, unlisted numbers may have slipped in.

After obtaining the address of a possible relative, resist the temptation to pick up the telephone. A letter can assure the person that you are related, and may elicit more information than a surprise call. If you don't get a response, follow the letter with a telephone call. Your letter will have introduced you and your purpose, setting the person more at ease.

The lack of a response to a letter does not necessarily indicate disinterest. Some hate to write. Your initial letter will, however, serve its purpose as an introduction.

# Consulting Your Local Library

The local library's holdings depend upon the size of the area. Although they may be too small to have books that would directly pertain to genealogy (see Chapter 8), they will no doubt have a number of traditional reference books that will be useful. Check the reference section. Besides the telephone books already mentioned, look for other types of directories that can be useful to genealogists.

## City Directories

Become acquainted with city directories, found in your library's reference section. You will use these extensively, in a variety of ways, as your research techniques develop.

City directories can be highly productive in tracing the earlier generations of your family. Early directories list the residents alphabetically and often included a cross-reference by street address. This provides important details—the neighbors. If the neighbors' families still live there, they may have known your family. If they were close friends, they may even have kept in touch and might provide you with current addresses.

Most cities have changed the format of their directories. They continue to provide a listing by street (called a householder's index), but they have eliminated the alphabetical name listing. Instead, they usually provide a cross-index by telephone number. Although some towns still retain the old-style alphabetical format, in most current editions you lose the ability to search by your family's surname.

Write to the library of the town or city where you believe your family lived. Ask them to search the current issue of the city directory or to photocopy the pages with the surname or street you are seeking. When you're asking for dates in the past, give them no more than one or two years, as most librarians are very busy. Offer to pay the costs, and enclose an *SASE*.

To obtain the addresses of libraries to which you can write, contact the reference librarian at your local library and ask the librarian to check the *American Library Directory*. Or go to www.americanlibrarydirectory.com and register for free. That will enable you to search for libraries, though on the free registration you will only be able to see the name and address. (Paid subscribers can access the complete listings of the libraries, which include a listing of the library's holdings.) In using their search feature, if you enter a city on the first line that shows "Library/Institution Name?", you will get only libraries starting with that name. If instead you choose to enter the city in the "City" field further down the search form, you will get all of the libraries in that city.

**Genie Jargon**

SASE (or S.A.S.E.) is a Self-Addressed Stamped Envelope. Due to the high cost of postage, many organizations (and individuals) will not answer inquiries if one is not provided.

Elizabeth Petty Bentley's *The Genealogist's Address Book*, or Juliana Szucs Smith's *The Ancestry Family Historian's Address Book: Revised Second Edition*, can assist with addresses, too, although the libraries listed in those sources are mainly those with genealogical holdings. Many small-town local libraries are not included in their books.

## Posting It

In determining ways in which you might find your lost relatives, consider the library bulletin board. The librarian may be willing to post a notice. Mention that your research is for genealogy and enclose a separate notice for posting. Keep it brief, but give enough details to identify the family you are seeking.

**Pedigree Pitfalls**

Never send a notice for posting on a library bulletin board with writing on both sides; it cannot be properly displayed. Be sure it includes your name and address and, if you have one, your e-mail address. (Your phone number is optional.)

Ask the librarian if the library maintains files of letters from people who have written the library for information, often referred to as "vertical files." A letter from your second cousin, also interested in genealogy, could be in that file waiting for you to find it!

## Sign In, Please

Visitor registers are popular in the genealogy section of the library. A bound volume (or loose leaf, or even 3" × 5" cards) is placed prominently for visitors to enter their names, addresses, and the surnames of their interest. The librarian may be willing to search it for the surnames of your interest. In some areas the genealogical society has even indexed such entries.

If you visit any facility with a guest register (courthouse, museum, library, historical attraction), take a few minutes to add your name. Your reward may be a letter or telephone call from a distant relative.

# The Hometown News

To locate living relatives, consider subscribing to the hometown paper. You will be amazed at the leads it can provide, particularly if it is a small community. Watch for family names in the social news, school news, church news, and even the advertisements. All will be of interest and might lead to contact with relatives. Be sure to note in which newspaper it was found, page number, and column. Try to get a microprint of the page while you are at it.

Don't overlook obituaries, particularly the part about "the survivors include …." It is common to include brothers, sisters, aunts, uncles, and children, and often their city of residence. This will help immensely.

Also try a "Letter to the Editor" of the hometown newspaper. This is especially successful in smaller communities. Make your letter brief but show clearly that it is a family local to their area and that your interest is genealogical.

*Sample of Letter to the Editor for inquiring to the newspaper about living relatives.*

---

Dear Editor,

My great-uncle John Jackson died 15 September 1925 in your town. At that time his obituary stated that he left two sons, Joseph and George, and a daughter Mary Jefferson. I am interested in contacting them as we are compiling our family genealogy. Can some of your readers put me in touch with them?

Thank you for your help.

Sincerely,

[Your name and address here.]

---

Don't overlook the use of the classified section. An advertisement under "Personals" may be seen by those who know your family. Give a few details so that the family can be quickly identified; ask to reach your relatives. Mention your interest in genealogy.

Take advantage of the online forums and message boards, too, especially those that are surname oriented. Post your query in a short but clear posting. Then wait and see what happens. Many have found "lost relatives" using this route. Don't be limited by surname forums—try also those that are locality oriented. If you know that the family lived in Monroe County, New York, then post to a forum for that New York area. It could yield excellent results for you.

Some of the better-known forums or message boards include www.genforum. genealogy.com and www.ancestry.com. There are others. See Chapter 5 for further discussion.

# After School: Alumni Records

Does someone remember that cousin Harry was a graduate of the state college? His brother attended Harvard? Check for a college alumni directory on your library's reference shelves or go the college's website for the school's address. Address your letter to the attention of the Alumni Director. The school may have alumni records with addresses. Harvard, for example, published in 1919 the *Harvard Alumni Directory—A Catalogue of Former Students Now Living: Including Graduates and Non-Graduates, and the Holders of Honorary Degrees.*

At the website www.distantcousin.com/Yearbooks, there is a search feature for many school yearbooks and directories, categorized by state. I quickly found in the Harvard directory more than one page of Walker alumni, living, in 1919, all over the U.S. and even in Canada. There is an amazing number of directories available on the Internet, for many such directories are out of copyright with no restrictions on posting to the Web. Also seek literature on school reunions. The newsletter after the event could include your relative's new location.

# The Genealogical Societies

When you have determined in which county your relatives lived, obtain the name of the county's genealogical society. There are a number of directories that could assist. *The Genealogical Helper* publishes annually a list of genealogical societies. Some societies are listed in Everton's *The Handy Book for Genealogists*; Ancestry's *Red Book*, or Ancestry's *The Source*; Elizabeth Petty Bentley's *The Genealogist's Address Book*; Juliana Szucs Smith's *The Ancestry Family Historians Address Book*; and a variety of other publications. Examine these for addresses of societies in other areas.

Alternately, use the Internet. Go to www.
cyndislist.com and scroll to "Societies &
Groups." Or make use of the USGenWeb
Project by going to www.usgenweb.com. This
amazing volunteer project strives to provide
websites for every county in the country. Each
website offers a diversity of information and
records, depending upon its *webmaster*. They
usually also list the libraries and genealogical
societies for their county.

Consider joining the genealogical society in
the county in which your relatives lived. As a
member of that society, you will have privileges.
You may find an interested volunteer who will
assist you. If the organization publishes a
newsletter, ask them to publish a notice in their
*query section*. One of your relatives may even be
a member of the society. Many such groups
solicit family charts from members. Request a
search of those charts for names of others
working on your family names.

**Genie Jargon**

A **webmaster** is the
main person in charge of the
website, and often is the one
who makes decisions on what is
posted to that site.

**Genie Jargon**

A **query section** in a
genealogical publication refers to
a specific section of the magazine set aside for submitted
inquiries. Almost all periodicals
have such sections, as do some
newspapers that carry genealogy
columns. They may limit the
length or have other restrictions.

# Periodicals Galore

Thousands of genealogical periodicals are published each year in the United States.
In addition to placing queries in those in the county you are researching, place them
in others that are published statewide or nationwide. Inquire about cost and whether
they require membership or subscription to use that service. Make some choices
depending upon your budget. Mention enough about the family in your query so that
readers can identify it.

---

Seeking descendants of John Masters

b. 15 April 1858 in Monroe Co., NY, m. there in 1888 to Mary
Adams. They moved about 1910 to Perry County, IL and had 3
ch., John b. 1912, Joseph b. 1915, and Agatha b. 1918 (who m.
John Davis). Wish to contact descendants.

---

*Sample of query to submit
for publication in genealogical periodicals.*

**Genie Jargon**

"b." is used for born, "m." for married, and "ch." for children. These are standard abbreviations used in queries to reduce space.

A number of national journals are connected to a society and are part of the society's membership benefits. You can subscribe to most whether or not you are a member. The New England Historical and Genealogical Society's *Register (NEHGR)*, The National Genealogical Society's *Quarterly (NGSQ)*, The New York Genealogical and Biographical Society's *Record* (NYGBR), The *Mayflower Quarterly*, and others are worth reading. Some national periodicals are subscription only, that is, not associated with a society. Three that have query sections are *Everton's Genealogical Helper*, *Reunions Magazine*, and *Heritage Quest*. Some subscription journals focus on articles but do accept a limited number of queries from members. *The American Genealogist* (known as *TAG*) is among them.

# Families That Stay Together

A valuable resource in your effort to locate relatives is a family association dedicated to the particular family name you're researching. These operate under a variety of names—society, clearinghouse, or others. Their purpose is to collect information on the family, share it, and preserve it. They may publish a newsletter, maintain a database for researchers, or offer search services. They are eager to hear from descendants. They may be able to supply the addresses of others in your family. If they publish a magazine, they can insert a query for you.

There are thousands of family associations, but many are short-lived. Others are so ill-manned that they often do not reply. Do not let the lack of a reply from one group influence your decision to contact another. Many hundreds maintain extensive archives and are eager to hear from you. Their records are valuable and sometimes are the only source for a particular photograph, a family Bible, or an old letter.

## Locating a Family Association

Although there are some directories listing groups, none are complete. *Everton's Genealogical Helper* for many years has published an annual listing. Also try www. cyndislist.com and go to "Surnames, Family Associations, & Family Newsletters." Or, simply insert the family name followed by "Family Association" in your Internet browser, for example, "Rose Family Association." That may turn up listings, but could miss some that don't have "Family Association" as part of their name. Try also a search using the surname plus "Newsletter" or "Society" or "Clearing House."

Elizabeth Petty Bentley compiled a useful *Directory of Family Associations* that is updated periodically. The disadvantage in using Bentley's *Directory* is that it includes many organizations no longer in existence, and in many instances, includes individuals who collect a name but who are not family associations. Despite these drawbacks, it can be helpful.

**Tree Tips** _____

If you have difficulty locating an association, insert a query in a national periodical inquiring whether an association for that surname exists. Or, go to a service such as www.genforum. genealogy.com, and then proceed to the message board or mailing list for the surname. Post a query asking if anyone knows of a family association for that name.

## A Rose Is a Rose Is a Rose

When using the resources of a family association, it is important to understand its focus. They differ considerably. They may include descendants of an ancestor who is not the immigrant, descendants of the immigrant, or descendants of the surname.

**Tree Tips** _____

Although most family associations do not require you to join for them to be of assistance, ask for a copy of their membership brochure. You may find it beneficial, depending upon their goals and services, to be a member of the group.

Those focused on the descendants of an ancestor who is not the immigrant, for example, may include all the descendants of the great-grandfather and his wife who settled in Des Moines, Iowa. In this case the association is probably named after that couple. Groups devoted to descendants of an immigrant usually carry the surname in their title and include all the male and female descendants of that immigrant. In the third type, the surname organization, anyone bearing the surname is traced. They may have no relationship to each other. Members do not have to bear the surname, but each trace someone carrying that surname.

Even surname organizations have differences. One may search all of the surnames in the United States, regardless of nationality. Another may focus on an ethnic group, such as those only of Scottish ancestry or only those of German ancestry.

Upon ascertaining the existence of a family organization, write or e-mail to them. Be specific in your request. Identify the family briefly (names, dates, locations, spouses, children), and ask if they can put you in contact with members of that family. Inquire also about publishing queries in their magazine or on their website.

# We'll Meet on the Fourth Sunday ...

Thousands of families hold family reunions each year, ranging from a picnic in the park to a major gathering in a large hotel. Watch for announcements in genealogical publications. No magazine includes all the reunions, only those for which they have received an announcement. Try to attend if possible. The contacts you make will surely evolve into wonderful friendships, and you will hear many stories you have yearned to know. The reunion might be small, organized by a local branch, or nationwide, involving hundreds of descendants. Some even plan overseas trips to the ancestral home.

# Using Social Security to Find Your Kin

In 1935 the Social Security Act was enacted. It generated an enormous amount of paper records, some of which can be used to locate your relatives.

## The Death Index

One especially useful resource is the Social Security Death Index (SSDI), previously available on CD-ROM and now available online at www.ancestry.com, at www. distantcousin.com, and other sites. It does have limitations. The database does not include all those who died with a Social Security number, only those whose deaths were reported to the Social Security Administration. Usually this occurred when the family applied for a benefit at the death of its relative. If the death was not reported to the Social Security Administration, the individual is not listed in this database.

The information contained usually includes the following:

◆ Social Security number

◆ Name (last and first)

◆ Birth date

◆ Death date

◆ Issuing location of the original card (by code)

◆ Zip code of last-known residence

◆ Zip code of recipient if a lump sum payment was made

**Pedigree Pitfalls**

Although some of the CD-ROMs and online databases are titled "Social Security Death Index," the database includes deaths that were *reported*, and therefore, are not complete. The database was started in the early 1960s.

Locating an entry on the Social Security Death Index can help find living relatives. For example, follow up on the date of death provided by obtaining the death certificate itself. The death certificate can lead you to living relatives by providing the place of death and the name of the informant who may be related. Then check a phone or online directory (see earlier in this chapter).

Whether you find a deceased person's Social Security number on the SSDI or some other way, perhaps on a death certificate, you can get a microprint of his or her Social Security application, the SS-5 form. The microprint will supply the birth date and place of the applicant and name of parents. This doesn't help in finding living relatives, because only applications of deceased persons can be obtained. It can, however, be tremendously helpful in tracing the family to earlier times.

If you found the listing on the SSDI, then you need only to send the current fee (available on the Social Security Administration's website) and the Social Security number of the deceased. Go to http://ssa-custhelp.ssa.gov and then go to "Ask a Question." Fill out the form and after you "submit," the answer will probably be immediately displayed online. For a small additional fee, you don't even need to supply the Social Security number to get the SS-5. If you found the Social Security number in some way other than on the SSDI and you can't find the name included in SSDI, then you will be required to submit proof of death. Requests for SS-5 should be mailed to this address: Social Security Administration, Office of Earnings Operations, Freedom of Information Officer, 300 N. Greene St., P.O. Box 33022, Baltimore, MD 21290.

# The Internet: Finding Cousin John

There is an explosion of activity on the Internet that can help the genealogist. Many forums are available in which users can post a notice of interest in certain families. Others can respond. If you are on the Internet, use these message boards to seek relatives. Some report astounding results, locating lost branches of their family whom they had never expected to find. Try www.rootsweb.com or www.genforum. genealogy.com. Each has an alphabetical index to the surname boards.

As always, be specific when posting. Asking to locate the relatives of "The Taylor family who lived in central Ohio" or posting the subject line as "Help" is too vague. It will be ignored or bring overwhelming responses asking for clarification. Inquire instead with precise details. Insert some idea of time frame and location. For example, if you post a notice with the subject stated as "George Taylor (1748–1810) Fauquier Co., Va.; Jefferson Co., Tenn." everyone immediately knows which Taylor you are tracing.

Use of extensive abbreviations in posting notices on the Internet is acceptable, but be sure you don't sacrifice readability. You want everyone to understand.

**Tree Tips**

For tips on preparing queries, go to www.cyndislist.com/queries.htm. Then go to "How to." Several articles there will assist. A well-constructed query can dramatically increase results.

# Not the End of the Tale

As your search progresses, you will constantly discover new ways to locate living relatives. A letter written by a descendant may be part of the military pension file in the National Archives and provide you with a location of family members. The state may maintain a statewide property index and allow it to be searched, sometimes even online. The voter registers may be open to the public. The possibilities are endless. You will be thrilled when your scouting turns up your people. Every success will energize you and fill you with the satisfaction of following clues. You're now on your way to the same addiction afflicting the rest of us!

## The Least You Need to Know

- Your library and the Internet have telephone directories, city directories, and other items to help search for your living relatives.

- Your ancestor's or relative's hometown newspaper can assist in the search.

- Use the genealogical societies and family associations, which can help locate living relatives.

- Send queries to genealogical publications and online message boards and mailing lists.

- The voluminous Social Security records are a wonderful tool for research.

# Chapter 7

# A Rose by Any Other Name ...

## In This Chapter

♦ Surnames change through time

♦ Changes—deliberate and accidental

♦ Spelling variants

♦ Handwriting complications

♦ Naming patterns

Surnames evolved to help distinguish one person from another. They were descriptive of relationships such as Thomasson (Thomas's son); of physical characteristics such as Petit (small) and Schoen (beautiful); of place names (Hill, Lea, Meadow); or of occupations (Carpenter, Hunter, Miller). Many of us are known by surnames that would surprise our immigrant ancestors. Surnames are not static through time, nor are they necessarily the same for an individual throughout a lifetime.

The spelling of names is phonetic, and the way the letters were arranged depended on the person writing the name. Most of us descend from people who were illiterate. Our ancestors couldn't write and didn't know how their names were spelled. They only knew how to pronounce their names as spoken by their families and neighbors.

# Variations Aplenty

Outside influences, unusual events, naming patterns, spelling variations, and misinterpretations by transcribers determined the surnames of our ancestors. Before searching for documents, consider that your ancestors' names may be different from what you were led to believe. The same surnames may be spelled so many different ways as to be unrecognizable by someone trying to trace the line. For example, in the following figure, each of these surnames was used by at least 100 people at the time of the census.

> **Tree Tips**
>
> Sometimes looking at other documents or entries written in the same hand makes the letters easier to read. Comparing the names in the county as written by two different people, let's say the county clerk and the tax assessor, may clear up problems.

Ministers, recording clerks, ship captains, and census takers wrote what they thought they heard. And what they heard was based on their knowledge and background. Language and spelling were not standardized even among the educated. Many times a name was spelled several different ways in the same document.

*Examples of name variations found in the first United States federal census, 1790.*

*Taken from A Century of Population Growth.*

> Fitzgerald, Fichgerrel, Fitchgearald, Fitchgerrel, Fitsgarrel, Fitsgerald, Fitsgerel, Fitsgorrel, Fitsjarald, Fitsjerald, Fitts Gerald, Fitzarrell, Fitzgarald, Fitzgarrold, Fitzgearld, Fitzgeral, Fitz Gerald, Fitzgerrald, Fitz Gerrald, Fitzgerrel, Fitzgerrold, Fitzjairald, Fitzjarald, Fitzjerald
>
> Rawlings, Raling, Rallins, Raulens, Raulings, Rawlins, Rollens, Rollin, Rolling, Rollings, Rollins
>
> Sinclair, Saintclair, St. Clair, St. Clear, St. Clere, Senkler, Sinekler, Sinclar, Sinclare, Sinclares, Sinclear, Sincleer, Sincler, Sinclere, Sinclier, Singclair, Sinklar, Sinklear, Sinkler

# Handwriting Further Obscures the Names

Letter formation often leads to difficulties in reading and interpreting surnames. Flourishes and curlicues can render letters nearly indecipherable. The letters I and J sometimes look very similar. A poorly written G can resemble an S. The letters R and K are often written similarly, and a capital B that is not closed at the bottom can be mistaken for an R. Other letters can be confused: M and N; N and H; V and U.

Indexers had difficulty interpreting the letters, too, so the name you are looking for may be alphabetized under the wrong letter. If you don't find Seemon in the "S" section, look under "L."

# Immigrating Changed Lives and Sometimes Names

Immigrants changed their names by accident or by design. Other languages had letter combinations not found in English, or letters pronounced as other letters in the English language. *F* sounded like *V*, so Freer was written Veer. *W* sounded like *V*, so Werner was listed as Verner. A guttural pronunciation made *G* sound like *K*. Letters were slurred, an *H* dropped. *Sch* sounded like *Sh*, so the *c* disappeared.

You can get some idea of how names changed and how a name change might affect the immigrant by reading letters culled from records of the Immigration and Naturalization Service at http://uscis.gov/graphics/aboutus/history/articles/names.htm. They describe situations in which the immigrant's name or that of his sons doesn't match the name on his naturalization papers, so they are not able to vote. In another, the immigrant dropped part of his name at naturalization, and then moved to another city and wanted to reinstate the suffix. These kinds of situations explain why we may have trouble finding our immigrant ancestors.

## The Wish to "Sound American"

Occasionally, the immigrant shortened or changed his name, but more often, the children of these immigrants Anglicized their names to better assimilate: Petrasovich became Preston; Noblinski became Noble; Savitch became Savage; Madsen became Madison.

Sometimes finding their names "different," immigrants chose to translate their names to the English equivalents. Blau and Bleu became Blue; Weiss, Blanc, and Bianco all became White. Occupational names were changed with Schmidts becoming Smiths and Kÿfers becoming Coopers.

If you are unfamiliar with the language of the immigrant, look for a dictionary that has both the foreign language and English. Perhaps the foreign language equivalent for the surname will be the one you need to further your research. Knowing that "Weaver" translates to "Weber" in German may be just the clue you need to find an earlier generation.

A wish to disassociate from "foreigners" made some families make the change. In Pennsylvania, Frank Nicotera felt the pressure of his Italian name. When he married a Collins, he registered at the union hall as Frank Collins. When his little brother was ready to go to work, Frank took him to the union hall where everyone assumed he was Nick Collins, not Angelo Nicotera. The family today goes by the name Collins. The grandchildren are unaware that the family's surname was Nicotera only three generations ago.

The following sample Declaration of Intention is an example of the name changes that often happened. The subject was born 20 October 1892 in Casal Velino, province of Salerno, Italy, according to his birth certificate, which names him as Florigio Cicerelli. He first immigrated (under that spelling) in 1910 with his father Saverio on the *U.S.S. Berlin*, arriving in New York City with a destination of San Jose, California. Returning to Italy, he was married under that spelling in 1922 to Carmela Spagnuola. When Florigio returned in 1930 from his fourth and final trip to Italy, the Arrival Certificate in New York shows him as Cicierelli. Three years later, when he filed to become a citizen, his name is shown as Ciciarelli. In the meantime, he also had adopted the more American sounding "Frank," and was known throughout the rest of his life as Frank Ciciarelli. His children's names bore that spelling, too. Similar changes occurred in thousands of families.

Families make unpredictable decisions that cause research problems for genealogists. Letters are added or dropped. Perhaps the name had a prefix that was later dropped: St. Martin became Martin; Van Hoorn became Horn. A generation later, someone chose to reinstate the suffix. One branch of the family may decide the name would be more aristocratic with a slight change. Even simple names are changed. Names abound where an "e" is added or removed: Brown/Browne, Green/Greene, Germaine/Germain, Low/Lowe.

---

### Lineage Lessons

There are families in which brothers have different surnames though they have the same father. One has decided to keep the old spelling, whereas the others have adopted a new spelling.

This can lead to two branches of the same family having very different surnames. In another case, a divorce in New York City in the 1820s resulted in the wife resuming her maiden name and her younger children taking that name, whereas the adult children retained the father's name.

TRIPLICATE
To be given to
declarant)

No. 5135

# UNITED STATES OF AMERICA

## DECLARATION OF INTENTION

(Invalid for all purposes seven years after the date hereof)

State of California

County of Santa Clara

ss:

In the ........ Superior ........ Court

of ... California ... at San Jose, Calif.

I, Florigio Ciciarelli

now residing at Route 2, Box 5, Los Gatos, Santa Clara, California

occupation Barber, aged 40 years, do declare on oath that my personal description is:

Sex Male, color White, complexion Medium, color of eyes Blue, color of hair Brown, height 5 feet 8 inches; weight 165 pounds; visible distinctive marks None

race Italian, North; nationality Italian

I was born in Casal Velino, Italy, on October 22, 1892

I am married. The name of my wife or husband is Carmela Ciciarelli

we were married on Oct. 2, 1923, at Casal Velino, Italy; she or he was born at Casal Velino, Italy, on July 17, 1900, entered the United States at New York, N. Y., on Jan. 16, 1950, for permanent residence therein, and now resides at Los Gatos, California. I have two children, and the name, date and place of birth, and place of residence of each of said children are as follows: Ranato, born Dec. 7, 1929, at Naples, Italy; and Angela, born Apr. 27, 1932, at Los Gatos, Calif.; both residing at Los Gatos, California.

I have heretofore made a declaration of intention: Number .... on Aug. 3, 1923 at San Francisco, California, in the U. S. District Court.

My last foreign residence was Casal Velino, Italy. I emigrated to the United States of America from Naples, Italy. My lawful entry for permanent residence in the United States was at New York, N. Y., under the name of Florigio Ciciarelli, on August 23, 1910 on the vessel Berlin

(If other than by vessel, state manner of arrival.)

I will, before being admitted to citizenship, renounce forever all allegiance and fidelity to any foreign prince, potentate, state, or sovereignty, and particularly, by name, to the prince, potentate, state, or sovereignty of which I may be at the time of admission a citizen or subject; I am not an anarchist; I am not a polygamist nor a believer in the practice of polygamy; and it is my intention in good faith to become a citizen of the United States of America and to reside permanently therein; and I certify that the photograph affixed to the duplicate and triplicate hereof is a likeness of me: So HELP ME GOD.

*Florigio Ciciarelli*

(Original signature of declarant without abbreviation, also alias, if used)

Subscribed and sworn to before me in the office of the Clerk of said Court, at San Jose, Calif. this 7th day of August anno Domini 33. Certification No. 22-12153 from the Commissioner of Naturalization showing the lawful entry of the declarant for permanent residence on the date stated above, has been received by me. The photograph affixed to the duplicate and triplicate hereof is a likeness of the declarant.

Henry A. Pfister

[SEAL]

Clerk of the Superior Court.

By ................................., Deputy Clerk.

Form 2202-L-A
U. S. DEPARTMENT OF LABOR
NATURALIZATION SERVICE

*A Declaration of Intention form filed in 1933.*

# Talking to Yourself

You may need to be creative to find other spellings of the surnames you are tracing. Think of the many ways a name could be pronounced and then think of the spellings. Say the surnames out loud and spell them phonetically. Look for records under any of those spellings. Could Stone be spelled Stoan? Charette could mutate to Shorett, Cayeaux to Coyer. To help you think of the spelling variants, examine the compilation of names from the 1790 census mentioned above. As you speak the names, you may get new ideas on how to spell the surnames you are researching.

**Tree Tips**

Ask your friends and associates how they would spell the surname you are tracing, based on its pronunciation. Ask children, who are much more phonetic and unbiased than adults. You may come up with some new ideas on variant spellings.

**Pedigree Pitfalls**

Never assume that the surname you are researching has stayed the same through the generations or even through a lifetime. How many times have you had to correct the spelling of your own name? Perhaps some of the misspellings will survive to someday confuse your descendants.

Names were often corrupted as immigrants interacted with their neighbors. Perhaps the individual giving information to the census taker was not your ancestor, but a neighbor who happened to be home when your ancestor wasn't. The census taker took the information the neighbor gave rather than revisiting your ancestor. And so Mr. Justice became Mr. Justis or Jean Christien became John Christian.

According to the 1850 census, Diana Drollinger's grandfather was born in North Carolina about 1800. A search of the North Carolina census and other records turned up no Drollinger/Drolinger/Drullinger families. Although census information is sometimes incorrect, other sources also suggested a North Carolina birthplace. The key to the puzzle was in the microfilmed pension records at the National Archives. Henry Drollinger states in his pension deposition that his name was Drollinger, pronounced Trollinger in the German style. A check of North Carolina records for Trollingers uncovered numerous families, and, eventually, Diana's great-grandparents.

# Different Record, Different Spelling

The name might undergo several transformations before it takes the familiar form you know. When the immigrant Weir/Weer accumulated enough money to buy a house, he recorded the deed in the county clerk's office where he became Wiere. Weir/Weer/Wiere moved west, bought some land, and this time the clerk wrote

Wear. Meanwhile, his account at the general store was under the name Ware, and that's the name the children learned to write when taught by the 18-year-old school-marm. So your grandfather is George Ware, but his grandfather was Samuel Weir.

# Naming Patterns

*Patronymics* were widely used in forming surnames. This was used to sort out the individuals in a community, such as Richard's son or Thomas's son.

Patronymics were particularly prevalent in the Scandinavian countries. At first it seems confusing to know that Mr. Jensen's sons all have the surname Ericssen. But as soon as you know that the surname is formed by adding *sen/son* to the first name, you can see how Eric Jensen's sons came to have the surname Ericssen. Daughters would have *datter* added to the father's first name, thus Eric Jensen's daughters would use Ericsdatter as their surname.

**Genie Jargon** _____

**Patronymics** are names derived from a father's name or paternal side of the family. For example, if your father was named "Tom," your surname might end up "Tom's Son" or "Tomson," which in turn might turn into "Thompson."

Other countries used the son suffix also, such as Williamson, Jameson, (also expressed as just Williams or James), but did not change the surname with every generation.

Other prefixes and suffixes were used to denote sons or daughters, among them, *O*, *Ab* or *Ap*; *Mac* or *Mc*; *Fitz*, *ich* or *itch*; *ev*, or *off*. The resulting names were sometimes altered with O'Brien becoming Obrien or Bryan, Ab Owen abridged to Bowen.

Several links to information on patronymics and other subjects regarding names can be found on Cyndi's List (www.cyndislist.com/names.htm).

# Religious Naming Customs

In some religions, it is customary to name children for dead relatives in a specific order. In other religions, it is the custom to name the first boy for the maternal grand-father and the first girl for the paternal grandmother. In others, it is the custom to name the first boy after his paternal grandfather and the first girl after her maternal grandmother.

**Tree Tips** _____

When working on a family you know to be a specific religion or nationality, learn the naming patterns common to that group.

# Individual Naming Patterns

Some families devise a naming pattern of their own that persists for several generations. The first male in every family is named Henry, perhaps, or James. Each generation perpetuates the tradition. When there are three or four first cousins all named William Smith, it can be difficult to sort them out, especially if all remain in the area throughout their lives. It may also be the family custom to name a child the same name as an older sibling who died in infancy.

### Pedigree Pitfalls

Never assume that you have the correct person if there are two or more individuals in the same area with the same name. It is necessary to gather the facts for each event they are connected to and make comparisons.

### Pedigree Pitfalls

Don't assume that a child's surname-sounding middle name is a surname in your direct line. I once found a child whose name was Diana Courll Drollinger. Courll was not Diana's mother's maiden name, as originally thought. Instead, she was named for her married aunt: Diana Drollinger Courll.

# Mother's Name Preserved

A mother's maiden name is frequently used as a middle name for either boys or girls. Other family surnames are used as well. Clark Stone Phillip's middle name is his paternal grandmother's maiden name. Mary Catherine Smith may be shown as Mary C. Smith in a record, but when she married John Jordan, she may be shown as Mary Smith Jordan, or Mary S. Jordan.

If your ancestors were creative, you may have to be creative. Strange things happen in genealogy. For instance, a contemporary family has two girls and two boys. The boys carry their mother's maiden name as their surname because the mother is from a family with no boys and she wants the name to be carried on. The girls have their father's surname.

# Given Names Giving Us Trouble

It is not only surname variations that befuddle us, but first names also. Is Katharine Shimmin the same person as Catherine Shimmin? This name could also be spelled Kathryn. First names could also be Anglicized. Katharine may have been Katrina, Katja, Catherina, Katrintje, or Tryntje.

## Five Children, Same First Name!

German children often had two given names, but were called by the second. Frequently, all the boys in the family had the same first name, or a variation of the same name, such as Johann/Hans, but were called by their second names. And the girls in the family might all have had the first name Anna or Maria. The children may have been referred to with both names or just the second. Different documents may use different names for the same child. You will wonder if you are dealing with one person or three, as you sort out Maria Elizabeth, Maria Christena, and Maria Caterina. This can be further confused by an adult returning to his or her first given name after being known by a second name as a child.

Today parents-to-be thumb through books of names looking for ideas for the baby's name. Although there have always been trends in first names, your ancestors didn't rely on book lists. They thumbed through the Bible, or they named their children for friends and relatives or famous people. Hundreds of boys went through life carrying the first and middle name of George Washington or Benjamin Franklin.

The romance of the west inspired one set of parents in the naming of their children. Their little girl Sierra Nevada is enumerated as Nevada one time, Sierra another, and on her marriage license she is Vada. As far as can be determined, her parents were never west of Indiana.

## He Was Called Billy; She Was Called Abby

Nicknames can throw you off the trail. If you always knew your great-aunt as Polly, you may be surprised to find that her name was really Mary. The Sally in a will may be the Sarah on a deed. William could be Bill, Billy, Will, or Willie. Bert can be a shortened form of Albert, Gilbert, Robert, and others.

Finding the name that the nickname stood for is not always obvious. This is especially true when the nickname is encompassed within a name, such as Gus for Augustus, Gum for Montgomery, or Fate for Lafayette. You may need to do some reading to know what names to look for. A particularly extensive resource is Christine Rose's *Nicknames: Past and Present.* The Connecticut State Library has culled some nicknames from their eighteenth- and nineteenth-century documents and put them online at www.cslib.org/nickname.htm.

## Double Trouble

It has been said that everyone has a double, someone else in the world who looks just like him or her. The same thing is true of names. In San Jose, California, a man who had voted regularly for years was cut from the rolls. John P. Taylor called the Registrar of Voters and found that he had been cut because he was listed at two different addresses. The computer matched the John P. Taylors' months, days, and years of birth, found them to be the same, and deleted one from the rolls. But there were actually two different John P. Taylors with the exact same birth date; one was John Paul and one was John Phillip, but they had both registered as John P.

Almost no one has a unique name. Names that are no longer common seem exotic to us, and we think the individuals will be simple to isolate. You may think that Tryphena Atherton should be easy to identify because, to you, the name is unusual. Early Vermont records have several Tryphena Athertons. You may think that the common name of Davis pared with Caleb is unique. In that case, you would be surprised to learn that there are at least four Caleb Davises on the 1840 census in New York.

Your ancestors went by many names, just as we do today. Some have different names at different stages of their lives. Some women change their names when they marry; some do not. Siblings may spell their surnames differently. In some families, one woman may hyphenate her maiden and married names, whereas others may not.

# Which Do You Pick?

When you begin to do genealogy research, you have the option of tracing any one of numerous surnames. How do you choose the one you want to work on? For many, this is a personal decision; for others, it is a matter of practicality. I began working on my maiden name because my father would never talk about his family, and I was very curious as to who they were. As I began to gather information from many family sources, I became interested in other lines because I had more information and a better chance of success.

Some may choose a surname to follow because of a family tradition connected with it: "Our family is related to Kit Carson." "Our family is connected to President McKinley." Maybe you have a desire to prove you are a Mayflower descendant, or the descendant of a Revolutionary War patriot. Maybe you seek admission to the Sons of the Republic of Texas. Perhaps you are eager to prove that you are a descendant of a Native American, a French trapper, or are eligible for a pioneer descendant certificate offered by many states.

Whatever surname you decide to pursue, one of the first things to do is to consider the different ways the name could be spelled.

## The Least You Need to Know

- Names could be spelled in a variety of ways.
- Ancestors may have translated their foreign name, or shortened it.
- Different branches could be using different variations of a surname.
- Customs among ethnic and religious groups can affect naming of the children.

# Chapter 8

# Getting the Most from Libraries

## In This Chapter

◆ Finding the genealogical collections

◆ Using the catalogs and indexes

◆ Finding family histories

◆ The different types of libraries

The previous chapter acquainted you with the diversity of written names. Now you're ready to tackle research in the array of books, websites, and special collections that can be accessed through libraries.

Libraries differ. So do their holdings. The small-town library has a limited budget to purchase books for special interests. However, if the local genealogy society is enthusiastic, their contributions, cake bakes, and book sales provide needed funds so that even small libraries usually have a few books on the subject. Check also the surrounding area. You may discover collections in nearby towns or cities, or even a regional repository in an adjoining county.

# The Bigger the Better

All states have a major repository. It may be a state library, a state genealogical society library, a state archives with a library, or a state historical society library. Some lucky states have all four. Each has its own strength, perhaps extensive newspapers or manuscripts or an extraordinary number of family histories. Become familiar with all the collections in the geographic area of your search. Larger facilities should have an inventory or guidebook, or at least a leaflet describing important aspects of their holdings. Though the state repositories have larger collections, the smaller local and regional libraries can hold magnificent treasures.

Make use of the Internet. Most libraries have websites. Some include digitized images, as well as indexes, historical background, and other worthy enhancements to your family's history.

**Genie Jargon**

An **online catalog** refers to a database that can be accessed by computer.

A **consolidated index** combines data from more than one source. For example, the indexes to five county histories might be consolidated into one.

## Making Your Way Around

You may be familiar with the standard card catalog with entries by subject, title, and author. But look also for catalogs of newspapers, schools, photographs, manuscripts, and other specialties. Many libraries have *online catalogs*.

While at the library also inquire about special collections. Volunteers may have indexed all the obituaries before 1920 or transcribed tombstones from three cemeteries. Other projects might include a *consolidated index* to names in the county histories.

# Winding Your Way with Books

One fundamental book to seek out is Val Greenwood's *The Researcher's Guide to American Genealogy*. It devotes chapters to sundry categories of records.

Another is Loretto Dennis Szucs and Sandra Hargreaves Luebking's *The Source, A Guidebook of American Genealogy*, which covers record types in detail. Turn to this massive book again and again as questions arise and as you need more help. And don't overlook the excellent *Red Book* edited by Alice Eichholz, Ph.D. Each state rates a chapter incorporating history and a useful discussion of types and locations of records, as well as courthouse addresses and data on the county's formation.

## Your Family on Its Pages

I was astounded the first time I saw a family history book among our family's books. I was so excited. Here was a book of genealogy all specifically devoted to our family! My surprise turned into amazement when I visited my first genealogical library and saw that there were hundreds, no, thousands, of similar books. These histories are usually devoted to one specific family or a combination of three to four families.

**Tree Tips**

Seasoned genealogists return often to in-depth guidebooks. These books are not meant to be read straight through, but rather, to be read in doses as you encounter new situations or unfamiliar records.

Because no collection is complete, check a number of repositories for a family history on your family. Enlist your reference librarian's assistance. Or from your computer, go to the websites of major genealogical libraries and look for family history books by entering the surname in their website search engine.

## Catalogs to Help

Many major libraries (Newberry in Chicago, New York Public Library, and others) have published catalogs. An example is the *Genealogies Catalogued by the Library of Congress Since 1986*, over 1,300 pages, listing many hundreds of books. None of the catalogs contain every genealogy book published, only what is in their collection. And they don't include the many books published since the publication date of their catalogs.

**Lineage Lessons**

When you find a family history on the surname you are searching, whether in book form or on the Internet, don't assume that everything in it is correct. Being in print doesn't make it true. If there are no citations included upon which you can judge the reliability, you'll have to do some independent research to establish that the facts are indeed correct.

# Magazines and Journals: Not at the Corner Newsstand

Family histories are not confined to books. Many periodicals and journals, particularly those national in scope, publish compiled genealogy articles. In some cases these are extensive and might be serialized in several issues. Others may be limited, perhaps covering just the immigrant and one or two generations. Significant finds (proving the English ancestry of a Mayflower passenger, or the maiden name of the immigrant's wife) appear often on their pages. Libraries frequently have a special spot for "newly arrived periodicals" in the genealogy section. Spend some time examining these to become familiar with what is available. Consider subscribing to those of most interest. In some instances you will obtain the magazine automatically by joining the associated organization.

## Crammed with Articles

How to find published articles that might lead to information on your family? Consult *PERSI* and *GPAI*.

*PERSI* is the <u>PER</u>iodical <u>S</u>ource <u>I</u>ndex published by the Allen County Public Library in Fort Wayne, Indiana. Their massive indexing project covers hundreds of periodicals in their library. Retrospective indexes in a number of volumes cover periodicals published from 1847 through 1985. Articles are indexed by subjects, locations, and surnames. Every year since 1986 *PERSI* has published an annual supplement, indexing periodicals published during that year. Look for PERSI in book form or CD-ROM at your library, or access it online as a subscriber of Ancestry.com. You can also access it at many libraries by going to www.HeritageQuestOnline.com.

After you have located an article you want to read, if you can't find that specific periodical at your own library, you can order a photocopy of the article for a small fee from the Allen County Public Library. Their library has a copy of every magazine they've indexed in PERSI because that index is built on Allen County Public Library's own collection. A handy form for ordering copies of the article is available at www.acpl.lib.in.us/genealogy/persi.html. There you will find a paragraph regarding the fee structure; click on the link provided there to order copies.

> **Lineage Lessons**
>
> In addition to the comprehensive periodical indexes, there are numerous consolidated indexes to specific periodicals, such as *The Virginia Genealogist* and *New England Historical and Genealogical Register*. Many periodicals are digitized on CD-ROM with a searchable feature that will take you right to the page.

Though no longer published, *Genealogical Periodical Annual Index* or *GPAI*, 1962 to 2002, is still valuable for locating articles published prior to their cessation. *GPAI* indexed genealogies, lineages, Bible records, source records, and book reviews that appeared in various periodicals. Use both PERSI and GPAI to get broad coverage.

# Not Always Bound

Libraries hold a variety of *original material*, some of it unbound. In a visit to The State Historical Society of Wisconsin, I located a Bible record from an early family of New England. The original pages, torn and deposited in the society's collection, were probably from a Bible that made its way west in one of the many migrations. It listed the father born in 1782, and the mother born in 1779. Included were their full birth dates, their marriage date, the wife's maiden name, their children, and much more. Letters written by early pioneers have made their way into similar collections. The business papers of a local merchant, a thesis for a college degree, original sheet music composed by an ancestor, a genealogy chart sent from the old country—any of these and more can be found.

**Genie Jargon**

When referring to manuscripts, **original material** can be loose papers, letters, photographs, diaries, and other items. It may be maintained in a separate manuscript section of the library with its own catalog.

# The Wonderful World of Reference

Don't stop at the library's genealogy room—keep walking, right into the reference section. Nationwide directories of funeral directors, of newspapers (with addresses, date formed, and other important details), of schools, and sundry others await your discovery. You'll need these as you write letters and check what's online. The reference section also holds the multivolume biographical dictionaries such as *Dictionary of American Biography* (New York: Charles Scribner's Sons, 1937, 20 volumes). These and other similar publications have marvelous biographies and pen sketches, and often signatures as well. Don't believe every word in them, but use them to guide you to supporting records.

In the following figure, this pen sketch and signature from *Lamb's Biographical Dictionary of the United States* (Boston: James H. Lamb Co., 1900) illustrate the marvelous reproductions you can sometimes obtain from biographical dictionaries. Their biographies often include details that help in tracking the families.

*Pen sketches and signatures adorn the pages of the biographical dictionaries, gazetteers, and atlases.*

# Webster Was Never Like This

In the library's reference section are numerous dictionaries besides the standard Webster's. Consider the multivolume *Oxford English Dictionary* when faced with archaic terms. This explains many words and phrases no longer in use that you may encounter, including tools, implements, diseases, and others. You'll find an array of other specialized dictionaries on a wide range of topics. Or go online and enter a term such as "archaic dictionary" in your Internet browser or favorite search engines for other choices. A few of the many specialized online dictionaries and lists are found at cyndislist.com and by scrolling to the subheading of "Dictionary & Glossaries." Here are some examples:

- Genealogy dictionary at http://home.att.net/~dottsr/diction.html

- Genealogy terms at http://homepages.rootsweb.com/~sam/terms.html

- Glossary of legal terms at www.mylawyer.com/glossary.htm

- Quaker abbreviations from meeting records at www.onealwebsite.com/oneall/quaker1.htm

- Abbreviations found in genealogy at www.rootsweb.com/~rigenweb/abbrev.html

# A Library Is a Library Is a Library

Wrong! The types of libraries vary considerably. Among those you will use are the following:

- Public and private libraries
- Genealogical and historical society libraries
- Lending libraries
- University and college libraries
- Ethnic and religious libraries
- Lineage society libraries

## Public and Private Libraries

Public libraries can be very small on the local level or very large on the state level. Most public libraries have materials that can be loaned out, though that service may be restricted to residents. Usually reference books, which may include genealogical material (or fragile or irreplaceable books), are not allowed out of the library. In private libraries some collections are severely restricted in use. In those, manuscripts can usually only be accessed by certain individuals, though their librarians may assist by mail. However, many private libraries do make their collections personally accessible to the general public.

## Genealogical and Historical Society Libraries

The genealogical or historical society library may be public, or it may be the private collection of a particular group. If it is the latter, restrictions may apply and a small fee charged for its use. In some cases, members have *open stack* privileges, whereas nonmembers do not. If it is closed stack, the books must be requested and then retrieved by the staff. There can be a delay (usually 15 minutes to an hour) before the book is delivered. Most libraries that are considered closed stack do have some of their more commonly requested books available on shelves.

**Genie Jargon**

**Open stack** refers to the use of the books. If the library has open stacks, patrons may freely examine books on the shelves.

## Lending Libraries

Genealogy libraries usually do not allow patrons to borrow the books, but there are exceptions. California's Sutro Library in San Francisco, for example, will allow some books out on *interlibrary loan*. Go to www.library.ca.gov and follow links. The large collection at the St. Louis County Library in St. Louis, Missouri, (which now includes most of the volumes from the old National Genealogical Society Library of Arlington, Virginia) will lend many materials. Visit their website at www.slcl.lib.mo.us. There are others. Ask the reference librarian in your own local library for assistance in ordering from other libraries. Borrowed materials normally must be used in the requesting library.

Though interlibrary loan is an advantage for those who cannot travel, the disadvantage can be that the book you want to view may be out on loan when you arrive. To avoid disappointment, call the library before making a long trip. If you are interested in borrowing books by mail, examine the list of lending libraries in Elizabeth Petty Bentley's *The Genealogical Address Book*. Sometimes loan privileges are based on membership to a society, while others may loan for a small fee. Some also lend microfilm or microfiche.

> **Genie Jargon**
>
> **Interlibrary loan** is a procedure in which one library lends a book or microfilm to another library for use by a patron.

## University and College Libraries

Among the least-used libraries in genealogy are those of the universities and colleges, though they hold some of our richest resources. In the Colson Library, University of West Virginia, I located fragments of an original deed that had not been recorded. This indisputably proved the parentage of a Virginian born in the mid-1750s. At the Bancroft Library at the University of California in Berkeley, I was thrilled to hold an account book written in the 1700s giving valuable information on the Thomas Jefferson family.

Almost all universities have websites describing their collections. Within those descriptions you'll find extraordinary websites such as "Making of America" (MOA), a joint effort of the University of Michigan and Cornell University. MOA brings us a digital library of thousands of volumes. Among them are

> **Tree Tips**
>
> When visiting a university library, inquire about their manuscript catalog. That's the most likely place where the "hidden" treasures will be found. Search it by surnames, by localities, and by subject.

images from the two multi-volume series *Official Records of the Union and Confederate Navies in the War of the Rebellion* (1894–1922) and *The War of the Rebellion: A Compilation of the Official Records of the Union and Confederate Armies* (1880–1901).

Locate them at http://cdl.library.cornell.edu and click on "browse." Once there, scroll down to the mentioned series. Enter a name, click, and presto!—view the actual page. This is just the "tip of the iceberg" of exciting finds at university sites. Collections such as these, available with a few strokes of our fingers, awakens us to the power of the Web to truly put "flesh on the bones" of our forebears. Go also to www.hti.umich.edu/m/moa for a number of other books at the MOA site.

## Family History Library

The Family History Library (FHL) is maintained by the Church of Jesus Christ of Latter-day Saints (Mormon) in Salt Lake City. As a result of their religious convictions, their genealogical collection is immense and worldwide. It is not limited to use by members of the church; the materials are available for research by anyone. Their library catalog and other computer projects make access to many of their records relatively easy. They maintain hundreds of Family History Centers across the country. Anyone can order microfilm for use in these branches.

**Tree Tips**

Use the FHL website's search engine to locate a Family History Center near you. Go to www.familysearch.org. Then click on "Library," then on "FamilySearch Center," and finally on "Family History Center." Or check your phone book.

The Family History Library's FamilySearch is an enormous collection of several genealogical databases. It includes the Family History Department's Ancestral File (data collected from church members and others), their International Genealogical Index (an international personal-name database of birth, christenings, and marriages about persons now deceased), and others. These are updated regularly.

One of the most useful segments of FamilySearch is the Family History Library Catalog with its listings of their extensive microfilm holdings. Most microfilm rolls can be borrowed for a nominal fee through your local Family History Center. You'll find microfilm for deeds, probate records, vital records, civil records, and much more, worldwide.

## Other Magnificent Collections

The Allen County [Indiana] Public Library at Ft. Wayne houses one of the largest collections of genealogy material in the United States. For years they have systematically added to their holdings, which are considered same of the finest in the country. Their strong collection of periodicals resulted in the development of the PERSI index previously described. Additionally, many thousands of genealogy books are available on their shelves. Access their catalog at www.acpl.lib.in.us/genealogy/index.html.

Other major collections are the New England Historic Genealogical Society Library in Boston, Massachusetts (www.newenglandancestors.org), and the New York Public Library in New York City (www.nypl.org), the Historical Society of Wisconsin Library in Madison, Wisconsin (www.wisconsinhistory.org), the St. Louis County Public Library in St. Louis, Missouri (www.slcl.lib.mo.us), and others. Their already extensive collections continue to grow as interest in genealogy escalates.

## Religious and Ethnic Libraries

Some churches and ethnic groups maintain libraries and archives. Their hours may be limited, so inquire ahead of time if you plan to visit. Check with your local reference librarian for guides that will lead to the location of many church archives. Also go to www.cyndislist.com and scroll to "Religions & Churches." Alternately, insert the name of the denomination in your browser, and add the word "archives" for listings. Enormous amounts of information exist on the websites—general background on the religion, descriptions of their library holdings, and perhaps even actual images of records. A few of the websites follow:

◆ Baptist: The Northern Baptist Historical Library and Archives at www.sbhla. org/archives.htm. Included is a list of microfilmed church records available for purchase. And they have a photo gallery and brief biographies.

◆ Catholic: cyndislist.com has links to websites of dioceses and archdioceses not only in the United States, but also in the world. One useful website is http://home.att.net/~Local_Catholic. This includes a guide to type and location of records, biographies, history, and others.

◆ Huguenot: The National Huguenot Society's website can be accessed at www.huguenot.netnation.com/general. The Huguenot Society of Great Britain and Ireland is at www.huguenotsociety.org.uk/resources. These sites include such informative material such as "Who Were the Huguenots," "Important Dates in Huguenot History," addresses of collections, and other aids.

- Jewish: The American Jewish Archives at www.americanjewisharchives.org/intro. html, and "Reading Hebrew Tombstones" at www.jewishgen.org/infofiles/ tombstones.html are both helpful.

- Lutheran: The Evangelical Lutheran Church in America has a website at www.elca.org/library/library.html. The Lutheran Archives Center at Philadelphia can be accessed at www.ltsp.edu/krauth/archives.html. These include links to other sites.

- Mennonite: The Mennonite Archives is available at www.mcusa-archives.org. Included is an amazing collection of "Mennobits," obituaries of thousands with a search feature. Try also www.ristenbatt.com/genealogy/mennonit.htm for background and links, and even tombstone inscriptions in a number of cemeteries.

- Methodist: The Methodist Archives & Research Center (England) at the John Rylands University Library of Manchester is at http://rylibweb.man.ac.uk/data1/ dg/text/method.html. The United Methodist Archives at www.gcah.org is another of the sundry Methodist research sites available online.

- Presbyterian: Presbyterian Historical Society at www.history.pcusa.org is a good place to start. Once there, click on "Presbyterians in America" for a number of good links including a brief history of the Presbyterian Church in this country, a Presbyterian timeline, and others.

- Quaker: The Friends Historical Library of Swarthmore College in Pennsylvania at www.swarthmore. edu/library/friends includes explanations of Monthly Meetings, description of the kinds of records Quakers kept, which monthly meeting to search, and more. Many other Quaker websites are available—enter "Quaker" in your browser and off you go!

**Tree Tips**

Most lineage societies are by membership only. If you have an interest in joining, and you qualify, an existing member can sponsor your membership. Lineage societies are requiring extensive proof of relationship accompanied by source citations, so prepare carefully.

## Lineage Society Libraries

The best-known and most extensive library in this category is the National Society Daughters of the American Revolution Library in Washington, D.C. Members of the NSDAR can use the library at no charge; others pay a small daily fee. It has considerable material, including Bible records submitted in support of applications. Go to their website at www.dar.org. An awesome database at their site at http://members. dar.org/dar/darnet.cfm indexes thousands of records in their Genealogical Records Collection (GRC). Use the search engine provided after you've read the "Index Overview" at the site. Check also Eric Grundset's *American Genealogical Research at the DAR*—it will provide many tips for successfully using this library.

Besides the well-known DAR Library, there are also others. Read the pertinent chapter in Ancestry's *The Source* or check www.cyndislist.com for Lineage Societies.

## The Library of Congress

The Library of Congress has a genealogy department, but don't stop there. Look for their rare books section, the newspaper collection and finding aids, photographs, and the map section; all will be important in your search. Consult James C. Neagles' *The Library of Congress: A Guide to Genealogical and Historical Research* for some understanding of the vast facilities.

And don't overlook the Library of Congress's extensive website at www.loc.gov. There is much of interest here, but especially, click on "American Memory" for a seemingly endless well of genealogical treasures. Photographs, images, sounds, background information, taped interviews (such as those with many former slaves), and much more.

## The Least You Need to Know

- Genealogical collections and repositories vary drastically in size. Most have websites.

- Many "family histories" are published in book form or posted on the Web. Verify them if proper citations are not included.

- Libraries have more than books; manuscripts, maps, newspapers, photos, and multimedia can provide crucial information in your search.

- There are notable genealogical collections comprising voluminous material both in libraries and on the Web.

# Chapter 9

# Your Family's Hometown

## In This Chapter

- Using the public library to find relatives
- Learning to recognize the records your family left
- How other types of county records can assist in the search
- Some of the treasures in the museum

You may be one of the fortunate people who lives in the same county where your family has resided for more than one or two generations. Within your family's own county, there are a number of repositories to assist in your search. You can become familiar with the records your family could have generated in the county in which they lived. If your family did not live in the same area in which you now reside, consider making a trip to where your parents and grandparents lived most of their lives. This chapter concentrates on what is available in the libraries and museums of your ancestors' hometowns.

Chapter 13 tells you how to prepare for the trip to your ancestors' hometowns, and Chapter 14 explains the materials available in the courthouses there.

Go to the public library where your immediate family lived. Ask if there is a genealogy section and a "local" history section. Both will be useful. The genealogy section may include "family histories," books devoted to the genealogy of a specific family, and other published and unpublished manuscript aids related to lineages. The local history section consists of books, pamphlets, scrapbooks, and other items pertaining to the county. Find out, too, if there is a separate genealogical society in the area. They may meet in the public library but often have their own headquarters and library.

Some of your family's records will be in their original form in the courthouse. Some however, may have been abstracted and published—those you will find in the library. The library may also have originals—scrapbooks, photographs, and others. In some cases, even "discarded" courthouse records have made their way to the local library collection.

# Getting Started in the Public Library

Take with you the names, dates, and locations of your family members who resided in the county. Your goal is to find their birth dates, marriage dates, spouses, and death dates as starters. Stay alert for records that mention the churches they attended or their religion. (Knowing that, you can later determine if the church left records naming them.) A record showing where they were buried can supply you with leads. Each major event in their lives that has associated records can help identify their relatives and reveal snippets of their lives.

Your purpose is to find everything that could bear on your family. Nothing is too insignificant to note. Write down fully in your notes the day of your library trip, the name and address of the one you visited, and in which book or file you found the information so that you can find it again. In library holdings you might learn the following:

**Tree Tips**

Ask at the library for the name of the official county or city historian. They, too, can point you to local collections, and may even be the custodian of some of the records themselves.

- Birth date and birthplace

- Names of parents

- Death dates and town or township

- Marriage date, place, and spouse

- Biography, possibly with photograph or pen sketch

- Military service

- Names and addresses of relatives and when they moved into the county or left the county.

- Occupations of parents and relatives

- Acreage owned by family members

**Tree Tips** _____

To access an alphabetical listing of public libraries nationwide, go to www.publiclibraries.com.

You may initially be unable to locate something specific. Stick with it. As you learn more about the records, your success will increase. And with each success, your enthusiasm for the search will increase, too.

# Shelves of Possibilities

After you start browsing the library shelves, you will begin to learn the many resources available. Books and finding aids of every description exist. Look for such things as these:

- Old Settlers' files

- Obituaries/necrology/funeral records

- Tombstone surveys

- Vertical family files

- County histories and indexes

- Published vital records

- Published deeds, probate and court records

- Scrapbooks

- Gazetteers and atlases

- Voting registers

- City directories

- School records

- Artifacts and photographs

## Old Settlers Remembered

Many counties have projects to preserve information on their earliest settlers in what are commonly called "Old Settlers' files." These may consist of recollections of descendants, biographies, or even taped interviews. Examine them for any of the surnames of your family who resided in the county. Note also the name and address of anyone who submitted information; they may be alive or might have family members still living. Contact with them could yield some wonderful memorabilia. Just remember not to accept what is written as "fact" until you have verified it.

**Genie Jargon**

**Necrology** is a list of people who died within a certain time frame, or a collection of obituaries. You may find the collection so titled in the library.

## Death Records

Many local libraries have indexed their early obituaries or established a *necrology* file. The content of the obituaries varies. Normally, those in smaller towns were more extensive than in larger cities. Check this file for members of your family. (See Chapter 16.)

## Vertical Files: Just Waiting to "Talk"!

As interest in genealogy intensifies, libraries receive letters of inquiry from all over the country. To preserve these, they often create *"vertical files,"* a set of folders stored in a filing cabinet usually by the family surname. Included may be letters, clippings, Bible records, photographs, research notes, charts, and others. These can yield new clues, and equally as important, may supply names of others seeking the family.

## County Histories: The "Mug" Books

Almost every county in the United States has had at least one county history published, and some have several. They vary in content. Those published in the late 1800s or early 1900s typically consisted of brief histories of each of their townships or towns, churches, lodges, medical profession, schools, newspapers, county government, and notorious happenings, and even those who served in the military from the county. They may include the name and place of origin of the early pioneers of the area—who established the first grist mill, the first physician, town officers, and other similarly valuable information. Consult P. William Filby's *Bibliography of American County Histories*. Or in your Internet browser insert "bibliography county histories," and listings for specific states will be displayed. Look in your library for town histories. Though town histories are not listed in Filby, many have been published.

The county histories are sometimes referred to as "mug books" because often they included biographies with photographs (or pen sketches) of the early citizens. The lack of a biography was no reflection on a person's standing in the community, however. The books were mostly on a subscription basis; those who paid were included, while others were not. To subscribe or not depended upon the frugality and monetary priorities of the individual. The histories published in the late 1800s were supplied by people far closer to the time of the events and should be (but aren't always) more accurate than recollections of present-day descendants.

View the mug books with caution. If the biography includes several earlier generations, there can be multiple errors caused by loss of memory or lack of knowledge of the family background. (Or even, sometimes, by a desire to elevate their standing in the community or to obscure details of a less-than-desirable past.) All facts must be confirmed. Nonetheless, the biographies are unique and provide an insight often lacking in any other source. You will learn of your ancestors' schooling, jobs, purchase of the farm, the church they attended, when they "found" religions, and other fascinating facts.

A common problem with published county histories is the absence of an index. Usually only the name of the subject in the biographies was listed; the other names within the sketch were not. And rarely were the names in the town and historical sections indexed. It can be a tedious process to locate your ancestor's name among the pages. Fortunately, many individuals or groups initiated projects to remedy this shortcoming. Even if an index has not been published, there may be a card index at the library created by locals for the histories of their own county.

**Genie Jargon**

A **vertical file** is a collection of resource materials, usually pamphlets, letters, clippings, and others. It is normally arranged in manila folders and filed in alphabetical sequence by subject or name.

**Pedigree Pitfalls**

Note the year of publication of the book; was your ancestor living then? If not, someone else provided the data and may have guessed at some of the facts.

**Tree Tips**

If you can establish the name of the community in which your family lived, first search those sections in an unindexed book. The location will give you a starting place.

## Vital Records: The Facts of Life

Vital Records—births, marriages, and deaths—are among the richest of documents that help build the family tree. Searching them may take some effort because it often requires going to a variety of locations. They can be scattered among the shelves of the courthouse, city hall, county health department, local historical society, and even church and state archives. First, check at the library to see if anyone has compiled or published any of the local vital records. Although you don't want to rely upon the published version (because of possible omissions and errors in transcriptions), you can use it to initiate the search. The preface of the book of vital records might explain where the various records are housed, available time periods, and which vital records, if any, have been destroyed.

## The Web Shines Here

The Internet provides a variety of ways in which you can supplement the search for a county's vital records. One valuable website is www.vitalrec.com. Or go to www.cyndislist.com, and scroll down to "Death Records," (or to any of the other vital records listed there).

Another alternative is to go to www.usgenweb.org, and use their links to get to the state and county of your search. Examine the county website carefully to see if any of the vital records have been posted, published, or microfilmed.

At http://home.att.net/~wee-monster/deathrecords.html is a nifty website "Online Searchable Death Indexes for the U.S.A." categorized by state. It includes obituaries, cemeteries, and the Social Security Death Index, in addition to death records.

## Local Records

If you are fortunate, your county may be one for which abstracts of other early records have been published. These might include an assortment of land records: deed abstracts, surveys, land entries, and others. Though you should also examine the originals in the courthouse, the published records have the advantage of an all-name index for the book, whereas the courthouse clerks only index the main parties.

A multitude of other published abstracts might be found: court minutes, order books, wills, inventories, and others. Look for mention of members of your family and clues to relationships. Later you will make your first trip to the courthouse and experience the excitement of using the original records. For now the published books can aid you in understanding the variety of available records.

# Local Scrapbooks

Preparing scrapbooks of local events was a pastime for some townspeople. It gave them a sense of community. Reading these scrapbooks you will get a sense of life in the community as it grew. Seldom indexed, the scrapbook pages can reward you with one or more articles involving your ancestor.

# Gazetteers and Atlases

The county gazetteer (a geographic dictionary) or atlas published in the late nineteenth or early twentieth century is a treasure. The pen sketches of the homes and farms are priceless. The wagons and farm implements in the yard, the crops growing—these reflect a way of life. Also included are township maps, many showing the name of the property owners on their section of land. Nearby cemeteries may be noted. These not only help in establishing the family's residence, but may also lead to the location of a family cemetery. Acreage, occupation, and even their place of nativity may be included. The names of the neighbors can also be helpful.

*The Historical Atlas Map of Santa Clara County, California*, published by Thompson & West of San Francisco in 1876, includes a Business Directory. Businessmen are listed by name, address, occupation, nativity, year they entered the state, when they came to the county, their post office, and the number of acres owned. You learn that Sheriff J. H. Adams came in 1849 from Illinois during the gold rush, and that Dr. Benjamin Cory of Ohio came even earlier, in 1847. These wonderful atlases are not to be overlooked. Some pen sketches measure 12" × 14" whereas others are 8" × 12" or other sizes. They are unique in design and historical significance. Some of the commercial companies, such as Thompson & West, Lewis Publishing, and others specialized in such histories, preparing them for many counties and states. The originals are collector's items.

If you can find a pen sketch of your family's home or farm in an early atlas, a good reproduction of it will be wonderful for framing. The following figure shows the office and residence of G. W. Breyfogle, M.D., at the corner of Third and St. James Streets in San Jose, California. This reproduction from *The Historical Atlas Map of Santa Clara County, California*, provides a wonderful sense of a bygone era.

**Tree Tips**

Can't find a location in the United States? Go to www.asu.edu/lib/hayden/govdocs/maps/geogname.htm for several links to sites to locate place names.

*The office and residence of one of San Jose, California's early physicians.*

On cyndislist.com scroll to "Maps, Gazeteers & Geographic Information" for numerous items of interest. Sometimes volunteers have transcribed the whole of an early voting register. Check out the marvelous site for Yuba County, California's voting register at www.cagenweb.com/yuba/registers/registers-index.htm for an example. Included are 1872, 1876, 1877, 1879, 1880, 1886, 1888, 1892, and 1894, with more in progress. All easily accessed through the search feature provided! You'll find entries for those whose nativity was England, Ireland, Scotland, Germany, and more, and virtually every state.

## He Voted with Pride

Some areas may have published their early voting registers. In California, the published registers of many counties before 1900 are in libraries. They include data not easily obtainable from other sources. The *Great Register for Santa Clara County* for 1892 includes age; physical description (height, complexion, color of eyes, color of hair); visible marks or scars, if any, and their location; occupation; country of nativity (usually shown as the state); place of residence; post office address; date when naturalized; place where naturalized and by which court; date of registration; and whether sworn.

A marvelous sense of the man—what he looked like, how he made his living, if he was an immigrant—are all revealed. John Cotler, a farmer, was age 58 and born in Ireland. He was naturalized 17 August 1855 in the U.S. District Court in Boston. His descendants now know where to find his naturalization papers. Charles Cranz, age

74, was born in Germany, naturalized on
10 April 1840 in Canton, Ohio, and now
lived in California. You learn, too, that he
was 5' 7" tall, with a light complexion,
blue eyes, and brown hair, and a farmer
by occupation. Though not all states have
such detailed registers, determine what is available for the county of your search.

**Tree Tips**

If you are unable to learn
about voting records at the
library, check with the county
registrar of voters.

## City Directories: Home Sweet Home

The availability of city directories varies. Larger cities, such as Philadelphia, Boston,
Baltimore, and New York have directories extant from the early or mid-1800s and
some from even earlier. Small towns may at first be included in the directories of
their neighboring cities but probably had their own in later years. Very rural and
sparsely settled areas might have all the towns in the county in one volume.

Want to know if there is a city directory online? Go to www.citydirectoryrecords.
com. Remember, no directory listing online is complete—find two or three others,
too, but this one will get you started.

It is unlikely that within a county, the city directories are all housed in the same
repository. In mid- and large-size communities, each has its own library and maintains a set of its own directories. After you establish where in the county your family
lived, determine if the town has its own collection. These directories will not only
place your ancestors in the county or town at specific times, but may lead you to the
old home, perhaps still standing.

Additionally, watch for the following:

- Others of the surname listed at the same address; they are relatives.

- Widow's listing, giving her deceased husband's name and occupation.

- Individual's first listing in the town, to indicate arrival or coming of age.

- Individual's last listing in the town, to indicate departure from the area or death.

If the directory has a reverse listing by street address (called a householder's index),
check for neighbors. Some may be married daughters (families often lived in close
proximity). After you learn their occupations, you can follow your ancestors from job

to job. Even the date of death might be pinpointed within a year or two if the husband and wife are listed in one directory, and if in subsequent directories only one appears as a widow or widower. If the whole family disappears from the directory entirely and does not reappear in subsequent issues, they probably moved from the area.

Another useful section in the city directories is that of businesses. If your ancestor was a tailor, examine the business listings of tailor shops. Also examine the advertisements. They are charming, and you may be rewarded with your ancestor's ad entreating the public to purchase the finery he or she offers.

---

### Lineage Lessons

Do not assume that the spouse died in the same year that the surviving spouse is first listed as a widow or widower. It may take a year or two for the directory listings to reflect such events. If a husband is shown in several editions with his wife, and then shown alone, he is likely widowed (though they could be separated). Watch for subsequent issues that might reveal the name of a new wife.

---

## Learning with School Records

If you know what school your family attended, and it is still in existence, contact them for school records. They may be reluctant to furnish records from their files but sometimes will if sufficient time has elapsed. If the school is no longer standing, try the county department of education. If you do not know which school they attended, examine the city directory for the appropriate time period and determine which schools are listed on nearby streets.

## She Grew Roses; He Went to Lodge

Clubs, lodges, and fraternal organizations may still hold records of your family. Some have national headquarters and will answer inquiries if an SASE is included. The published county history, previously discussed, may give some information on the organizations that existed when your ancestors first lived in the area. Determine if any are still in existence. Many have websites.

If your ancestor was a member of the Chamber of Commerce or other civic organization, get in touch with them. Even if they don't maintain records of past members, they may remember them and offer some recollections. They may have retained newsletters or minutes of their organization that can add pizzazz to the life history you are building.

The women might have joined garden clubs, knitting circles, reading circles, and church-affiliated groups. Try to find them. It will give you a glimpse of their personalities to know their interests and hobbies.

**Tree Tips**

To locate schools that may have existed in your family's neighborhood, obtain a detailed street map of the town and use it together with the city directory and telephone book.

# Artifacts and Memorabilia

Museums can vividly depict how your ancestors lived. Relics from the early times of the community—photographs, sketches, portraits—all assist in portraying your ancestors in the community. If there was musical talent in your family, you will enjoy seeing the old instruments they played. If Great-Grandpa was a druggist, some of his own paraphernalia might be included in the museum's display.

Be sure to inquire about indexes to manuscripts or photographs or other holdings of the museum. If your ancestor was a collector of anything—postcards, thimbles, or fans—see if the collection was donated to the museum. Such collections are often annotated with intriguing bits of

**Tree Tips**

For a listing of hundreds of online museums in the U.S., go to http://icom.museum/vlmp/usa.html.

information about the donor. When the Arizona State Historical Society wrote to me to inquire about a quilt in their collection donated by a descendant of the town's jailer (related to my husband), they were able to supply a fascinating tradition of the quilt being stitched by the girls at the Bird Cage Saloon in Tombstone, Arizona. It was said to be their gift to the jailer's baby daughter.

## Photographs: A Peek into the Past

Perhaps one of the most treasured finds in local museums are the photographs. Families who long despaired of ever finding a likeness of their great-great-grandfather may find his class photograph framed and displayed in a case. Museums normally have indexes to such collections and can assist you in locating them. Consider paying them to have a copy made.

## The Least You Need to Know

♦ The library in your ancestors' hometown has numerous manuscript and published records.

♦ If your family lived in your own town, you will find vital records, court records, funeral records, and much more in your own backyard.

♦ Additional records for search can include such diverse sources as school, city directories, and voting registers.

# Part 3

## Following the Trail

It's time to start searching for your family in the census, and, through it, follow them in their journeys north, south, east, and west as they migrated. The thrill of finally finding your family on the census, and realizing that probably at least one of them was there at the very time the census taker was writing down the information, will make you feel very close.

You may be like many others and hate to write letters. How to start? What to ask? This will be easier with the guidance you read here. You will find some tips to increase the power of your letters, making the most of every one of them.

# Chapter 10

# Have You Done Your Homework?

## In This Chapter

- ◆ What is the census and why is it important?
- ◆ Preparing for the first records research
- ◆ Understanding the Soundex code
- ◆ Coding your surnames

Most genealogists start their records' research with the U.S. federal population census, a count taken every 10 years since 1790 to determine the number of congressional representatives for each state. Our forefathers didn't know that they were laying the foundation for one of the most fundamental research documents for genealogy.

## Census Importance

Why are the *censuses* so important to your quest for information on your ancestors, and why are they among the first records to search? Widely available, they place your ancestors in a specific place at a specific time, and the related information on them leads you to other locations and records.

**Genie Jargon**

A **census** is an official population count that often includes related information used for government planning.

The objective of the census is to account for every individual living in the United States on a designated day. The chances are good that your ancestors were enumerated if they resided in the United States on the day the census was taken. Later chapters give suggestions to help you find them if they seem to be missing.

---

**Lineage Lessons**

Even if the enumerator did not visit every residence in his area on the date deemed census day, he was to collect the information as if he were there on that day. Let's say the census date is 1 June, and the enumerator doesn't get to a household until 13 June. The baby born 2 June should not be listed on the census because he or she was not in the household on the census date. Similarly, if an individual died 2 June, the person should be listed on the census because he or she was alive on 1 June, the designated date.

---

What can you learn from the census? At various times the census questions pertain to military service, citizenship, marital status, and other topics. Some responses will surprise you. Thinking the family 100 percent Southern, you may be flabbergasted to find that Great-Grandpa was a Union vet from the Civil War. If family tradition says that your third great-grandfather was born in Ireland, but the census information says he and his father were both born in Virginia, then you have a discrepancy to check.

The census may be the first place you find your ancestors in their family groupings. Maybe Grandma is older than you thought, or your mother has an older brother no one mentions.

# Preparation Saves Frustration

Before you go to your computer or head out to a repository to search the census records for your family, do your homework. Make a list of the likely heads of households (person in charge of the family unit, such as husband/father, grown son, or widow) for whom you have gathered some information from talking to your relatives and going through all the material you found at home. Be sure to include any variant spellings of the surnames.

For each individual on your list, add a time period (the estimated dates of their life spans based on what you already know) and a probable state and county of residence.

For example, take a look at the following sample of a census search:

| Abraham Gant | 1930 | Morgan Co., KY |
| | 1920 | Morgan Co., KY |
| | 1910 | Estill Co., KY |
| | 1900 | Estill Co., KY |
| | 1880 | Orange Co., VA |
| Joseph Jaspers | 1930 | Monroe Co., NY |
| | 1920 | Monroe Co., NY |
| | 1910 | Monroe or Erie Co., NY |
| | 1900 | Erie Co., NY |
| | 1880 | too young |

The approximate birth dates of the individuals on your list will indicate a starting point for the census search. (The 1890 census is omitted from the list because it is virtually nonexistent.) Which ones would likely be on the 1930 census? Which on the 1910 census? If your parents were children in 1920 or 1930, they will be enumerated with whomever they were living with at that time: parents, grandparents, aunts and uncles, orphanages, or other.

Unless you suspect otherwise when you begin, assume that ancestors under ages 18 to 21 were living with their parents, and start your research with those parents. Group your list of individuals by the areas where you expect they were living.

> **Lineage Lessons**
>
> In the pursuit of your family history you will do a great deal of census research. The pending research lists you prepare and the transcripts of your census work are best managed on printed or electronic forms. Using electronic forms is most efficient because the data can be sorted and manipulated in many ways.

## Where Did They Live?

The county is the division of government where you begin to look for your ancestors in official records, so first determine in which counties your ancestors' towns belong. If their town has disappeared from current maps, look up the town in a gazetteer. There may be several towns of the same name; be sure to get the one in the area where your ancestors lived. Gazetteers can often be found in state or university libraries. An 1895 United States gazetteer is online at www.livgenmi.com/1895. For more resources, check Cyndi's List under "Maps, Gazetteers & Geographic Information."

**Tree Tips** _____

Review the material you already have on your ancestors. You may find the county of residence among the family papers, on death certificates, in obituaries, or in city directories.

The closer you can locate the residence for your ancestors, whether street address, township, or ward, the more quickly your search is likely to go. However, don't be discouraged if those are the very things you are hoping to uncover by searching the census. You will be successful; it will just take a little longer. If you are unable to zero in on a county, the search is not hopeless. Examine the state census indexes carefully for your ancestors' surnames. You can often determine the county from those indexes by noticing where there are clusters of the surname. The addition of searchable online census indexes makes it possible to sometimes find an ancestor even if you do not know the state. However, be aware that if the name is a common one, you may get too many returns to narrow down to a reasonable number to check.

## Which Census to Search First?

Because of privacy laws, the latest census available for research is the 1930 census. Generally, you will start your research with the most recent censuses, 1930, 1920, 1910, or 1900, and track the individuals back through each census taken during their lifetimes. The objective is to conduct a complete census search for each individual on your list. You may wonder why you need to keep getting additional censuses when you found them in one census listing. There are three main reasons: You want to compare the data you find, the composition of the household may change, and each census has different information that can lead you to other records.

## Last Touches for Your List

Your research list should now be a list of individuals with some indication of the census years in which you may find them listed, the probable counties and states in which they lived during those years, and the most recent available census on which you might expect to find them. At this point, to prepare for your search for the actual census enumerations, it's time to code the surname for each individual on your list that you will be searching for in the censuses of 1930, 1920, 1910, 1900, and 1880. (The 1890 population census is virtually nonexistent, nearly all of it having been destroyed by a fire, January 21, 1921, in the Commerce Department building.)

# Cracking the Code

Federal indexing for the 1880, 1900, 1910, 1920, and 1930 censuses is based on a phonetic system called the *Soundex* (or a similar one called *Miracode*). It was devised to overcome the vagaries of spelling by grouping together surnames that sound alike, but are spelled differently. In the Soundex, Bream, Breem, or Briem will be found in indexes under B650; Wier, Weer, Wiere, and Ware would be W600.

**Genie Jargon** _____

**Soundex** is an indexing system based on the phonetic sound of the consonants in the surname. Each name is assigned a letter and three numbers. The letter is always the first letter of the surname. The **Miracode** for the 1910 census uses the same sound system but arranges the resulting lists by the visitation number assigned by the enumerator, rather than page numbers of the census schedule as in the Soundex.

The 1880 census was Soundexed only for households having children under the age of 10. (These children were the first to become eligible for old-age benefits in 1935.) This does not mean that other households were not enumerated. It does mean that if your ancestor was not in a household with children under the age of 10, he or she will not be on the Soundex indexes, but will be in the census itself.

# Those 1880 Children Retiring

With the passing of the Social Security Act in 1935, the government had to determine who was eligible for benefits. Those eligible needed to prove their ages. If they had no birth record, they could help substantiate the birth by a census record. The government, realizing that the first group of applicants was born before there was statewide registration of births, needed an efficient way to locate individuals on the census for verification of the birth. The only ones in the household that were important to the government in this initial Soundex were those who were under 10 in 1880. It was that group who would be applying for Social Security.

## Learning the Soundex System

Applying the Soundex code to the surnames on your list before you go to the repository will speed up your census research when you get there. Table 10.1 explains the code.

### Table 10.1    Soundex Coding Key

| Number | Letter Equivalent |
| --- | --- |
| 1 | B P F V |
| 2 | C S K G J Q X Z |
| 3 | D T |
| 4 | L |
| 5 | M N |
| 6 | R |

The letters A, E, I, O, U, W, Y, and H are disregarded. To apply the Soundex to your surnames, follow these steps:

1. Use the first letter of the surname to begin the code.

2. Cross out all the vowels and the letters *W*, *Y*, and *H* in the surname.

3. Using the table, assign an equivalent number to the first three letters left in the surname.

4. Disregard any remaining letters in the surname.

If the surname has fewer than three letters left, assign zeros to those places.

Further refinements include the following:

- Double letters are treated as one and coded with one number; thus 2 *L*s will be 4, not 44.

- Two or more letters with the same code number that appear in sequence in a surname are assigned one number; thus *CK* in Dickson is coded as 2, not 22, and Szalay is S400.

- Two consonants with the same code number separated by a vowel are both coded; thus Svoboda is coded S123, not S103.

- A name that yields no letters is assigned 3 zeros, thus *Chu* becomes C000.

- Code names with prefixes, such as Van, Von, De, Le, with and without the prefix. You may find it either way in the Soundex.

- When two consonants with the same code number are separated by either an H or W, only the first is coded with the second being ignored; thus Burroughs is coded B622, not B620.

---

### Lineage Lessons

The last refinement in the Soundex coding rules is a reference to the "lost H and W rule," which is very important for researchers looking for surnames with either an H or W in them. For a period of time, those preparing Soundex coding erroneously treated H and W as they did vowels. That is, they used them as separators, so letters having the same value in the code were coded as one letter. When "the lost H and W rule," also called the "Ashcraft rule," was rediscovered, coding reverted to its original rules. Researchers tracking surnames with the letters H or W in them should look for them under both codes. For example, if the surname is Halkowski, look for it under H422 as well as H420.

---

Examples using these rules are shown in Table 10.2:

## Table 10.2   Soundex Examples

| Name | As Soundexed |
| --- | --- |
| Aguilar | A246 |
| Mendelsohn | M534 |
| Beebe | B100 |
| Li, Lee, Law | L000 |
| Flick | F420 |
| Von Kemp | V525 or K510 |

## Soundex Puzzlers

There are some nuances to Soundex coding that affect names that may be on your lists. Men and women in religious orders were usually coded as if Sister, Brother, or Mother were their surnames. Indian and Hawaiian names may be coded as if they had a surname. Running Bear may be coded as B600 and then alphabetically as if his first name were "Running." For more information about special situations, consult Kathleen Hinckley's *Your Guide to the Federal Census* and Tony Burroughs article "The Original Soundex Instructions," published in the *National Genealogical Society Quarterly*.

Names that sound the same, but begin with different letters such as Courll and Kurl, or Fillip and Phillip, can give researchers problems because they will be coded differently. In cases like these you may need to use both codes to be successful.

Eastern European names did not always fit the Soundex coding system. Same-sounding names might be spelled differently enough to code differently, making it difficult to find the individual sought in indexes. Names such as Moskowitz and Moskovitz sound the same, but their codes are M232 and M213, respectively. To remedy this situation, two researchers devised a modification of the Soundex known as the *Daitch-Mokotoff Soundex System*. It is not used for the federal census indexes, but reading about the system may provide new ideas on what variations of your surnames you need to know for successful census searches. A good place to begin learning about the system is at www.jewishgen.org/InfoFiles/soundex.html.

**Genie Jargon**

**Daitch-Mokotoff Soundex System** is a modification of the Soundex System used to accommodate Eastern European names in some indexes, but not those for the census.

---

**Lineage Lessons**

Although the Daitch-Mokotoff Soundex System is not used for federal census records, this modification of the Soundex can be used to search the Ellis Island Immigration database and numerous Jewish databases. Researchers tracking Slavic and Germanic surnames will want to become familiar with this phonetic system. Coding chart and rules are online at www.avotaynu.com/soundex.html.

---

## Shortcut Coding

Many genealogy programs will generate the Soundex codes for every surname in your database. Also, there are Soundex code generators online in which you enter a surname and the code is generated for you. One (http://resources.rootsweb.com/cgi-bin/soundexconverter) is a RootsWeb page that will return not only the code for surname you enter, but also a list of other names with the same code. Some online code generators such as www.stevemorse.org/census/soundex.html will return the surnames with both the Soundex and Daitch Mokotoff Soundex codes.

Math teachers often express concern when students use calculators for all their arithmetic work, wondering if they understand the underlying concepts. The same is true of using these generators. They are convenient to use, but it is important to understand the basic systems of coding as well.

## Soundex Codes and Online Indexes

Although Soundex codes are not necessary to use online indexes to censuses, understanding the Soundex and applying it to the surnames on your list is still important. You may be unable to find your surnames with a simple alphabetical search, in which case you will want to use the Soundex code search option. Also, other online indexes, particularly those for ships' passenger lists, use Soundex codes to increase the chances of success in finding the person whose name was not spelled the way you thought it was.

# Indexes Before the Soundex

There are various published indexes for the 1790-through-1870 censuses before the first Soundex of 1880. Although most indexes cover an entire state, others are regional. Occasionally, an individual or a genealogical society prepares an index or a transcription of a census for one county. Copies of these indexes and transcriptions may not be widely distributed. Nonetheless, check for indexes at all the libraries and repositories where you look for other sources.

With the help of CD-ROM technology, consolidated comprehensive indexes for all years and all states were created by commercial enterprises. Some may be available in a nearby library or for sale on various websites, such as www.heritagecreations.com and www.genealogy.com. These CD-ROM indexes have been supplanted by online indexes that enable nationwide searches with the click of a mouse. Comprehensive online indexes are most often subscription services, sometimes accessible through your library.

Indexes of a more specialized nature are frequently prepared and posted by volunteers, and are available free of charge. Be sure to check www.cyndislist.com to see if there are special-interest indexes online for any of the places you are researching. Perhaps the Indiana 1820 index of males in Orange County www.usgennet.org/usa/in/county/orange/censtate1820.htmwould be useful to you, or maybe the 1840 index for Bloom Township, Fairfield County, Ohio, at www.foorgenealogy.com/1840cen.html would have some clues. Also, check the USGenWeb www.usgenweb.org for states and counties of your research focus to see if any indexes for them have been posted online.

No matter how good the index, some mistakes are made. If you don't find your family on a particular index, do not assume that they are not on the census. They may have been missed in the indexing, alphabetized incorrectly, or you may be looking in the wrong geographic location.

# Locating a Copy of the Census

After you have your list of individuals with their states and counties of residence, their names Soundexed for 1880–1930, and a list of censuses you expect them to be on, you need to know where you can find the actual census records. Remember, up to this point you have only been using an index.

Microfilmed copies of the federal census are available in many locations. The National Archives and its regional branches have full sets from 1790 through 1930, with many (though not all) existing indexes. Large libraries and repositories often have complete sets, although some have only the series for your state. Your local library might have selected censuses for your county. The Family History Library has a complete collection, and their copies may be borrowed and viewed at their Family History Centers. Other copies are available through rental services.

Images of all the federal censuses are online at various subscription services. Because the subscription services differ somewhat in their coverage, indexing, search capabilities, and image quality, you may be successful only after checking more than one. If you do not subscribe to more than one site or do not subscribe to any sites, check to see if your library subscribes. Many do. These services are also accessible at the Family History Library in Salt Lake City and at some Family History Centers.

# Is It True?

Keep in mind that census information needs to be corroborated with other records for reasons that are discussed in Chapter 11. Don't be misled by accepting the census information as completely accurate. Use it as a guide.

You will return to the censuses again and again as you discover new individuals, or as new information calls for a reevaluation of your earlier work. Each time you discover a new surname, conduct a complete census search on that family.

---

### Lineage Lessons

Even when information on the census is accurate, it can be misleading. On the 1870 census, Lewis Dunn's birthplace is listed as West Virginia, but the 1860 census shows Virginia as his birthplace. Which is correct? As it turns out, both are correct. The actual place of his birth is in an area that was once a part of Virginia, but became part of West Virginia when that state was admitted to the Union in 1863.

---

## The Least You Need to Know

- List and Soundex the surnames you are researching.

- Determine the probable states and counties where your ancestors lived.

- Start your census research with the most recently available census, where you can expect to find the families you are researching.

- Census records are available on microfilm and online.

# Chapter 11

# Making Sense of the Census

## In This Chapter

- ◆ The search path for locating the census record you need
- ◆ Variations in the federal population schedules
- ◆ Using the census for clues
- ◆ Deaths and Civil War veterans from the census

Your ancestor's family is sitting around the kitchen table at their farmhouse, talking to the census taker. The baby is crying in the background, while two-year old Hannah is chasing the cat under the table. When was little Jake born? Where was Grandmother born? How old is Mattie? I often imagine these scenes, and wonder how long it took the census taker to elicit all the information he needed on the large family of parents, 12 children, the grandma living with them, and assorted farm hands and helpers. What the census taker wrote down forms the basis of the federal population schedules—one of the most frequently used sources in genealogy for both beginners and experienced searchers.

# Counting All Those People

The federal censuses from 1790 through 1930, taken every 10 years, are available for public perusal. The original schedules are normally not available for study and although some have been destroyed, all were microfilmed. In some cases they were scanned and are available for viewing on the Web. Though states had significant losses of early census records, the only serious loss for a whole census year was the 1890 population lists, destroyed in a 1921 fire. Only a very small portion was saved, available on National Archives' micropublication M407.

> **Lineage Lessons**
>
> Because of privacy laws restricting access to the census for 72 years, the 1930 census was only released in 2002. Its importance to twentieth-century researchers has been significant.

## Index Information

Except for a few instances when the census taker recopied the lists alphabetically, the census lists in early years were written in order of visitation. This made the schedules time-consuming to use; a researcher had to conduct a page-by-page search in the county's listings to find a particular family. Various commercial companies and individuals in the past 50 to 75 years have remedied this situation by creating indexes and making them available in book form and later on CD-ROMs. These have now been superseded in large part because of the availability of census records on the Internet. Many have been digitized and indexed; in some cases, these are every-name indexes, not just head of household. Availability on the Internet is largely by subscription. In other instances, some specific locality censuses may be at a state or county website, such as those at http://history.vineyard.net//edgcen50.htm for the 1850 census of Edgartown, Massachusetts. A number of others exist but they are few compared to what is found at the subscription websites.

**Pedigree Pitfalls** _____

Many indexes published in books were entered into a computer and then sorted. Names typed incorrectly were sorted incorrectly. Andrew Williams, mistyped "Willaims," or John Smith, mistyped "Simth," will not appear in their proper sequence in the publication. Consider all possibilities. Most of those now appearing on the Internet subscription websites have been reindexed, eliminating many of the previous errors but in some cases creating new errors.

From 1790 through 1840 the head of the household was the only one listed by name; others in the home were categorized by gender and age only. Thus the indexer could not include the names of all those residing in the dwelling. If your ancestor was a child during the 1790-1840 census, you won't find the child by name but will have to search for the head of a household in which that child may have lived.

The censuses of 1850 and later did include all individuals living in the dwelling, but most of the early indexers only picked up the head of the household for the index. This is being remedied. For example, Ancestry at www.ancestry.com, a subscription service, has created all-name indexes to some years and is working to complete others. See cyndislist.com under the sub-heading "Census" for census availability of selected locations.

No matter how complete the index, you will have to be creative in searching it. The name of the head of the household could have been mistyped in the preparing of the index in the twentieth century, or the indexer may have misread it. Or the census taker could have erred. Remember that many inhabitants were unable to read or write. Census takers spelled the names the way they sounded. This problem was compounded by the heavy accents of immigrants. Check all variations of the name.

The head of household is not necessarily the father. It could be a widowed mother, relative, guardian, or other person. Occasionally there was a separation and you will find both the father and the mother as heads of separate households.

## Search Path 1880-Through-1930 Census

Let's consider the search path to find a listing from 1880 through the 1930 census.

Step One (using Soundex):

- Code the surname (Chapter 10).

- Determine at least the state and, if possible, the county.

- Use a catalog to determine the appropriate Soundex microfilm and roll number depending on the coded name.

- Find the entry on the Soundex microfilm.

- Copy all the data shown, particularly the county, E.D. (Enumeration District), and page (sheet) number.

Step Two:

 ◆ With the numbers you found on the Soundex, return to the microfilm catalog. Look for state and county (and E.D. if the county is on more than one roll) to find the proper roll on which to obtain the full listing.

 ◆ Using the microfilm roll, find the family's full listing on the microfilm.

 ◆ Copy all the data shown.

# Search Path 1790-Through-1870 Census

Locating the census you need in a repository which holds the microfilm is a simple process:

1. Determine the state and, if possible, the county.

2. Locate published indexes; find the head of household noting the state, county, township, and page number it lists.

3. Using the information you found in the index, check the microfilm catalog for the appropriate microfilm and roll number.

4. Using the page number and township or ward from the index, find the family's listing on the roll of microfilm.

5. Copy all the data shown.

---

### Lineage Lessons

In the 1930 census there is Soundex available for only 10 states and partial indexes for 2 states. Complete indexes exist for Alabama, Arkansas, Florida, Georgia, Louisiana, Mississippi, North Carolina, South Carolina, Tennessee, and Virginia. A few counties are available for Kentucky and West Virginina. Unless you subscribe to Ancestry.com, which has developed an every-name index, for the rest of the 1930 census it will be necessary to ascertain the address of the person you are seeking, perhaps through an old telephone directory or city directory. Armed with that information, use *Enumeration District Description Maps for the Fifteenth Census of the United States, 1930* (National Archives micropublication M1930) to pinpoint the enumeration district.

## Soundex (Index) Microfilm 1880 Through 1930

You already have the Soundex code for the surname from reading Chapter 10. You need that code to find the indexed listing. The Soundex microfilm is arranged as follows:

◆ First by state

◆ Second by surname code

◆ Then by first name

Because the Soundex brings together all similar-sounding surnames, there will be many different surnames listed within that code. After you find the code on the microfilm, you will find that within the code that it is sub-indexed by the given name of the head of household. That cuts the search time considerably. For example, you code your surname and search the Soundex for that code. Once there, you observe that to find the surname with the first name of Thomas, you can roll the film to the first names starting with T, and quickly locate any Thomas.

# Let's Practice

At the repository, ask to see the microfilm catalog. You coded the surname Carlson as C-642; you want to find Charles Carlson who lived in North Dakota. The catalog shown in the next figure indicates that the 1920 North Dakota Soundex is micropublication M1580, and that the code C-642 is on rolls 8 and 9. Because you are searching for Charles Carlson, you will examine roll 8 because it includes code C-642 through the first name of Katherine. (If you were searching for Martin Carlson, you would examine roll 9. That roll starts with code C-642, first name of Lars, and continues through the rest of C-642 codes and on to the next numerical codes.)

Using the same example, find roll 8 of micropublication M1580 of the Soundex. Note that there are "title cards" at the beginning of each of the codes, so you know when the code on the film changes. Find C-642 and then start watching the alphabetized first names. You want Charles Carlson, so proceed to the first name of Charles. Remember that all the surnames sounding alike will be together; there could be a number of surnames coded as C-642 that show a Charles as a given name. But not all will be for Carlson. If you do not find Charles Carlson, don't give up yet. Was his full name Charles William Carlson? Because this is in strict alphabetical order by the given name, you have several alternatives: C. W., Chas., Charles W., Charles William, and even Chuck or another nickname.

*First 10 rolls of North Dakota Soundex from the catalog.*

## NORTH DAKOTA M1580

1. A-000 Irak—A-536 Bunt O.
2. A-536 C.—B-200 Isebell
3. B-200 J.B.—B-356 William
4. B-360 A.J.—B-531 Thomas L.
5. B-532 (N.R.)—B-625 William O.
6. B-626 (N.R.)—B-653 Willie
7. B-654 Agathe—C-462 Winnie
8. C-465 Adelade—C-642 Katherine
9. C-642 Lars—D-400 Iva
10. D-400 J.C.—E-200 Tonnes

## What Will It Show?

There are four different census cards that appear in the various Soundex: the Family Card; the Continuation Card (when the family doesn't fit on one card); the Individual Card (for those who lived in a home in which the head of household bore a different surname); and the Institution Card. Certain items from the full listings were extracted and entered onto these cards to form this Soundex index. You will be particularly interested in the Family Cards and the Individual Cards. If your ancestor, Jonathan Carlson, was living with his grandfather Jackson Martensen, Jonathan would be listed on an Individual Card. That card would include the name of Jackson Martensen and the reference numbers of the Martensen household so that you could then obtain that listing.

| Lineage Lessons |
| --- |
| There is an easier way to get to the 1880 census listings. You can bypass the Soundex and find every name listed simply by going to the Family History Library's website at www.familysearch.org. Click on "Search," and then on "Census." Select the 1880 United States census. Fill out their search form, and end by clicking "Search." This will lead you to every person named in the 1880 census. |

The census lists the head of the household with his or her age, birthplace, and citizenship. This is followed by the city, street, and house number. Then those living in the same home are listed, along with their relationship to the head of household, age, birthplace, and whether they are citizens. But most important to you right now is the upper right-hand corner, where you will find Vol. [Volume], E.D. [Enumeration District] number, Sheet [Page] number, and Line. You particularly need the E.D. number and Sheet number to find the whole listing. Remember, the Soundex is only an index coded by sound of the surname; it does not contain everything that is available in the full listing. It is important to copy those references from the Family Card; you will need them to obtain the full listing on another set of microfilm.

**Tree Tips** _____

The Family Cards and the Individual Cards for the 1880, 1900, 1910, 1920, and 1930 censuses differ slightly.

A shortcut is online at the subscription-based www.ancestry.com where there is an index to the 1920 census for every home Use their search engine for easy access. Also at this site is the previously mentioned every-name index to the 1930 census, as well as various others.

## Using the Microfilm Catalog

You used one set of microfilm to access the Soundex and to get the needed reference numbers. Specifically, you now know from the Soundex the state, county, enumeration district number, and page number. Go to the microfilm catalog again. This time check the section in the catalog that

**Tree Tips** _____

Do not confuse the Supervisor's District on the census sheet with the Enumeration District right below it. It is the latter (E.D.) that you need in order to find the full listing on the film.

is for the full 1920 census (not the Soundex). Determine the micropublication number and the roll you will need. If there is more than one roll for the county, watch for the roll with the enumeration district number you found on the Soundex.

*From the 1920 Federal*
*Population Census Catalog.*

**NORTH DAKOTA**

1330. Adams Co. (EDs 1-11), Barnes Co. (EDs 1-19), Benson Co. (EDs 20-35), Billings Co. (EDs 12-20), and Bowman Co. (EDs 21-31).

1331. Bottineau Co. (EDs 36-56), Burke Co. (EDs 32-41), Burleigh Co. (EDs 57-69, 267, and 70-76), and Divide Co. (EDs 42-49).

1332. Cass Co. (EDs 1-2, 12-21, 5-11, and 22-26) and Dickey Co. (EDs 77, 257, 78, 260, 79, 259, 80-82, 258, 83, 84, 262, 85, 256, 86, and 87).

1333. Cavalier Co. (EDs 27-42), Dunn Co. (EDs 50-59), Eddy Co. (EDs 88-95, 266, and 96), Emmons Co. (EDs 97-113), and Griggs Co. (EDs 121-128).

1334. Foster Co. (EDs 114-120), Golden Valley Co. (EDs 60-68), Grand Forks Co. (EDs 54-65, 43-53, and 66-72), and Grant Co. (EDs 69-81).

1335. Hettinger Co. (EDs 82-89), Kidder Co. (EDs 129-134, 261, and 135-140), Logan Co. (EDs 155-162, 263, and 268), La Moure Co. (EDs 141-154), and McKenzie Co. (EDs 90-106).

1336. McHenry Co. (EDs 163-178, 264, and 179-182), McIntosh Co. (EDs 183-191), McLean Co. (EDs 107-124), and Mercer Co. (EDs 125-133).

1337. Morton Co. (EDs 134-152), Oliver Co. (EDs 167-172), Mountrail Co. (EDs 153-166), and Nelson Co. (EDs 73-83).

1338. Pembina Co. (EDs 84-101), Pierce Co. (EDs 192-201), Ramsey Co. (EDs 102-117), and Renville Co. (EDs 173-181).

1339. Ramson Co. (EDs 118-128), Stark Co. (EDs 197-210), Richland Co. (EDs 129-148), and Sioux Co. (EDs 182-187).

1340. Rolette Co. (EDs 202-211), Sargent Co. (EDs 149-158), Slope Co. (EDs 188-196), Sheridan Co. (EDs 212-220), Steele Co. (EDs 159-163, 211, and 164-167), and Towner Co. (EDs 168-175, 212, 176, and 177).

1341. Stutsman Co. (EDs 221-226, 269, and 227-243), Traill Co. (EDs 178-189), and Wells Co. (EDs 244-247, 265, 248, and 255).

1342. Walsh Co. (EDs 190-210), Williams Co. (EDs 239-256), and Ward Co. (EDs 211-217).

1343. Ward Co. (EDs 218-238).

# There They Are!

You now have the roll of microfilm in hand. Finally, you can locate the full family listing. Proceed to the county you need on the film. Look for the Enumeration District (E.D.) number you obtained from the Soundex. The E.D.s will be arranged numerically, usually in the upper right hand of the census page just below the Supervisor's District. Then proceed to the page (sheet) number you found, and look for the listing.

One of your most exciting moments will be in locating your first census record. There they are—the whole family, Grandpa, Grandma, and all the children, including your mother when she was a child. It's fun to imagine Grandpa and Grandma trying to remember their former homes so that they could give the birthplace of each child, along with answering the census taker's other questions.

After the census listing is found, hand copy it in its entirety. Census forms like those shown in Appendix C are useful. Census forms are also available online at www.genealogy.com/00000061.html or www.ancestry.com/trees/charts/census. Electronic spreadsheets for recording census data can be downloaded from www. censustools.com.

When viewing census, copy the entries exactly. If it shows Jas., don't write James. If it shows William, don't write Wm. If it shows John Charley Harvey, don't write it as John C. Harvey. If you wish to add a note, add it in brackets so it is clear that this was an addition. Be sure to include the gender. You may think it is obvious that John is a male and Ann is a female. But what about Willie? Later you may wonder if that was a daughter named Wilhelmina or a son named William. Nothing is too minor and can later be helpful. If there is a microfilm reader/printer, make a micro-print or copy it all carefully. Note the neighbors, too.

**Tree Tips** _____

Even if you know that there is an error in the listing, copy it exactly as it appears. Be sure to include everyone listed in the home, such as boarders, servants, and so on. You may later realize that there was a relationship.

# Using the Pre-1880 Schedules

Indexes for censuses from 1790 through 1870 are not available in Soundex. They have been indexed by a variety of indexers, however, and are available in published books and online. Though indexes vary, they usually show the name, county, township, district or ward, and a page number.

After you have the indexed entry, determine from the catalog which roll you need. For any pre-1880 census, you will not need to determine an enumeration district; they are indexed by the page numbers (and townships), which will lead you to the listing. In a few minutes you'll find that long-sought listing.

**Tree Tips** _____

Often there is a stamped page number, as well as one or two handwritten page numbers. Some indexers used the stamped page numbers, while others used those that were hand-written.

# The First in 1790

Marshals were required to list the number of inhabitants within their districts. They were to omit those Indians not taxed (those who did not live within the towns and cities) and list those who were taxed. They listed free persons (including *indentured servants*) in categories of age and sex. The rest were counted as "all others," that is, slaves.

**Genie Jargon**

An **indentured servant** is one who entered into a contract binding himself or herself into the service of another for a specified term, usually in exchange for passage. The number of years could vary; usually it was four to seven years.

**Tree Tips**

When the census schedules show age brackets such as males 10 to 16, males 16 to 26, and so on, the ages included within the category are actually one year under the next category. For example, males 10 to 16 includes males through age 15; males 16 to 26 includes males through the age of 25.

Free white males in the 1790 census were listed by two age groups, those of 16 years and upward, and those under that age. The total free white females were listed with no age distinction at all. Only the head of the household was listed by name. John Jackson, who was age 40 and who had a son, age 18; a son, age 12; a wife, age 38; and two daughters, ages 8 and 10, would be listed as two males 16 or over, one male under 16, and three females.

In 1908, the federal government transcribed and printed the 1790 census for all available states: Connecticut, Maine, Maryland, Massachusetts, New Hampshire, New York, North Carolina, Pennsylvania, Rhode Island, South Carolina, Vermont, and the reconstructed census of Virginia. The 1790 census for Delaware, Georgia, Kentucky, New Jersey, Tennessee, and Virginia were lost or destroyed. The printed 1790 census is available in most large libraries. A reprint edition by Genealogical Publishing Company in 1952 made the set widely available.

## Creatively Using Sparse Information

Let's say you are tracing Jonathan Calavary who was born, according to a Bible record, on 3 March 1783. You find him in census records in 1830, '40, and '50 as head of household. But who is his father? He was only about seven when the 1790 census was taken. He should therefore be listed as a male under 16 in his father's home in 1790. Search the 1790 census for the state for the name Calavary. You may find a family with a male listed as under 16. With that unusual surname, there won't be many and it will be a starting place for the search.

# 1800 and 1810 Census

The 1800 and 1810 censuses were more expansive. The head of the family was listed; the free white males and free white females were listed by age: under 10, 10 to 16, 16 to 26, 26 to 45, and 45 or older. They also included the number of other free persons in the household (except Indians not taxed), the number of slaves, and the place of residence.

In some early censuses, the lists were copied and rearranged alphabetically by the census taker. This loses the advantage of listing the family with neighbors. However, most often the lists are in the order that the families were contacted by the census taker.

> **Lineage Lessons**
>
> Since only the head of household is actually named in the censuses of 1790 through 1840, it isn't possible to determine with certainty which are family members. Some of the others listed by age may not be part of the immediate family. Another relative or a helper could have been living in the home.

# 1820 Census Adds Males 16 to 18

The 1820 census included the same questions as in 1810. It also added a category for males 16 to 18, while retaining the 16-to-26 category. Other questions included the number of those not naturalized; the number engaged in agriculture, commerce, or manufacturing; the number of "colored" persons; and the number of other persons, with the exception of Indians.

> **Tree Tips**
>
> In 1820 the males listed in the 16-to-18 column are also included in the 16-to-26 column. Keep this in mind when you are figuring the total number of people living in the household.

# 1830 and 1840 Censuses Narrow Age

In 1830, the age categories were narrowed, enabling researchers to establish ages with more precision. The categories for males and females were as follows: under 5, 5 to 10, 10 to 15, 15 to 20, 20 to 30, 30 to 40, 40 to 50, 50 to 60, 60 to 70, 70 to 80, 80 to 90, 90 to 100, and over 100. The number of those who were "deaf, dumb, and blind" and the number of aliens were listed. In addition, the number of slaves and free "colored" persons were included by age categories.

The 1840 census contained the same columns as 1830, with an addition important to genealogical research. A column was added for the ages of military war pensioners (usually for Revolutionary War service). Also added were columns to count those engaged in agriculture; mining; commerce; manufacturing and trade; navigation of the ocean; navigation of canals, lakes, and rivers; learned professions and engineers; number in school; number in family over age of 21 who could not read and write; and the number of "insane."

The value of knowing the age of pensioners in the 1840 census is immense. The pensioner might have been the soldier, or the widow, or other entitled person. You will find that Mary Conklin at age 97 was living with Mary Montanya in Haverstraw, Rockland County, New York. John Jones of Metal, Franklin County, Pennsylvania, was living at the remarkable age of 110. This listing of pensioners was extracted and published by the federal government in 1841, with a reprint by Southern Book Company in 1954 and subsequent reprints with an added index by the Genealogical Publishing Company.

# Everyone Has a Name in 1850

The 1850 census was the first to require the name and age of *everyone* in the household. Its value to genealogists increased dramatically as a result. A dwelling number and family number was assigned to each listing in the order of visitation. Questions included name, age, sex, "color," occupation, value of real estate, birthplace, whether married within the year, whether attended school within the year, and whether they could read or write (if over the age of 20). Additionally, whether any were deaf-mute, blind, insane, "idiotic," or a convict.

The census is useful for clues in naming patterns, in identifying the household as of a certain date, occupation, and migration. The value of real estate gives some idea of the worth of the family and is an additional clue that there could be land records available in the county.

## Those Others Living with the Family

Those living with the family should be carefully noted because they might be relatives—a mother-in-law or a married sister. And very important, the families enumerated a few listings before and after the family should be noted because they, too, may be related. If not, they may still assist the search because families usually did not move in isolation. When migrating from one area to another, they were often accompanied by family or friends. That information can lead you to a prior residence.

Let's say you are tracing a family listed in the 1850 census of Montgomery County, Tennessee, and note the older members of the family were all born in North Carolina. You know that they moved between 1844 and 1846, because a child was born in Tennessee in 1846. The surname is common. Where in North Carolina to look? Check the neighbors. You notice that some of them were also born in North Carolina and, judging from the birthplaces of the children, seem to have moved around the same time. Look in the 1840 census index of North Carolina for the surname, *and the surname of the neighbors*. This may help narrow the search when you find similar names grouped together in one of the North Carolina counties.

---

### Lineage Lessons

The occupations listed in the census can help. If there were several by the surname in the county who were cabinet makers, you might suspect a relationship. If they were farmers, look for land transactions. If your nineteenth century ancestor was a doctor, perhaps the medical school he attended has data. The census can even point you to military records when it shows "sailor" or "Col., U.S. Army" as the "occupation."

---

## Slaveholders and Slaves

There were separate slave schedules taken with the 1850 census. The name of the slave owner was given, the number of slaves owned, and the number of former slaves now freed. The slaves, however, were not listed by name. These schedules have been microfilmed.

# Leads and More Leads

The clues that result from the use of a census listing are many. Your family was listed in 1850 Pennsylvania and part of the information shown was as follows:

| Name | Age | Sex | Birthplace | Occupation | Real Estate |
|---|---|---|---|---|---|
| SMITH, Jonathan | 39 | m | Virginia | Farmer | $100 |
| Mary | 37 | f | Virginia | keeping house | |
| Barnabus | 11 | m | Virginia | | |
| Catharine | 9 | f | Maryland | | |
| Joseph | 7 | m | Pennsylvania | | |
| Martha | 3 | f | Pennsylvania | | |
| Jessie | 1 | f | Pennsylvania | | |
| JORDAN, Barnabus | 65 | m | Virginia | retired | |

How does this help? You now know that Jonathan Smith was born ca. (about) 1811 in Virginia, and that his wife was born ca. 1813 in Virginia. Their son Barnabus was born ca. 1839 in Virginia. Catharine's birthplace indicates that they moved to Maryland between about 1839 and 1841. However, soon thereafter, they moved to Pennsylvania, in time for the birth of Joseph ca. 1843, followed by Martha and Jessie. You now have an idea of the migratory pattern of this family. In addition, because Jonathan Smith was a farmer and had real estate valued at $100.00, you can check for a deed on the farm. Even the township is helpful. Using that, county histories can be consulted for early inhabitants. Newspapers can be examined for their community columns.

### Lineage Lessons

In using the census to establish an approximate birth, if the daughter is eight in 1850, show that she was born "ca. 1842." Do not show it without the ca. (meaning *circa*, or about) because the year may not be correct. In 1850, the census year was measured from June 1, 1849, through May 31, 1850. The actual month of birth affects the calculation of the age. Aside from that, there are many errors in ages.

What about Barnabus Jordan, aged 65, living with the family? You note that he was born in Virginia (as was Mary Smith, Jonathan's probable wife), and that Jonathan and Mary Smith named a son Barnabus. Possibly Barnabus Jordan is Mary's father. Though this census does not give the required proof, it is another "lead" to follow.

Do you stop here? No. Check the listings before and after Jonathan Smith. Two listings before is Martin Smith, age 69, born in Virginia, and Mary Smith, age 67, born in Virginia. Could they be Jonathan's parents? Three listings after Jonathan is

Thomas Gordon, 40, and Matilda Gordon, 35, both born in Virginia. Among their children is a son, *Barnabus* Gordon. Perhaps Matilda is a sister of Mary. The name similarity of the child Barnabus, together with the ages of Mary, 37, and Matilda, 35, both born in Virginia, would suggest that they might be sisters. Although it will need further investigation, you have another clue.

# The 1860 and 1870 Censuses

The 1860 census contains information similar to that of the 1850 census, but adds a column for the value of personal property and a column for those who were paupers. There were also separate slave schedules, as in 1850.

**Tree Tips**

Use the address provided by the 1880 census to examine the city directories for a few years before and after the 1880 census. You may find relatives living with or near the family during some of those years.

In 1870, a column was added for Father Foreign Born and another for Mother Foreign Born. (If marked, this can lead to a search of naturalization records and ship passenger lists.) Also, if an individual was born or married within the year, the month of the event was to be recorded.

# 1880, 1885, and 1890 Censuses

The 1880 census adds the birthplace of the father and the mother (state and country only) in the population schedules. This has created an important resource, but it must be used with caution. Often the person did not know where his or her father or mother was born, so only guessed. The 1880 census added another entry important in your search: the relationship of the person listed to the head of household, such as "wife," "brother," "mother-in-law," "boarder," and so on. Whether they were single, married, widowed, or divorced was noted. Another helpful addition is the address of those who lived in cities or urban areas.

## Special 1885 Federal Census

Five states and territories conducted an 1885 census partly funded by the federal government: Colorado, Florida, Nebraska, Dakota territory, and New Mexico territory. These are at the National Archives in Washington, D.C.; only those for Colorado and Nebraska have been microfilmed.

## Special 1890 Civil War Census

With a few minor exceptions, most of the 1890 federal population census was burned. A special census taken that year for Union soldiers, however, was only partially destroyed. It is missing states and territories from A through Kansas and part of Kentucky, but the rest survives and includes the soldier's rank, company, regiment or vessel, enlistment, discharge, length of service, post office address, and some other remarks. This is available on microfilm in the National Archives.

# Changes in the 1900, 1910, 1920, and 1930 Censuses

The 1900 census has the month and year of birth in addition to age and the number of years married. The mother was required to list how many children she had borne and how many were still living. For immigrants, the year of entry, the number of years in the United States, and whether naturalized were noted. The census also included various other questions.

In 1910, refinements were made. One of the most important additions was the question of whether the males were Union or Confederate veterans. This can lead you to military records.

### Lineage Lessons

A serious deficiency exists in locating families in 1910 microfilm, because only 21 states have a Soundex or Miracode. For the other states, you must do a page-by-page search in the counties of interest, or use the subscription services of Ancestry.com or HeritageQuest.com for they have this census indexed. If you can establish the physical address of the family, you can shorten your search by using National Archives micro-publication T1224 to establish the enumeration district.

In addition to names, ages, and so on, the 1920 census adds the year of immigration, whether naturalized, and the year of naturalization, as well as other important information.

In 1930 the census had interesting questions such as whether individuals owned a radio set. Besides personal questions such as sex, race, age, marital status, and occupation, they were asked if they were veterans, and if so, of which war. If an immigrant, the enumerator inquired as to year of immigration, naturalization, or whether an alien. All these details are important in weaving our ancestor's lives.

# Mortality Schedules

Starting in 1850, a listing was made by the census taker of those who died during the previous 12 months (June 1, 1849, to May 31, 1850). This mortality schedule is an important search record. It includes the name of the deceased, sex, age, "color," whether widowed, place of birth, the month in which the death occurred, profession (or occupation or trade), the cause of death, and the number of days ill. The originals of these are not centrally located. In addition to the 1850 mortality schedules, the 1860, 1870, and 1880 censuses included similar lists with a few changes. In 1870 the census included the birthplace of the deceased's parents. Mortality schedules were also taken with the special 1885 federal census. Greenwood's *Researcher's Guide to American Genealogy* has a listing of mortality schedules and the physical location of these important records.

The Family History Library has some of the mortality schedules on microfilm and a microfiche listing of those available in other locations. Look also for the index to the 1850–1880 mortality schedules by Accelerated Indexing Systems, and the online listings at www.ancestry.com.

**Tree Tips**

Some nonpopulation schedules are available for agriculture (where you might learn the amount of a crop your ancestor produced in the preceding year), manufacturing, and so on. A good discussion of those will be found in the chapter "Research in Census Records," by Loretto Dennis Szucs, in Ancestry's *The Source*.

**Lineage Lessons**

In addition to the federal government taking censuses, a number of states conducted a state census. These are not centrally located. The best source for information on these records is Ann S. Lainhart's *State Census Records*, widely available in libraries. It explains the differences between the state and federal censuses, questions asked, and the location of these records.

# Can You Trust These Old Records?

You might be perplexed when you find that the census listings you obtained from 1850, 1860, 1870, and 1880 all conflict. "How can that be?" you wonder. The problem is that you do not know who supplied the answers. Perhaps the father did not remember the exact ages of the children. Perhaps the mother was shy and became confused. Perhaps one of the children supplied the information. Add the possibility that the census taker made an error or that he entered the data incorrectly. Also, some problems exist on individual rolls because of pages skipped when microfilming, or because of poor quality of microfilming when the project was started.

If these weren't problems enough, some of the census returns had two additional handwritten copies made from the original. The copies were distributed to other agencies depending upon the year of the census. Now the chance of error was multiplied. The person writing the copies could have skipped an entry, erred on reading a name, or made any number of other errors.

# Now You've Got Something to Work With

Obtaining census records starts to lay the foundation for the documentation you build on your family. By comparing the listings in the various census years, you can reconstruct a fairly accurate list of the family members and the places in which they lived. You can even determine something about their background through questions on naturalization or military service. You will get further insight as to their worth, those in the family with afflictions, and other details. Always get all the available census records for your ancestors, not just one or two. Every listing is a potential source of important leads and will help to construct that solid, documented line for you. For additional reading, consult *Guide to Genealogical Research in the National Archives,* Chapter 1.

## The Least You Need to Know

- In the censuses from 1790 through 1840 only the head of household was listed by name.

- From 1850 on, the census names each person in the household.

- In 1880 the census lists the birthplace (state or country) of the parents, and the relationships to the head of the household.

- Though anyone can use census microfilm in major libraries or National Archives branches, there are also subscription services online with digitized images.

- Census records have many errors created by faulty memories or lack of knowledge by those who supplied the information.

# Chapter 12

# Corresponding Effectively

## In This Chapter

- The importance of knowing where to write
- The letter that will bring a response
- Samples of concise letters
- Some cost-cutting ideas

Writing letters will substantially aid your search. Sooner or later everyone needs to do it. Contrary to popular belief, not everything is on the Internet!

You may have gotten away from letter writing and rely either on email communication or the telephone. There are times, however, when a letter is more effective. This is especially true when you are contacting a busy office. If you interrupt a hectic workday, it is too easy for someone to give you a negative answer on the telephone. Many times, short of going to a location personally, a letter will have to do.

Keep in mind your goal and the goal of the responder. You want some data. The person responding wants to supply the data with the least effort and time as possible. Your letter will be far more effective if you remember certain basics. Clearly state what you want, send it to the right place, and make a good impression so that it will be taken seriously.

Here are other considerations which we'll discuss more fully later in the chapter:

- Use full-size (8.5"×11") paper

- Eye appeal (wide margins, space between paragraphs, no smudges)

- Include your name and address on the letter

- Be concise

- Enclose an LSASE (long self-addressed stamped envelope)

- Address the right facility

- Know the date when state registration of vital statistics started, so that you don't write to a state for a 1875 death certificate if their statewide registration began in 1911

- Know the holdings of the repository

- Offer to pay

- Don't unnecessarily limit your request

- Supply variant spellings for the family name

# The Mechanics of Correspondence

Before we get into what to say in a letter requesting information, let's talk about some basics that should be a part of every letter.

## Making It Look Neat

Use standard letter-size paper when writing. If the recipient files the letters, standard-size paper makes it easier, especially if they use a two-hole punch at the top. Smaller-size paper tends to get lost in the stacks or slip between larger papers.

Make your letter attractive. Crowding the page leaves the impression that reading it will be a chore. Leave sufficient margins on all sides. And leave a blank line or some space between paragraphs to set them off. If you do not have a typewriter or computer, take care to write legibly, neatly, and briefly.

In this electronic age, many letterheads are prepared on the computer. Use a large-enough font of type. Those with poor eyesight may mistake the 1 in your letterhead for a 7 if it is fancy script or too small.

**Tree Tips**

Keep a copy of the letters you send, at least until you get an answer. On the computer it is easy to create a file or document of "outgoing mail" and just add each letter as it is written. Periodically you can delete older letters that you don't need to keep, though the small amount of computer space may make keeping them indefinitely a better choice. When you need to refer to a stored letter, use the "find" feature of your word processor, inserting a few keywords that you recall (such as the name of the recipient, the address, or the subject).

## Including Your Contact Information

Include your name and address on the letter, and e-mail address if you have one. Letters can get separated from an envelope. Without an address, the letter you spent so much time composing may never get a response. Position the address at the top of the first page, not at the end of the letter. When it is answered or filed, the responder can then immediately identify the sender without having to shuffle through the whole letter. Small courtesies that lighten the responder's load put you in a more favorable position for a reply.

Invest in a small rubber stamp with your name and address. You will use this often. When you write to someone and include enclosures, rubber-stamp the enclosures on the front so the recipient knows at a glance how to reach you. If the recipient photocopies your enclosures and sends them to someone else, that person also needs to know who supplied the data. (Alternately, use small stick-on mailling labels.)

## Spelling It Correctly, and Getting the Right Zip Code

It is disappointing to have the letter returned in a few weeks because you misspelled the street name or inserted the wrong house number. Recheck the address. If in doubt, use a telephone book or online directory (see Chapter 6). The post office has assigned four additional numbers to zip codes to assist in getting the mail to its destination. Go to www.usps.gov and click on "Find a Zip Code."

**Pedigree Pitfalls** _____

Keep it brief! And keep it focused. This is probably the most difficult part of letter writing. You are eager to give details. But you soon learn that the shorter your letter, the more successful it is. The key is to be concise. Don't use ten words when five would do. At first you may need to do a draft and then rewrite. As you develop the skill you will experience an increased success rate. If you have a computer, you can create some "boilerplate" paragraphs that you can insert in letters. One might be to introduce yourself, another might be to request a search for an estate, and so on.

## An SASE for Reply

Many repositories and individuals will not answer letters unless you enclose an SASE. While you are at it, make it an LSASE (Long Self-Addressed Stamped Envelope). The responder may have important data to send that will not fit into a smaller envelope. The responder is forced to prepare a long envelope, put postage on it, and hope for some other use for the smaller stamped envelope you sent. Your request might be set aside and forgotten. Or the responder may opt to send you a brief reply that fits the smaller envelope and decide not to include copies that could have been easily slipped into a larger envelope.

# What Should You Say?

When you are seeking information about your ancestor, be specific. A "Please send me everything you have" letter, whether to a repository or to a relative, will almost certainly remain unanswered.

To develop the technique of writing an effective letter to a business or repository, consider your goal. What is it you want? Information about the parents? Children? State your desires clearly. Different records need to be examined, depending on your goal. If you are searching for Ezekiel Madison's parents, you might try for an obituary, death certificate, birth record, marriage record, and various others. To find Ezekiel Madison's children, his obituary could help, but his death certificate, birth record, or marriage record would not disclose that information. Each request involves different search techniques. Responses will be more on target if the responder understands your goal. Before you write, decide on one or two things that you are hoping to find. Then, state them clearly.

# "Dear Courthouse"

Writing to a courthouse is somewhat different from writing to an individual or a library. In writing to a courthouse, keep your requests separate. If you need a marriage record and a will, write two different letters. This is not the time to save postage. If those documents are in two separate offices, you will also be dependent upon a clerk to fulfill your order and then transfer your request to another office. A glitch can develop. If, however, you are ordering two of the same type of document, such as two marriage records, include both requests in the same letter; the same clerk will be handling them both. Always limit any request; if you need more than three or four documents, even if they are of the same type, order the additional ones later. Otherwise, a busy clerk will process simpler requests first, setting your more extensive one aside and perhaps forgetting it.

## Alternate Spellings

The clerks of the courthouse will not know that the surname you seek can be spelled in a variety of ways. They will look only for the name you request. If you write for the will of John Critchfield, show it in your letter of request as "John Critchfield (Scritchfield, Crutchfield)" and any other spellings you have encountered. Otherwise, the clerk may miss the record.

**Tree Tips**

Don't know the exact title of the office you want? Write on the envelope: "Probate Office" (for estates) or "Marriage Record Office" or "Deed Office." It will reach the appropriate clerk.

## Writing to the Right Place

You want to obtain a deed from Groton, Connecticut. Should you send your request to the registrar of deeds addressed at "County Courthouse"? You need a will from Lynchburg, Virginia; send the Campbell County Courthouse a letter? In both of these instances, your letter would have been unsuccessful. Each would have cost you two stamps (for your letter, and for the SASE you enclosed. If you don't get a response you might assume the information is not available. All the while, the records could be on shelves of the appropriate keeper of records.

What went wrong? Connecticut does not keep such records in county courthouses; they have town halls where the deeds are recorded. You wrote to the wrong place. And Lynchburg is one of around 30 independent cities in Virginia which have their own courthouse and are not a part of the adjacent county. The use of a guidebook or online website to determine the appropriate jurisdictions is important.

Several books will assist you in these determinations: Everton's *Handy Book for Genealogists*, Ancestry's *Red Book*, and Marcia Wiswall Lindberg's *Genealogist's Handbook for New England Research*.

**Tree Tips** _____

*Ancestry's Red Book* describes some of the collections. Many state repositories now have pages on the Web that describe their own collections. Also try www.usgenweb.com mentioned previously for an organized volunteer effort to provide information by states and counties.

In writing to local governments, keep these points in mind:

♦ In some New England states, the document you want may be in the Town Hall, or in a probate district office (encompassing several towns).

♦ In Virginia, it may be in the courthouse of an independent city. (There are a few other independent cities in the United States, too, such as Baltimore and St. Louis.)

♦ The county may have more than one courthouse.

To find the addresses of other places to write, use the many directories available in your library; there are directories of funeral homes, newspapers, libraries, and others. *Directories in Print* will open your eyes with the listings it includes. Also helpful is Elizabeth Bentley's *The Genealogist's Address Book* as well as Juliana Szucs Smith's *The*

*Ancestry Family Historian's Address Book*. Or go to the website of the county or town—usually the addresses are listed there. Start with www.usgenweb.org, then click on the state, and then the county. Use these resources to determine the correct address; you want the letter to get there on the first try.

## State Registration of Vital Statistics

All states eventually provided for registration of vital statistics on the state level. The beginning dates varied from state to state, but most are in the first part of the twentieth century. Before that time, most counties maintained their own registers, but the starting dates of those also varied. Without knowing the beginning date of state registration, you will be guessing whether to write to the State Department of Health or to the local government. A handy website for checking on vital records of states is that of the National Center of Health Statistics at www.cdc.gov/nchs/howto/w2w/w2welcom.htm. There you can get information on cost, address of where to order, and other helpful information. Or check "Where to Write for Vital Records" in Ancestry's *The Source*.

## What's on the Shelves?

When writing to a repository, knowing its holdings will increase your success rate. Which of the state repositories has the best newspaper collection for an obituary? Which is more likely to have the military muster rolls of the state? Look for published guides, which might be available in your library.

# What's It Going to Cost?

It is normally a good practice to inquire about the cost of a document or service in advance of placing an order. If you don't, you may be surprised with a fee higher than you had expected. For mail-order requests, some New York counties, for instance, charge $25.00 to search a record under 25 years old, and $70.00 for records over 25 years old. Their photocopy charges by mail can be as high as $3.00 per page. When you write, first explain what you need, and then add, "Please quote for a copy of these records before proceeding." The alternative is to send a small check (perhaps for $5.00), with the notation, "If it is higher, please let me know before proceeding."

## Offering to Pay Promptly

When writing for a record for which payment will be required, you have options.

◆ Enclose a check with the exact fee.

◆ Offer to pay upon being advised of the charges.

◆ Send a check for a small amount and ask them to advise you before filling the request if more payment is required.

◆ If you are ordering a birth or death record, or some other record with a standard fee, the guide books or websites may provide the amount of the fee. If so, enclose a check or money order for that amount with your request.

**Tree Tips**

Some repositories accept credit cards. If you are in a hurry for the information, you can call to inquire.

If you do not know the amount, you can insert a clause, such as, "I will pay the cost immediately upon knowing the charge." This may delay fulfillment of your request because the responder then has two options:

1. To send you the information with the bill.

2. To write to let you know the amount.

Never, never, send cash. You may feel it is such a small amount that if it should get lost, it isn't a problem. But this creates an awkward situation; the recipient may feel that you will question his or her honesty if the funds happen to get lost.

# Sample Letters

Letter writing is a skill that you can master. When you see the high success rate that results by observing a few "rules," it will encourage you to explore what can be accomplished by mail. The following examples of letters demonstrate the technique of keeping requests simple but to the point. Develop a few letters of your own and save them as templates to use when you write future requests.

## Trying to Find a Will

In the first example, you are writing to get some information from an estate. You are hoping that your great-grandfather left a will. But don't limit yourself to requesting the will. If he died without a will and had sufficient property, there still could be an *administration*. Depending upon the reply to the letter shown below, you can follow up with a request for additional documents.

---

### Lineage Lessons

An **administration** is normally an estate in which there was no will. The administrator was appointed by the court to handle the estate. Some counties will have a document, called a **petition for administration**, setting out the name of the heirs and possibly their addresses. It depends on the state and the time period. The administrator's bond is more widely available. This was required as security for the performance of administrative duties in handling the estate. Though the genealogical information on it is less than you will find on a petition, it still provides clues.

---

[Your name and address]

[Date]

Probate Office
[address here]

Dear Clerk of the Probate Office:

I would like to obtain a photocopy of the will of:

John W. Jorgensen; died 3 March 1842

If he did not leave a will, I would like to obtain a photocopy of the petition for administration and the administration bond.

Please let me know the cost for photocopies, and I will send the fee immediately. Enclosed is an SASE.

Thank you for your assistance.

Sincerely,

As you dig deeper, you will find that there are many additional papers involving estates that can help. For now, writing for a will or administration will get you started. See Chapter 14 for more information about the additional paperwork you may find.

## The Obituary

Obituaries are of tremendous value to your search, but obtaining them seems to be a stumbling block. First, determine not only the county but, if possible, also the town or township within the county in which the family lived. The county may have had more than one newspaper; if so, you want to find the one that covered their home community. Then, write to the local library where they lived or the public library of the county seat to see if they have copies or films of the newspapers that they can check.

> Suzy Que
> 1111 Apple Blossom Court
> Anywhere, MO 12345-6789
>
> Public Library
> [address here]
>
> Dear Librarian:
>
> I would like to obtain a photocopy of the obituary of:
>
> Joseph H. Johnson, who died 14 April 1892 in the town of Sunshine.
>
> [Here include a paragraph as to whether you are enclosing some funds, or "Please let me know the cost and I will remit promptly."]
>
> Thank you for your assistance.
>
> Sincerely,

## Ordering a Vital Record

If you are writing to the county for records created before state registrations were required, try the example shown below. Don't unnecessarily limit the date when requesting a marriage record. Judge a span of time from the birth dates of children but allow enough leeway, perhaps 5 to 10 years.

> [Your name and address}
>
> [Date]
>
> Register of Marriages
> [Courthouse Address here]
>
> Dear Marriage Registrar:

I would like to order a photocopy of the marriage application (or license) and certificate for:

Joseph Cruse (or Kruse) to Virginia Malley, about 1860–1867

Please let me know the cost and I will remit promptly. [Or, if you prefer, enclose a small check.]

I enclose an SASE for reply, and thank you for your assistance.

Sincerely,

## Dear Cousin ...

If you are writing to a relative for the first time, introduce yourself. Let them know your purpose and what it is you are seeking. You could include a family group sheet with the letter, which may pique interest, but don't flood the cousin with data at this point of the contact.

[Your name and address]

[Date]

[His or her name and address]

Dear [   ],

I have been working on the family history for two years, and just found out from a relative that you and I are related as second cousins. We both are great-grandchildren of George Milliken and his wife Susan Masters. My family is through their daughter Jane, who married Jesse Cooper. My mother told me that she lost track of your family after your parents moved—about 30 years ago. I am delighted to now be in touch.

I was told your grandparents passed away many years ago. Can you tell me when and where they died, and where they are buried?

I have also been hoping to find someone with a photo of our great-grandparents, George and Susan. Do you have one that can be copied or do you know of anyone in the family who does?

It would be a delight to hear from you and to exchange information about our families.

Your cousin,

# A Penny Saved ...

The cost of letter writing has escalated. Not only do you pay more for postage, but also for paper, envelopes, and supplies. You want to make those letters count. If they do not achieve your goal on the first try, the cost of producing the letters again, and the time expended, must be considered. Be sure you know the current postal rates not only for the first ounce, but also for additional ounces.

Invest in a postage scale. The small scales go to one pound, or, for a slightly higher cost, you can get a two-pound meter. It will not take long for you to recoup your investment. Without a meter, you probably often guess at the weight, adding additional postage "just to be sure."

**Tree Tips**

Keep the Post Office 1-800 number close by, and use it to inquire about rates when you are in doubt. Request the basic leaflet on postal rates from your local post office so that you can refer to it as needed. Or go to www.usps.gov and click on "Calculate Postage."

## The Least You Need to Know

◆ Everyone needs to write a letter at some time; it's not possible to do all genealogical research online.

◆ The concise letter will bring more results.

◆ Don't combine a variety of different requests in the same letter.

◆ Keep the letter appealing to the eye.

◆ Addressing the letter properly will ensure that it gets to the right place.

◆ Knowing the proper rates and weight will reduce postage costs.

# Part 4

## In Your Ancestors' Footsteps

Grab your suitcase; we're going on the road! In Part 4, you'll visit the areas where the family lived. You'll walk the same ground they walked so many years ago. You'll learn to use the courthouse records, to visit the cemetery and glean new clues, and to search the fascinating newspapers while there. You'll also learn of the marvelous military records that await you on the trip to the National Archives or its branches. And you'll weave Internet resources into your trip preparations.

Excitement beckons—start packing! Even if you don't plan a personal trip in the near future, the advice and techniques in this section take you further down the road in your pursuit of your ancestors.

# Chapter 13

# A Little Traveling Music, Please

## In This Chapter

- ◆ Planning a research trip
- ◆ What to take
- ◆ What to do before you leave
- ◆ What to do when you get there

You've read some genealogy guide books, researched a number of census records, corresponded with relatives and repositories, and developed a familiarity with the kinds of records that will advance your knowledge of the family. Soon you will be eager to travel to certain counties for a first-hand look at the records created by and for your ancestors. Some of the most exhilarating experiences in genealogy result from delving into original records (rather than published or filmed ones) and from walking the roads trod by your ancestors.

Decide which counties are likely to produce the most information on the most people. Review the information you've accumulated and narrow the possibilities for the first trip. Your decision will be influenced by many things: time, distance, and cost of travel; priorities, such as a family reunion or an elderly relative in poor health; a burning curiosity about one ancestor in particular; and other personal issues.

# Counties Have Ancestors, Too

Before you go too far in planning your trip, be sure you are headed for the right county. Counties are the political subdivisions of states. Their current boundaries are not necessarily the ones they've always had. New counties were carved out of one or more old ones, or counties were absorbed by adjacent counties. Disputes and/or new surveys redrew the lines between counties. Why should you care? Because the records of your ancestors are in the counties as they were when they lived there.

Some states have forms of government other than counties. Connecticut is organized around towns, rather than counties. In Virginia there are numerous independent cities, completely autonomous from the counties they adjoin. Louisiana counties are called parishes. Read up on the political divisions of the state as you start your research there. Skipping lightly over the preparation can lead to many disappointments, not the least of which is to find that you are in the wrong county.

**Genie Jargon** _____

The **parent county** is the county from which a present-day county was formed.

**Genie Jargon** _____

**County seat** is the town that is the administrative center for a county. Don't assume it is the largest town in the county. A few counties even have two courthouses.

Your ancestor may have spent a lifetime on the same piece of land, yet may have resided in two or more counties due to boundary changes. If you don't know about the *parent county*, you can miss all the valuable records your ancestor left there. To know where to look, you must find the dates that the counties were organized and the names of the parent counties.

To find parent counties, consult Everton's *Handy Book for Genealogists* or *Ancestry's Red Book*. For boundary changes in census years, see William Thorndale and William Dollarhide's *Map Guide to the U.S. Federal Censuses, 1790–1920*. Checking the county's website on USGenWeb, (www.usgenweb. com) may be another source of information. Niche software AniMap (www.goldbug.com) shows every county's boundary change from colonial times, not just from the census years.

While you are zeroing in on the county, also find the *county seat;* that's usually where the county records are kept.

# Do Not Pack Lightly

Old admonitions about packing lightly for travel do not apply to genealogy. At the minimum you need these reference materials to make your research trip effective:

◆ Pedigree charts

◆ Family group sheets

◆ Research calendar

◆ Your notes

◆ Listing of county formations and parent counties

◆ Maps of state and county roads

◆ Prioritized checklists

◆ Lists of facilities' addresses, phone numbers, and hours

◆ Names of possible contacts

**Tree Tips**

If you belong to a genealogical society, pack your membership cards. Some states require membership in a genealogical society in order to use certain records.

Also useful are travel guides, such as those from the American Automobile Association and state genealogical guides. Excellent genealogical guides have been published for many states. They usually provide historical background, overviews of the state's court systems and laws, and sections covering each county's repositories and records. Read them for background information before your trip.

# Packing Those Technology Marvels

Do consider taking your laptop computer, digital camera, and, of course, your cell phone. You may feel that you don't want the extra gear, but it is advantageous to do your note-taking on the computer rather than waiting until you get home. Also if you use a genealogy program, you can quickly check names and dates you didn't bring, thinking that you'd not need them on this trip. If your travel accommodation provides Internet connection, you can continue your research online after the local facilities shut down for the day.

Record custodians sometimes allow documents too fragile to subject to copiers to be photographed with digital cameras. If you have learned to photograph microfilm records, you can save the cost of copies. The instant feedback of photographing cemeteries or landmarks with a digital camera prevents the agony of getting home without the sharp photo-documentation you thought you had.

# Preparing a Packet and Checklists

For each surname you are researching on this trip, prepare a packet or notebook that includes the pedigree charts, family group sheets, research calendars, and your notes. Review this material, looking for the gaps in your information, and start some lists of what you want to know.

**Pedigree Pitfalls**

Never take original documents in your travel packet. They can be lost or destroyed. Instead, take *copies* of anything that you think will be helpful.

Put in your packet the checklists covering what you are missing and the priority of the information you need. Are you trying to locate the deeds you think must exist because on the 1860 census Grandma is listed as having $1,000 worth of real estate? Are you missing a marriage date? Are you trying to prove a death date? Missing a wife's maiden name?

Decide which of these you want to tackle first and what records you need to see. Are you most interested in deeds? Estate records? Marriage records? Perhaps you are trying to locate a hard-to-find family history, or you want to search for obituaries in the local newspaper. It's a rare genealogist who has time to exhaust all the possibilities on the first onsite research trip, so decide ahead of time what is most important to you. Go through the list again and add an "if time allows" list.

Have alternate names or ideas, because your original plan may be thwarted when you get to the courthouse. At a courthouse to search the 1870 tax records stored in the attic and inaccessible without an escort, I arrived to learn that the escort's mother had died the previous night. The office was shorthanded due to vacations and no one else could help. The trip would have been wasted if I hadn't had a secondary set of objectives.

# Mapping Your Strategy

Become familiar with the county you're interested in and its surrounding counties by studying several kinds of maps before your trip. You need present-day highway maps to find your way around and to give you an overview of the local scene. But even if your ancestor's town still exists on present-day maps, try to find maps contemporary with his life.

The Atlas and Gazetteer Series produced by DeLorme for all 50 states combines detailed maps with lists of historic sites and museums, natural features, scenic drives, wineries—whatever is pertinent to that state. They list the covered bridges, ferries, and lighthouses; the scenic-drives section features Amish sites and heritage tours, or suggests traveling the Old National Road. Look beyond the road map for historical perspective on your family. DeLorme maps can be ordered from their website www.delorme.com.

Try to determine where your ancestors lived in relation to the county seat. Then remember the conditions they faced in trying to get to the courthouse to conduct official business such as recording a deed or getting a marriage license. If they had to navigate some rugged terrain, they may have opted to delay recording the deed. If they lived near the border of another county or state, they may have records in the other location. This can be crucial to your finding the records. Mystified as to why there was no marriage record for a couple I was sure must have married in a particular county, I expressed my puzzlement to the clerk. I learned that couples sometimes took the train 18 miles to a town in the next state to marry because there was no waiting period and the age limit was lower.

## The Lay of the Land

*Topographic maps* are another helpful aid to secure before you travel. The detail on these maps may literally take you in a new direction. Farm roads, cemeteries on private lands, and churches are all usually marked on these maps prepared by the U.S. Geological Survey. Done on scales such that it takes several maps to cover one county, they are more useful for research purposes than the usual county maps of today. Seeing a now-isolated family cemetery once accessible by a farm road can lead to a sought-after burial site.

**Genie Jargon**

A **topographical map** is a detailed, precise description of a place or region. It will graphically represent the surface features, such as elevation and creeks.

You will enjoy poring over the maps, locating the creeks and ridges and comparing the features with the deeds you find at the courthouse to determine the location of your ancestor's land. When the deed reads "under and on the great mountains on the branches of Rockey Creek," you'll know where to look.

**Tree Tips**

Always seek permission before venturing onto private land. A simple explanation of your purpose will usually get you access.

The maps, also called quadrangle maps, are available for a nominal fee from the U.S. Geological Survey Map Distribution Center. Ordering them is a two-step process. Write first for the free index and catalog booklets for the states you are researching.

Then use the descriptions to order the maps you need. Quadrangle maps can also be ordered online at http://store.usgs.gov, but finding the one you need is cumbersome because the corresponding indexes are not online.

In the following section of the topographic map, from the Baldwinsville Quadrangle, New York, note the cemeteries shown.

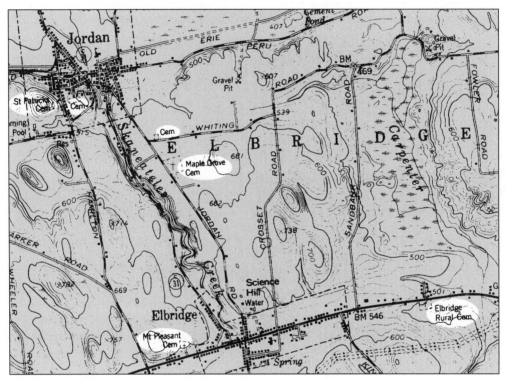

*From a topographic map in New York.*

## Contingency Plans

Another map for your travel packet is a simple outline map of the state with only the counties and their county seats marked, such as is found in *Ancestry's Red Book* or in the computer program AniMap. You may need to refer to this map for ideas of other counties in which your ancestor's records might be found. If you are researching in Noble County, Indiana, and you find a deed that says your ancestor was "of LaGrange County, Indiana," you'll want to look at your map to see where that is and consider the possibility of going there on this trip.

If your research trip is in a county bordering another state, be sure to take a map of the nearby state. You may uncover leads that take you into that state, and you don't want to spend time hunting down a map. With Internet connections commonly available at libraries nationwide, you can probably check for information on research facilities at that next destination and soon be on your way.

## Calling Ahead

This cannot be overemphasized. Make a list of all the places in the county that you want to visit; you can get ideas from state guides, comprehensive guides dealing with all states, and directories that list museums and historical societies. Try to determine what special collections of materials may be in the county. Call each and ask their hours and whether the records are open to researchers during those hours. Be sure to ask if there are holidays, special events, or unusual circumstances that will interfere with your access.

**Tree Tips**

Never assume that you will be able to have immediate access to public records. Hours and rules for access change. Always call to check before making a special trip to a distant repository.

Even if the county or historical society has a website with hours and accessibility, confirm by phone. The website may be outdated or not cover irregular events.

Imagine my surprise to find a handwritten sign on the courthouse door saying, "Closed Monday for Deer Day Holiday." This rural county closed government offices and schools on the first Monday of the hunting season! Another time, I called ahead but didn't ask the right questions. The courthouse was open on Columbus Day, but I did not ask if I would be able to research that day. Unfortunately, the small room housing the old records I needed was closed for research because county officials were counting absentee ballots in there. Another time, records I particularly wanted to see were inaccessible because they were being microfilmed.

**Tree Tips**

Take rolls of quarters and dimes to use for parking meters, vending machines, and perhaps copy machines. Larger facilities often use copy cards, but usually maintain one machine that takes small change from individuals not wishing to purchase a card.

## Packing for Research

Pack comfortable shoes. You may have to do much of your research while standing. Old courthouses have limited research space and high counters. You may have to climb a ladder to reach the earliest volumes stored near the ceiling. Clothing should be "business casual." You'll have better service if you are not in sweatshirt and jeans. Take clothes that won't show the dirt; old records are dusty and stored in areas that are rarely cleaned.

# Now You've Arrived

You always have a tight schedule on a research trip, so use your checklists and the information in Chapters 9, 14, and 15 to make a tentative work plan for each day. Courthouses usually open and close early, but libraries often have evening hours. Small museums and historical societies may have very limited hours; to visit them, you have to plan around their schedules.

Most research facilities are closed on Sundays. Use that day to visit the cemeteries, attend the church services at your ancestors' churches, find the old home place of your ancestors, and visit with distant relatives you may find. Reflect on your feelings as you gaze at the same mountains your ancestors saw, walk the creek bank where they fished, or sit in the church pews they once occupied.

## Engaging People

Talk to the individuals providing services for you: staff members at the courthouse, the libraries, and the Chamber of Commerce; the volunteers at the museum; and tour guides. They may know of a source, record, or individuals that you would not find on your own. In one courthouse a clerk produced an interim report of the survey of the county's historic properties. This working document with its detailed maps, photographs, and historic background of the county's communities was an outstanding research aid, one that I would not have found in the normal course of quiet research.

**Tree Tips**

Remember that the details of your family history usually interest only you and your relatives. Simply mention the purpose of your trip and ask if there is anything you've overlooked.

## Old-Timers Can Tell It All

Often, there are individuals in town who knew your ancestors. They were their neighbors or their fathers were in business with them. Their mothers were in the same church groups. These old-timers are delighted to reminisce with someone who has not heard their stories dozens of times. They may also tell you things that the family won't: "Your grandpa was quite handsome, and he got around some."

The old-timers may have photographs of your family. Ask if you may get them copied while you are in town. Or if you have a digital camera, photograph them on the spot.

Small towns and rural communities may have an unofficial historian—someone who seems to know all the old stories about the area. That individual can be eager to show you where the old tavern stood or tell you that your aunts and uncles and other children from the farms were picked up in a covered wagon and driven into town for school.

**Tree Tips**

Check the telephone books for surnames you are researching. There may be descendants still living in the area. If you can't contact them on this trip, you may be able to reach them when you return home.

## While You're in Town

Buy the local newspaper. You may get an idea for another source of information from something you see in the paper. Perhaps there is a farm auction or an estate sale; old books, such as county histories and old photographs often turn up at these sales. It may be worth your while to inquire.

Check the bulletin boards at the library. Local genealogical societies often have no office; to reach them you must know the officers. Meeting announcements or flyers about their services are often posted in public places. Even if you don't contact them now, you may want to engage someone from the society to follow up on something when you get home.

Pick up any brochures on local historic sights. The information in them will add flavor to your family history, making your ancestors more "real" to you.

## Getting Religion

If you have determined your ancestor's religion, try to locate the meeting place. Your ancestors usually did not venture too far for religious services. Check city directories and old maps to help locate places of worship closest to your ancestor's residence.

Investigate the possibility that the religion is still active in the local area. Call the church or synagogue offices to locate the old records. There may be membership lists, participants in ceremonies, or a history mentioning your ancestor as a founding member. More often, the structure is gone and the archives, if they survive, have been transferred to the library or a central repository.

## Being a Tourist

Absorb the atmosphere. Read the historic plaques. Buildings that your ancestors saw every day will help you visualize their times. When was the courthouse built? Your ancestors may have walked up these very steps to get their marriage license. Take a walking tour of town. Look for monuments inscribed with names; your ancestors' names may be on a war memorial.

**Tree Tips**

Many cities renamed or renumbered streets and houses as the city expanded. Before hunting for your ancestor's house try to ascertain if that particular area had changes. Sources for this information may be the county assessor's office, the city planning office, or the local historical society.

Does your ancestor's house still stand? Perhaps you'll have time to drive by. Check first to see if the neighborhood is a safe one, as neighborhoods change. Use caution if you want to photograph the house. The current residents may not understand a stranger's intent when they see a camera pointed at their home.

Drive the country roads. Imagine the days of times long gone, preserved in such serene scenes as the one in the following figure. Visit the old home place if it still exists. There may be a McDonald's on the spot now, but let your imagination replace that with the pictures you saw at the museum. Visit the cemeteries. Information and ambiance await you there. Chapter 15 details how to make the most of this part of your trip.

Before taking off on this trip, immerse yourself in the names of your ancestors and their associates. You want the names of associates in your subconscious so that they jump out at you if they are mentioned—they may lead you to your ancestors. You don't know what you will find when you get to the county, so anything you have tucked away in a corner of your mind may be useful.

*A wonderful scene from* History of Oneida County, New York.

## The Least You Need to Know

◆ Advance planning is the key to making the most of your time and money on a research trip.

◆ Maps are some of the best investments for your research trip.

◆ List what you want to know, and learn where the answers are likely to be.

◆ Call ahead to check the hours of the places you want to visit.

# Chapter 14

# Courthouses: Gateway to the Past

## In This Chapter

- ◆ Using the indexes to find documents
- ◆ What to look for in the documents
- ◆ Letting documents tell the tale
- ◆ Finding courthouse records on the Internet

I always feel a thrill when entering a courthouse. It never diminishes. There is excited expectation of what might be on the shelves or stored in a dusty attic. Walking up the stairs, worn with the steps of those who have entered for decades, I am swept with a sense of history. Visions of those family members who might have climbed the same stairs as they came to pay their taxes or to settle their grandfather's estate come to mind. I wonder if I will find a forgotten record stuffed in one of the metal boxes in the clerk's office that will solve a long-standing genealogical problem. In this chapter, we'll teach you to find *your* history under all that dust.

# What to Expect

Some courthouses have made an effort to carefully preserve their records. They have flattened the original papers and now store them in file folders. Some have even laminated the registers. Others, due to lack of interest or lack of funds, have done little. The records may be in deplorable condition. Be prepared for anything.

Another problem is the burned courthouse. Many were destroyed during the Civil War, or the old structure caught fire perhaps from an overheated potbellied stove used for heat. Some were purposely set afire. The clerk tells you, "The courthouse burned in 'The War.'" Don't become discouraged. I've found that a few additional questions may have surprising results. The first is, "Which records were destroyed?" followed by, "Which were saved, and where are they stored?" It is amazing how often certain records were saved, but the clerk may not offer that information. Ask the right questions!

*Typical courthouse shelves, with heavy books and metal boxes.*

**Pedigree Pitfalls**

Women should wear flat shoes. Men should not wear slick-soled shoes. Floors are often uneven, and stairs can be narrow. Sometimes you'll even need to climb a ladder. Many early records are copied from the originals into large, heavy, bound books. If you are unable to climb stairs or handle the books, bring someone who can.

# The History of the Farm

Be sure to take with you the names of the people you are seeking, the records you hope to find, and an idea of the time period. Perhaps at the top of your priority list you noted your desire to examine the deed to the old family farm. If so, your first step is to locate the office that holds the land records. There are a variety of offices in the courthouse: the County Clerk's office, Circuit Court Clerk's office, County Recorder's office, and others. Check the directory that is usually posted on the wall near the front door to find the right office.

Deeds have almost always been indexed. Land was important. A way to keep track of who owned it was essential. A deed was signed by the seller, who gave it to the buyer as proof of the sale. The buyer usually then took it to the courthouse. The seller or the witnesses came in to court to verify that the grantor signed it. This created a notation in the court minutes (a book recording a day-by-day account of what happened in court) that it was acknowledged, and the court ordered the transfer of property to be recorded. Usually, the original deed remained with the clerk of the court for several days, or even weeks, until he had a chance to transcribe it into one of the deed books. The original deed was then returned to the new owner.

**Tree Tips**

Land transfers were not always recorded. The land may have been inherited rather than transferred by deed, or deeds among family members may not have been taken to the courthouse in order to save the recording fee. Diligent searching, however, should produce something, perhaps even years after the original purchase, when the land was sold out of the family.

**Lineage Lessons**

Sometimes the buyer never returned to the courthouse to retrieve the now-recorded document. The original deed of your ancestor's property may be in that old box marked "original deeds" or "unclaimed deeds" on the top shelf, gathering dust.

## The Approach to the Clerk

When you enter the deed office, a clerk will offer to assist you. Do not go into the details of your family's history. The clerk is no doubt busy with the day's current activities and has no time to get involved. Instead, because you know what you want, simply say, "I would like to see the deed indexes for 1800 through 1875" (or whatever records and time period you are seeking). The clerk might take you into the *vault* and show you where to find the indexes, or just point you to the vault and let you proceed on your own.

**Genie Jargon**

The record books are normally stored in **vaults**— fireproofed rooms designed to help prevent destruction of the books in case of a fire.

## Indexes Tripping You Up!

Enter the record room and look around for the index books. Deeds are always indexed under both seller and buyer. There might be separate indexes: one for grantor (seller), sometimes called a Direct index, and one for grantee (buyer), sometimes called an Indirect index. Alternatively, the grantors and grantees may be listed together in one book called a General Index. If so, the grantors may be in the front part of the book, and the grantees in the back. In other variations the left page could be the grantor index, and the right page the grantee index. Or they may simply be intermingled, entered as they were recorded. In this case an additional column shows "to" or "from," indicating whether it was a grantor or grantee. Each index book covers a period of time. Index Book No. 1 may be for 1802-1840, Index Book 2 for 1841-1890, and so forth.

For example, if the clerk transcribed the original deed into Deed Book A, page 121, he would then index the deed in an index book under the name of the seller and under the buyer, and show the book and page reference in the index. If there was more than one seller or more than one buyer (perhaps the property was owned jointly by John Mathews and his brother-in-law David Donaldson, and sold to George Graham and his wife Martha Graham), the deed was then usually indexed in each of the sellers' and buyers' names. There are exceptions.

### Lineage Lessons

A court clerk might suggest that you need only look at the grantee index, and not the grantor index. Don't listen! There can be a variety of reasons why the purchase was not entered in the grantee index, although later the sale appears in the grantor index. The first deed may have been a patent or grant from the state or federal government, inherited, overlooked when the index was prepared, or just not recorded. Always check both indexes.

Sometimes the record was indexed only under the name of the first grantor (seller) or the first grantee (buyer) listed on the document, with the notation *et al.* (*et alii*, meaning "and others") or *et ux.* ("and wife") following. If it shows only "John Mathews, *et al.*" or "George Graham, *et ux.*," be sure to follow through and locate the actual deed. It will reveal the names of the rest of those involved (referred to as the *parties* in legal documents). Any record in which there are multiple parties should be carefully examined; often it is a transaction between family members.

## Making Sense of the Index

Open the index book, and see if it is a standard index and easily understood. There should be a diagram or chart and an explanation of the indexing system used in that county. Read it carefully. If, after a few minutes, you are still unsure, ask the clerk to explain the system.

In the following figure, using the so-called Russell system of indexing, go to the index book with the initial letter of the surname you are tracing. Then determine the first key letter as listed at the top of the figure (*l, m, n, r,* or *t*), to find where in the deed books the surname is indexed. For example, if the surname is Martin, then you are searching in the *M* index. Ignoring now the initial letter of the surname (you are already in the *M* book), search for the first key letter. The next letter is *a*, not one of the key letters (*l, m, n, r,* and *t*), so it is ignored. The next letter, *r*, in Martin, is the first key letter of that name. Looking at the columns, you note that Martin is therefore indexed on pages 14, 24, 34, 44, 54, and 64.

In the left column of the same figure, the letters ABCD, EFGHI, and so on, represent the initials of the given name. If you are searching for Abraham Martin, go to page 14 of the index. If you are searching for Mary Martin, proceed to page 44 of the index.

If you are searching a name such as Rowse in the Russell system of indexing, because there are no key letters (*l, m, n, r,* or *t*) following the initial letter of *R*, you would use the Miscellaneous column. (Anything not falling within the key letters is considered miscellaneous.) Abraham Rowse would be on page 16, while Mary Rowse would be on page 46. The Russell index, though prevalent (and still in use), is only one of numerous types of indexes.

*Sample of the Russell index, arranged by certain key letters.*

# TO LOCATE NAMES IN INDEX

Determine first key-letter following initial letter in Family Name. Find section number in the column headed by said key-letter, opposite given name initial desired. Names not containing a key-letter will be located under "Misc." Corporations, etc., will be located under the first key-letter following the initial letter in the first word of the name, or if no key-letter, under "Misc." Always omit the article "The."

| Given Name Initials | Key Letters and Section Numbers | | | | | |
|---|---|---|---|---|---|---|
| | **l** | **m** | **n** | **r** | **t** | **Misc.** |
| ABCD | 11 | 12 | 13 | 14 | 15 | 16 |
| EFGHI | 21 | 22 | 23 | 24 | 25 | 26 |
| JKL | 31 | 32 | 33 | 34 | 35 | 36 |
| MNOPQR | 41 | 42 | 43 | 44 | 45 | 46 |
| STUVWXYZ | 51 | 52 | 53 | 54 | 55 | 56 |
| Corps., etc. | 61 | 62 | 63 | 64 | 65 | 66 |

## What Should You Note?

After you determine how to use the index, look for entries that involve your family. The indexed entry will include the name of the grantor and grantee along with the date of the document, date recorded, type of document, book and page where it is recorded, and perhaps a very short property description showing the township, lot number, waterway, or other brief designation.

While you search the index, note the column that designates the type of deed. Typical designations might be warranty deed, deed of trust, gift deed, power of attorney, partition, or others. Each is a specific way of conveying land or rights. You will, in the course of your research, become familiar with all these terms and understand the value of each.

Be sure to note the reference given in the index: the book or volume number and the page number. You will need this to find the document. Note, too, the type of document.

### Lineage Lessons

When you find the book and page reference, take note of any abbreviations that appear immediately *before* the volume number. There may be separate volumes for specialized records. For example, "PA" (Power of Attorney), "DT" (Deed of Trust), or some other designation, might precede the volume number.

## Search Strategies in Deeds

While you are working with the deeds, take some time to copy all the index entries for your surnames of interest in the appropriate time period. If, after you return home, you find that you need another deed, you can order it by mail, citing the book and page number. (Or you may be able to order microfilm of the records from the Family History Library.)

Be particularly alert to indexed entries that appear to involve several people. They could be family members. The words *et al.* ("and others") can be a tip-off to such transactions. If the document is designated Power of Attorney, Gift Deed, or Partition (involving divisions), or if an estate is mentioned, then you should take the time to examine it. These types of documents often show familial connections.

## Is He Augustus W. Redman, A. W. Redman, or Gus?

Consider possible alternate versions of the first or given name. This will include initials, first and middle name reversed, and even nicknames. George Washington Smith may be found as George, as Washington, G. W., George W., Washington G., W. G., G. Washington, and Wash. It will be important to know all the variations. If you don't know that Patsy was a nickname for Martha, Nabby for Abigail, Jane and Jennie for Virginia, Polly for Mary, and others, you may miss the listing you are seeking. Christine Rose's *Nicknames Past and Present* includes many hundreds of nicknames, all cross-indexed.

## It's There Somewhere

You searched the index and noted a deed to what appears to be the old family farm, listed as Book B, page 510. Look around and see if you can find some books that are marked on their spines with the word "Deeds." Watch for Books A, B, C, and so on.

It is permissible to remove a deed book from the shelf and put it on the counter for examination, but be sure to put it back (in the same spot) when you are finished. The counters on which you will be working are usually high and slanted. Other researchers (perhaps title searchers from the local land title companies, attorneys, or other genealogists) will be working there, also.

**Tree Tips**

If the early deed books started with A, B, and C, the set following after the letter Z may begin with 1, 2, and 3; or, it may begin AA, BB, CC; or even 2A, 2B, 2C; and so on.

Use as little counter space as possible. If you have a coat, hat, umbrella, or briefcase, find a spot off the counter to place them; counter space is generally limited.

## Finally ... It Is in Hand

After you find the Deed book you seek, turn to the page you noted from the index. The document you want should start on the indexed page. Follow it through to the end, which may be several pages later. In Chapter 3 you learned about transcribing and abstracting. Use those techniques to get the information, or if you wish to have a copy of the entire document, ask the clerk about photocopying costs and procedures. The fees vary but usually are nominal.

> **Lineage Lessons**
>
> Good abstracting techniques enable you to keep your photocopying costs to a minimum. A disadvantage of relying on photocopies without making an abstract is that you (or the clerk) may inadvertently cut off some words from the side or bottom of the copy, or a key date in the binding edge may be blurred. Abstract it while you have the whole record in front of you.

# Success at Last!

You are now looking at the deed. What to do? First, you need to read through the document. Until you become familiar with old handwriting and terminology, this will be a slow process. However, it is through such readings that experience develops. You are seeking certain bits of information from the deed:

- Name of the parties (grantors and grantees)
- Residences of the parties
- Occupations of the parties
- Consideration "paid"
- A description of the property being sold
- Names of adjoining property owners mentioned
- Any special wording that might help in identification of the parties or the property

- Signatures or marks exactly as they appeared

- Names of witnesses exactly as they appeared

- Date and place the deed was acknowledged in court (or sometimes before a Notary Public if they moved to another area)

- Who acknowledged the deed

- Date of the deed, and date the deed was recorded

Copy names exactly as they appear (Chas., Rebeckah, and so on). Residences are important; they may even include mention of a former or later location: "John Gott, formerly of Lebanon, Connecticut" or "Richard Smith, now of Marion County, Indiana." Occupations are not only of personal interest, but can be used to segregate the records of two people with the same name.

The "consideration," (that is, what was given by the buyer to the seller to obtain the property), may be monetary. It might also be something else of value, such as "love and affection" (plus a token amount of 5 shillings or $1.00), or five horses, or anything else that the parties agreed upon.

The property description in the document will help you to locate the land. Additionally, it can provide clues through proximity. If someone of the same surname lived on the adjoining farm (mentioned in the property description within the deed), note it. Even if they did not have the same surname, neighbors might have been related, or they might have been former neighbors who moved with the family from another area and thus can provide clues to the family's original location.

## I Saw It Myself

All deeds had to be acknowledged, either personally by the seller or by the witnesses who testified that they saw the seller sign the deed. (In some areas the term "proved" was used, though strictly speaking on deeds it is an acknowledgment.) If the seller moved and personally went into court to acknowledge the deed in another county or state, you have clues to a possible new residence.

---

**Lineage Lessons**

The signatures in the transcribed deed books are not the original signatures of your ancestors. The clerk copied them and often tried to duplicate the appearance. If the seller signed with an X (or other mark), the clerk tried to duplicate that, too. This can be important. Two men with the same name who left records in the same area can be distinguished by their signatures or marks. One might be able to sign his name, while the other always signed with an X.

---

The date of the deed is important, as well as the date it was recorded. Often a deed is not recorded until years later. The delay can have special significance. Perhaps the father died and his widow received her *dower third*, with the remainder to go to the children. She continued to live on the property, undisturbed, and after her death 10 years later, the children sold the property. A document's recordation date many years after the date on the document should alert you to a possible change in the family status: the death of the mother, a parent's remarriage, or children coming of age. Watch, too, for special clauses in the deed that might help with relationships: "I give and convey … the land I inherited from my father Joseph Schneider …." Important relationship clauses such as this are best quoted in your abstract so that there are no misinterpretations.

**Genie Jargon** _____

The law usually allowed the widow a **dower third** (or some other portion, depending upon state, time period, and other factors) in the land. She not only received a dower third upon the death of her husband (he could not will it away from her), but if, during his life, he sold property, she usually had to sign a release of her dower interest. If she was unable to travel to the county seat, court-appointed representatives visited and questioned her, asking her whether the property was sold with her consent.

## Moving On

Work with the land records for as long as your time allows. They are one of the most valuable resources you can use, often showing relationships and yielding clues. If you don't have time to finish abstracting, you will at least have the information from the deed index. You may find that the Family History Library has microfilmed some of the records you need, and after you return home you can order some of the film.

# Those Departed Relatives

After you've tracked the deeds of your family in the courthouse, you'll want to do some research with *estates*. Estates are the whole of one's possessions, especially the property and debts left by a person at the time of death. They are another valuable source of clues. Relationships are often specified. Normally, those you first encounter will involve estates of decedents, (that is, people who died).

**Genie Jargon**

To reach the **age of majority** is to become of legal age. This usually was 21 for a male, and 18 or 16 for a female, but the age differed from state to state and in different time periods.

There are other types of estates. Perhaps a minor inherited some property and the court appointed a guardian to manage his or her estate until the *age of majority*, or, you might find the estate of an incompetent who was in need of a guardian.

## More of Those Indexes

Sometimes the clerks have created a consolidated index of the early estates, which includes a variety of estate documents. There may also be individual indexes for wills, administrations, bonds, and other records. Sometimes the only indexes available are those in each individual book. Will Book A has its own index, Will Book B has its own, and so on.

## Died With or Without

Basically, you seek two kinds of decedents' estates: testate and intestate. People dying with a will are referred to as dying testate, those dying without a will die intestate. If the person died leaving *real* or *personal property* that needed to be settled, an estate proceeding was filed in the county of residence. Some people, however, did not have sufficient property (determined by the state laws) to necessitate a court proceeding, so you may never find an actual record.

**Genie Jargon**

**Real property** is immovable property: land and, generally, what is erected or affixed to the land. **Personal property** is generally money, slaves, or goods: those items that are movable and tangible. Animals, furniture, and merchandise are personal property.

## Taking Charge

If your ancestor left a will, he or she usually named within the will an *executor* to handle his or her affairs. This created a *probate* proceeding. If the person died without a will, the court appointed an *administrator* to handle the estate; the process referred to as the administration. There are variations: the court may appoint an administrator to handle a will if the executor named did not want to serve, or if the executor died or moved to another state. You will learn these important refinements as you use the records.

## The Probate Process

Probate, the action to prove and admit a will, was initiated (usually by a relative or creditor) after the death of the testator. Notice was given by the clerk of the court that the will would be heard on a particular day; anyone contesting it could appear. At the time of the hearing, the court required proof, by testimony of the witnesses, that the will was signed by the deceased and was signed of his or her own free will. If the court approved the probate, the will was transcribed by the clerk into a Will Book in much the same manner that a deed was transcribed into a Deed Book. The will was assigned a book and page number, and was indexed under the name of the deceased. The original will also remained in the courthouse records; it was not returned to the family, as was an original deed. That original will, and other loose documents that would be created in the following months, in many states created a "probate packet," which is hopefully still in the courthouse. If so, the index should have a column for *File Number* so that the packet can be located.

**Genie Jargon**

**Probate** is a process of legally establishing the validity of a will. An **executor** is someone designated by the person making the will to handle his or her estate, as set out by the will, after the death of the **testator** (the person who made the will). An **administrator** is appointed by the court to handle the estate of a deceased person who has not left a will.

**Tree Tips**

It may be worthwhile to have the complete probate packet photocopied. Sometimes items from the packet are lost, or the entire packet itself can be mislaid or misfiled. Get them while you can!

The original loose papers in the probate packet should always be examined, if they do exist. Here you will find the original will (important to your search if the clerk's transcribed copy in the Will Book has an error). If your ancestor could write, the original packet might reward you with his or her original signature. The heirs may have signed receipts for their portions of the estate, providing additional signatures. If an heir was a married woman, the receipts often give the name of her husband, because he signed "in right of his wife" since by law he controlled the couple's assets. Other valuable documents are also included.

## But He Didn't Leave a Will ...

If the person died intestate (that is, without a will), the first record was usually when a relative (or creditor) came into court and requested permission to administer the estate. A variety of records could be generated from such actions, but these were not always indexed. To find them, you might have to do a page-by-page search of the record books. Search also for an administration packet, similar to the probate packets already mentioned. The index should have a file number to these records.

## Checking the Estate Records

Keep in mind that you are seeking one of two types of records: a testate estate (with a will), or an intestate estate (without a will), often called an administration proceeding.

Each generates a variety of additional records. You may find a petition to initiate the estate process, bonds for the executor or administrator in case they don't fulfill their duties, inventories of the decedent's estate, accounts listing all that was owed and due to the estate, petitions for the sale of the real estate of the deceased, estate sales when the property of the estate was sold at public auction, distribution of the estate, receipts of the heirs for their portion, and others. Each can provide wonderful leads, and a rare insight into the lives of your ancestors. The inventory may, by the tools listed, give clues to the trades of your ancestors; you'll be provided a glimpse into their education by the books they owned; and you'll find other intriguing bits of information.

## Letting the Published Indexes Assist

The classic in published estate indexes is Clayton Torrence's *Virginia Wills and Administrations 1632-1800*, (Baltimore: Genealogical Publishing Company, 1965), published as an index to the early estates of Virginia. Others have created indexes to some other states: the wills of North Carolina, the estates of Ohio, and so on. Look for them in libraries.

# I Do Take Thee As My Lawful ...

Find out which office holds the marriage records. Ask to see the marriage indexes. In most cases, they will be open for inspection, although some states do not allow access to the actual records. There may be a separate index for grooms and brides, or there may be an index only to males.

After you locate the book and page reference in the index, check to see if the marriage books are available for use. When you find the record you seek, take down all the pertinent information, including the names of the bride and groom, residences, ages, occupations, date of the license, date of the marriage, who performed the marriage, witnesses, consent if either was a minor, and so on.

Nothing on the record is too insignificant; the smallest detail can lead to further records or identification of the individuals. The witnesses may be related to the bride or groom. If either the bride or the groom was a minor, a parent's or guardian's consent will be valuable. Finally, the name of the person officiating might help to identify a church and lead to further sources.

**Tree Tips**

If there is only a groom index, check to see if the marriages of the county were published. If so, the published book should provide an index to brides.

Marriages generate a variety of documents: marriage bonds, licenses, applications, consents for the marriage of a minor, and certificates or "returns" showing that the marriage took place and who officiated. Sometimes these are in separate books with separate indexes, or they might be combined into the same record. What is available depends on the time period, laws, and local customs.

In addition to the bound marriage books, in which the clerk entered the details of the marriage, you may find original, loose marriage bonds. In earlier times, a bond was given by the intended groom. If he changed his mind and did not marry the intended bride, his securities on the bond had to pay the amount of the bond. As an option to taking out a bond, he may have had the *banns of marriage* announced.

---

### Lineage Lessons

The **banns of marriage** was an announcement, usually in church, of an intended marriage. Normally, it was announced successively for three weeks. In some areas this was the prevailing custom. A marriage bond necessitated paying a fee to the clerk of the court, so the alternate method of "publishing" the banns of marriage was an attractive substitute. The banns may be noted in church minutes but are not recorded in the county record books.

# The Tip of the Iceberg

On subsequent trips to a courthouse, you will find records you did not think to examine the first time. Look at a document with a view toward deciding if there could be other documents connected with the same action. If so, pursue those, too. They may have the answer to the relationship you have been pursuing.

There is no substitute for "hands on" use of the records. In the office of deeds, there can be survey books, plat books, mortgages, oil leases, power of attorney books, tax books, and a variety of other related records.

In the probate office you will find court minutes, court-order books, inventory books, bond books, account books, settlement books, estate packets, and others. If they have been preserved, you may also find the packets of the originals of the court documents.

> ### Lineage Lessons
>
> The laws vary as to the beginning date when birth and death registrations were required by each state. Prior to state registration, the counties normally maintained their own birth and death registers. Check for their availability at the courthouse. The information may be minimal compared to present day records, but if they exist, they will be enormously useful.

In the civil-records office there will be papers involving small and large claims: citations, debts, attachments, levies, summons, divorces, notices required to be published in the newspaper, and depositions, just to name a few.

For detailed discussion of courthouses, see Christine Rose's *Courthouse Research for Family Historians: A Guide to Genealogical Treasures.* This discusses every phase of courthouse research, with numerous examples and an extensive glossary.

# Are Courthouse Records on the Internet?

Every genealogist who has started research first on the Internet must eventually go beyond what is available from that source. That is especially true when working with courthouse records. Though there are isolated cases of digitized court records being available on the Web, the vast majority are not accessible in that form. The Internet, however, can help in related ways.

A useful site is the State and Local Government on the Net (SLGN) website at www.statelocalgov.net. Experiment with the options given. These websites won't have the actual records, but will provide some helpful aids, such as historical background, maps, hours and location, or others.

Another type of website is the Massachusetts Registry of Deeds at www.mass-doc. com/land_registry_dir.htm. This one takes you to a page with links to maps of the state's towns/cities and counties, plus links to counties. From there you can access the county courthouse information.

The site at www.co.ulster.ny.us is for the Ulster County, New York, local government website. Substitute the name of another county in the URL, such as www.co.ontario. ny.us and off you go to that county where you'll find maps and more.

These are just a few examples. There is an extraordinary number of sites that are available to help you when researching local government.

Will these websites serve as a substitute for utilizing the records within a courthouse? No. Some of the sites may have digitized a few of the records, some may post a few indexes, but this is miniscule compared to what is available. In no case are all the valuable courthouse records, or even a majority of them, available on the Internet.

---

### Lineage Lessons

One of the biggest fallacies of genealogy is that "everything is available on the Web" or on microfilm or in books. Not so. There is much, much more. Researchers posting messages on the bulletin boards often lament that they have a "brick wall" problem when in reality they have many clues to pursue. The answers just are not online. Nor are they all in published books or microfilm. Ultimately, it will be necessary in many cases either to visit the courthouse personally or write them a letter, or else hire someone to go there for you.

---

Each trip you make to the courthouses will bring new memories and experiences. You may be offered coffee or you may be ignored. Either way, remain courteous and friendly, and thank the clerks when you leave. The impression you leave will influence treatment of the next genealogist who arrives. You will remember each experience: the strawberry festival in the courthouse parking lot, going down three subbasements and through three locked doors to work in the old deeds, or finding another visitor there working on the same family. You may stop and consider, in awe, that you are actually holding in your hands a document that was written during the Revolutionary War, or a 1720 document signed by your ancestor dividing his few possessions. He was holding the very same paper you now have in your hand.

I'll bet that you, too, will become addicted!

## The Least You Need to Know

◆ The books in the courthouse are large and heavy; bring someone to help if you cannot lift them.

◆ Have an idea of which records you would like to access, and the time period you're seeking.

◆ Start your search with the indexes; use the references there to find the record book.

◆ Carefully abstract the records you find. Be alert for any clues to relationships.

◆ To compile a thorough genealogy it will be necessary to go beyond the Internet and even beyond books and microfilm. Many records are available *only* in the courthouse itself.

◆ If you can't go personally, write a letter!

# A Picnic in the Cemetery

## In This Chapter

- ◆ Cemeteries for research
- ◆ Finding the records
- ◆ Locating the cemeteries
- ◆ Recording the information

Cemeteries are quiet, peaceful places for contemplation and remembrance. They are also an excellent source of genealogical information. Plot placement, tombstone inscriptions, and records can fill in blanks, lead you in new directions, or add insight to your knowledge of your ancestors as people.

Why should you visit the cemetery if you already have a death date? Because you never know what you will find. Here are two children who died in infancy who you never knew about. Grandma's tombstone has an inscription that moves you to tears. Grandpa's marker is engraved with a Masonic symbol suggesting other records to check.

# The Chicken or the Egg?

Cemetery research has two goals: to find the cemetery and to find the records created by the ending of life. Whether you look first for the cemetery or the records is like the chicken and egg problem. Without knowing the cemetery, you'll have trouble locating the records; if you haven't found the records, you may not know which cemetery or where in the cemetery the grave is located. Different circumstances require different approaches. You decide the best approach based on the information you have.

# The Usual Preparation

On your trip to the area where your ancestors resided, allow time to search for burial records and for the cemeteries. You are already prepared with the background information you need on the surnames and any variants, and the approximate dates of death, as well as names associated with your family. You may have the name of a cemetery from a death certificate, an obituary, or interviews with family members. Your library research may have turned up cemetery surveys that list your ancestors, or you may have clues from a county history.

**Pedigree Pitfalls**

Confirm the accuracy of published cemetery tombstone surveys. Mistakes can be made in the original survey and in the copying of the survey notes to the typewriter or computer.

Courthouse research on the trip will turn up deeds so that you can locate your ancestors' residences. Where your ancestors lived in the area often influenced where they were buried. Travel was limited, and people were usually buried close to the home place. In many cases, they were buried on the home place.

After you locate your ancestors, look at your county and topographic maps to find possible cemeteries. Numerous burial grounds can be found within small geographic areas.

# Cemeteries Alive on the Web

Incorporate online resources into your work, to help with identifying cemeteries or gathering information about a particular cemetery. To learn about cemeteries in a geographic area, try searching by state, county, city, or town. Search USGenWeb.com and RootsWeb.com lists.

If you have the name of a cemetery, check for a Web presence. Cemetery websites range from the minimal to the expansive. Some have a history not only of the cemetery, but of the entire area. Others are lavishly illustrated with drawings and photographs. The site for Cypress Lawn Cemetery in Colma, California, www.cypresslawn.com has brief biographies of the notables buried there, a veritable who's who of early San Francisco and northern California. Many sites include detailed maps of the cemetery, whereas others offer access to records. Maple Grove Cemetery, Wichita, Kansas, (http://maplegrovecemetery.org) answers genealogical inquiries free of charge.

There are veterans' cemeteries, state hospital cemeteries, poor farm cemeteries, and slave cemeteries. There have been burials in cemeteries on Indian reservations, military bases, and in World War II internment camps. All manner of cemeteries have Internet sites. A search for "pioneer cemeteries" quickly yields well over 11,000 leads. Using "ghost-town cemeteries" as the parameter at Google.com results in at least 32 sites.

The government helps pinpoint veterans' gravesites with its national grave locator at www.cem.va.gov. Its lists of national and state veterans' cemeteries include contact information. Background details about Arlington National Cemetery, its rituals and traditions, as well as biographies of many who rest there, can be read at http://arlingtoncemetery.net.

A particularly interesting website is www.epodunk.com. Enter a state and then the name of a community. The resulting profile of the community is replete with statistical information and numerous links, one of which is to cemeteries in the community or within a few miles. Even tiny communities, such as Essex, Illinois, with its 2003 population of 651, have their own page with the latitude and longitude. Select the cemetery link to find the area cemeteries (14 for Essex) or the county cemeteries (48 in this case). Clicking on the topographic map link takes you to a USGS quadrangle map at www.topozone.com where you can see the exact location of the cemetery.

Another useful feature of epodunk.com is its link to funeral homes. Although the listings are geared to present-day needs, such as sending flowers for a pending funeral, the lists provide addresses and phone numbers you may find useful in your search for burial records. If your ancestor was involved in politics, check The Political Graveyard www.politicalgraveyard.com. This ongoing collection includes close to 150,000 federal and state officeholders and candidates, party officials, judges, and some mayors.

# Kinds of Cemeteries

Both the cemetery and its records are important to your research, and they may not be in the same place. There are several kinds of cemeteries: public, private, family, religious, and fraternal. Everything about their records varies: the information, the location, the accessibility. Cemeteries change hands; a commercial venture goes bankrupt and a municipality takes over, or, conversely, the county can't afford the upkeep and sells the cemetery to a business enterprise. Cemeteries are abandoned when all descendants in the family are gone. Or the town is down to 200 residents who no longer bury their dead in the town cemetery and have no wish to keep it up.

> **Tree Tips**
>
> Large cemeteries may have ethnic sections established by tradition, covenants, or discrimination. They might have a "Potter's Field" where the poor or unknown are buried; often no records are kept on the individuals buried in this section.

**Public cemeteries** are owned and maintained with taxpayer money by a governmental jurisdiction (county or town). Their records may be at the courthouse, city hall, or in an office on the cemetery grounds. Their records, occasionally difficult to locate, are usually open to the public.

**Private cemeteries,** or memorial parks, are for-profit businesses. Although their records are private, most are willing to help researchers.

**Family cemeteries** range from a few gravestones in a corner of the pasture to larger cemeteries, where not only the extended family was buried, but also others from the community who had close ties to the family. These records, if they exist, are usually more difficult to find; they may have been deposited at the library or historical society, or they may have been handed down through the family to someone who left the area. In some cases, the deed to the property made a provision to preserve the family burying ground.

**Church cemeteries** may adjoin the church or may be located some distance away. Church burial registers may take some digging to find. They may be at the church, but in many cases they moved with a minister or are archived at another location such as a regional church archive or a university collection.

**Fraternal organizations,** such as the International Order of Odd Fellows (I.O.O.F), also maintain cemeteries, sometimes adjoining another cemetery. A fraternal organization may also have a special section within a cemetery.

# When the Cemetery Moves

Public-works projects, such as dams and highways, sometimes make it necessary to move cemeteries, or the government may decide to consolidate several military cemeteries. In these cases, attempts are made to identify all the burials and move the remains to another location, but the original relationship of the graves to each other may be lost in the move. Occasionally, developers are unaware of, or disregard, the small cemetery on a property, and all records, both paper and stone, are obliterated.

Burial space in the churchyard may become full, forcing the church to start a new cemetery. You may need to search both. Sometimes churches remodel and build over an old, unused cemetery. Churches merge or split; this, too, affects the cemeteries and their records. Sometimes the cemetery doesn't move, but its name changes.

# Sexton's Records

Both public and private cemeteries have *sexton's* records. These are the records you want to see. Some cemeteries have a small sign at the entrance with instructions on how to reach the sexton. For others, call the listing in the telephone book. In very small towns or rural

**Genie Jargon**

A **sexton** is a caretaker responsible for burials and maintenance of the cemetery.

areas, there may be no telephone listing. Ask local people for the name of the custodian of the records. The records of cemeteries no longer in use or abandoned are somewhat harder to find. Check the libraries and historical societies for leads.

In a small cemetery, the sexton may do everything: dig the graves, cut the grass, maintain the records, sell the plots. The records may be in his home. He can be a valuable resource if he has lived in the community a long time.

Large cemeteries usually have an office where the records are maintained. This does not always hold true, however. At one large cemetery I visited, the sexton maintains his records in card files at his florist shop across the street from the cemetery gates.

Sexton's records vary, but may include burial registers, plats, plot records, and deed records for the plots. You may also find records of grave openings, indicating an ordinary burial, that a body was exhumed and shipped elsewhere, or that someone else is buried in the same grave. Don't expect to find complete records; it is unusual, especially for long-existing cemeteries.

## Burial Registers

These will be in chronological order by the date of burial, and may be indexed. If not, you will have to search through the lists based on the estimated date of death. The burial register may have only the name, burial date, and plot. Others are more extensive, listing age, birthplace, marital status, death date and place, and cause of death.

## Plats

The plat maps of the cemetery show grave locations and plot ownership. Active cemeteries keep these up-to-date in order to know which plots are for sale. Usually there are no dates, and if the plot owner's name is different from the surname you are researching, these may not help you. However, the plats can help you figure out where in the cemetery the graves of interest to you are located.

# Plot Records

These are usually card files with the name of the plot owner, date of purchase, and names and dates of burials in the plot. If the plot is in perpetual care, which requires a yearly maintenance fee, you might be fortunate enough to find a present-day descendant on the records. You can usually assume that everyone buried in the plot is related. However, assumptions can set back your research. When my husband and I visited the cemetery where his grandparents are buried, we saw a marker for someone no one in the family had mentioned. Suspecting a scandal of some sort, we asked my mother-in-law. She replied that Grandma was a kindly soul and when a stranger in town had dropped dead and no one knew his kin, she had him buried in the family plot.

As with other land transactions, the cemetery plot owner receives a deed. It is recorded in the cemetery records by the sexton, and in some areas, is also recorded in a special county deed book.

# Do You Need to Visit?

Yes, do visit! The sexton's records do not describe the monuments, nor do they tell you who is buried in proximity to your ancestors.

There is no substitute for strolling through the cemetery. Your ancestors walked this very ground. Grandma wept as she buried her third child during the smallpox epidemic. Grandpa chose to lay his parents to rest at the top of the hill overlooking the lake. Sons and daughters planted trees in loving memory—those same giant trees with roots now threatening to topple the monuments.

# Locating the Cemetery

The libraries and historical societies in the counties of your ancestors may offer finding aids for the cemeteries. These aids vary from a simple map showing the major cemeteries in the county to printed abstracts of one cemetery's records. In a tiny one-room historical society in Illinois, there are dozens of binders for the cemeteries in three contiguous counties. Each binder has a short history of the cemetery, a map, photographs, and an indexed list of the tombstone inscriptions found there. Similar records exist elsewhere.

**Tree Tips** _____

Civic groups may know cemetery locations from their work on Spring "clean up" days. Farmers and hunters may know of "lost" cemeteries.

# Follow the Money

Who paid the bill for the funeral? Funeral homes and morticians can be your biggest allies in finding the cemeteries and their records. They keep records, and usually they work enthusiastically with you to find information.

Families traditionally return to the same morticians for all funerals, so the funeral directors are often well acquainted with many family members and may be able to refer you to relatives still in the area. They also know all, or most, of the cemeteries in their county and many in adjoining counties.

> **Lineage Lessons**
>
> Although most funeral homes willingly work with you to find information, they are not compelled to do so. Funeral homes are private businesses, sometimes owned by large corporations. In our litigious society they may strive to protect themselves and their clients by treating all information as confidential. When seeking records, remain courteous and understand their position.

In more modern times, the funeral director collects the information for the death certificate and the obituary. These records can give you birth dates and places, siblings, and children, as well as occupations and other personal information. Remember, though, that the information was given by someone other than the deceased, so it may not be accurate. The stress of the occasion may befuddle bereft survivors. The informant may be unrelated to the decedent, an in-law, or a distant relative unfamiliar with the deceased's biographical details. Even if the death took place before death certificates were required, the funeral records are worth pursuing. For listings of morticians and funeral directors, consult *The Yellow Book of Funeral Directors* or the *National Directory of Morticians*. If you can't find these in your library, try your local funeral home. Although both publications have an online presence, the morticians' directory www.funeral-dir.com is the only one available to nonprofessionals in the funeral industry.

If a funeral home is no longer in business, contact other funeral homes in the area. They often know where the records are and may even have the records themselves. Conscious of the value of the records, many funeral directors make it a point to preserve old records whenever possible.

**Tree Tips**

When funeral homes consolidate or become custodians of defunct mortician's records, they may archive old records in an off-site facility and need to recoup their expenses by charging you for a search whether or not anything is found.

# Procession to the Cemetery

The absolute best time to visit a cemetery is on Memorial Day, formerly known as Decoration Day. Traditionally, this is the day when all the family gathers to spruce up the burial grounds, plant shrubs, and put out fresh flowers and flags. Cousins play hide and seek among the monuments while the old folks reminisce about days gone by. I remember these gatherings well from my childhood, with my father trimming the grass around his grandparents' and baby sister's graves and my mother tending to her great-grandmother's plot.

All family cemeteries are different, from the imposing monument in the cemetery in the following figure of the Hon. Joseph Bush family in *History of Chenango and Madison Counties, New York* (Syracuse: D. Mason & Co., 1880) to a cemetery full of mostly field-stone markers surrounded by a barbed-wire fence. No matter the kind of cemetery or whether you go on Memorial Day or some other day, here are a few steps to success:

- Dress appropriately; you'll be out in nature.

- Take pencil, paper, and digital camera or traditional camera with plenty of film.

- Plan your route to take in several cemeteries.

*The Bush family cemetery.*

## No Fashion Statements

The well-dressed cemetery researcher wears long pants, long sleeves, and old shoes or, preferably, boots. Cemeteries are well known for their abundant flora and fauna, especially chiggers, gnats, ticks, snakes, and small rodents. The grasses may be high and full of burrs, the ground uneven and full of small depressions. Don't let these things deter you, but do be aware of the hazards.

### Pedigree Pitfalls

When you are actually ready to visit the cemetery, it is prudent to take someone with you. Cemeteries are often in isolated spots; use some caution. Your companion can help you hunt for names on the markers if you do not have a map of the cemetery.

## A Picture Is Worth a Thousand Words

Whether you are a skilled photographer or strictly amateur, photograph the cemetery. Try to get a few panoramic shots, then focus on plots, and then the markers. Write a complete description of the cemetery: name, location (explicit enough so that you can find it again), and overall condition. Sketch the plots that are meaningful to your research and tell where they are: "Between the first two lanes to the east of the entrance, middle row, large double granite marker facing west with the name Harcourt. Nearby are Waggoners and Ballards." If you have the plot description from the records, use it. It will be something like Section A, Block 6, Lot 2.

## Mark Your Maps

You have a limited amount of time; make the most of it. Plan an efficient route so that you don't waste time zigzagging back and forth throughout the county. If the cemeteries are on private property, get permission before opening the gate and crossing the field.

# Engraved in Stone

The highlight of cemetery visits is reading the tombstones. The variety is astounding. From huge monuments to simple wood plaques, all were placed in loving memory of individuals who had strengths and weaknesses, as do we. They are teeming with information about our ancestors if we will only read them.

The inscription may be only a name and range of dates or it may be akin to a family group sheet in marble with information on the parents on the front of the marker and all the children and their birth dates on the back. Relationships are engraved on the stones: "Wife of John A. Davis," "Son," "Beloved husband." One of the most important finds may be the inscription on a woman's tombstone that says "Daughter of" and names her parents. This may be the only record you will find of her maiden name.

The stone you find may be only a chiseled stone as in the following figure (from a gravestone in the small family cemetery at *Bellevette* in Nelson County, Virginia).

Perhaps you'll find some sentiment.

There may be a reference to a Bible passage, or the entire inscription may be in another language. Look carefully at any symbols or emblems on the tombstone. They represent membership in fraternal, patriotic, civic, religious, and veterans groups with records regarding your ancestors. Learn to recognize the more common ones, and sketch unfamiliar ones to research.

*A chiseled stone in a family graveyard.*

 **Pedigree Pitfalls** _____

> Be aware that some monuments are placed in memory of someone who is buried elsewhere. Monuments might also have been placed many years after a death, when the family was finally able to afford the cost. You may find family members or interested associates replacing crumbled markers with new plaques. In all of these cases of stones erected later, there is more chance of error in the information.

## Reading the Markers Can Be Difficult

Sometimes the bottom part of the marker has sunk into the ground or the words are eroded. Weeds and tall grasses may completely obscure the marker. Dirt cakes in the letters; lichen creeps over the symbols.

For cases like these, it is useful to have with you a few tools: a trowel, grass clippers, stiff brush (*never* a wire brush), rags, and clear water. With these you may be able to clear away enough debris to make out the information.

**Pedigree Pitfalls** _____

> Never use harsh chemicals or abrasives on tombstones. Their damage is irreparable. Attempt only gentle cleaning.

In the recent past, genealogists were encouraged to take rubbings of the tombstones, but that practice is now out of favor. Tombstones are now an endangered species needing protection from the elements and genealogists.

---

**Lineage Lessons**

The impermanence of tombstones means that the record you make today may someday be the only evidence that this marker ever existed. Take photographs, but also make it a habit to record the information carefully and completely. Don't depend on the photographs alone.

---

## Sometimes You Are Disappointed

Age, environment, neglect, and vandals all take their toll on cemeteries. Many tombstones were made of sandstone and they are crumbling to dust. Years of freezing and thawing cracks the stones, and pieces are missing. Weather erodes the inscriptions. Vandals may have tipped over the markers. In one cemetery, dozens of stones were in a pile at the base of a tree. I could have cried as I realized there was no way I was going to know whether my ancestor's stone was in that big pile.

# Don't Leave Yet

Look carefully at the tombstones in close proximity to your ancestor's burial place. Relatives were often buried in clusters, and you might recognize some names.

The tombstones tell of great sorrow as you find a family burying babies year after year. Look at the dates on tombstones throughout the cemetery. You may find many families burying children on the same days. Suspect an epidemic such as diphtheria or influenza. In 1918, "Spanish flu" decimated whole families.

A clue to the cause of death of women is often revealed on the tombstones: "Mary Smith, died 6 October 1878, age 22." Next to her is "Sarah, infant dau. of J. A. and Mary Smith, 7 October 1878." Mary no doubt died in childbirth.

Last, spend a little time communing with your ancestors. They want to be remembered. You are their ticket to immortality.

## The Least You Need to Know

- Search both the cemetery and the records to get a more complete picture of your ancestors.
- The Internet is a rich resource for locating cemeteries.
- Information in the records and on the tombstones is from an informant and subject to error.
- Take a companion to the cemetery with you.

# Chapter 16

# More Than News in the Newspaper

## In This Chapter

- ◆ The differences among newspapers
- ◆ The variety of notices they carry
- ◆ The finding aids: indexes and inventories
- ◆ What's of value in the notices

In 1855 your ancestor left the hometown to join a wagon train to Oregon, noted in the local newspaper. Another wrote home in 1862 after a major battle of the Civil War and made the local news when he related details in that letter. In 1920 an old-timer wrote his lengthy reminiscences of the history of the town he helped settle in 1885. Newspapers are crammed with fascinating tidbits. You will be enthralled when reading the news and the quaint notices preserved on their pages.

# Dailies, Weeklies, and More

Not all newspapers are the same. They differed then and differ now in frequency of publication and in their focus. They include these:

◆ Daily newspapers: published in larger communities

◆ Weekly newspapers: small-town newspapers or a local competition to the daily

◆ Ethnic newspapers in native languages

◆ Religious newspapers

◆ Legal newspapers containing legal notices and court calendars

Seldom will you be accessing the original newspapers. Because of their size, the fragile newsprint, and the scarcity of copies of early issues, access to the originals is usually restricted. Libraries across the country have microfilmed many of their holdings; these are often available on interlibrary loan.

# Newspapers in the Area

Many newspapers have undergone numerous ownership changes. Others are no longer published, but their back issues may be preserved. Try the latest edition of *Gale Directory of Publications and Broadcasting Media* (formerly *Ayer Directory of Publications*). It will lead you to newspapers still in existence and provide background on their predecessors. If the newspaper you seek has gone out of business, it will not be listed in *Gale* but might be in a former *Ayer list*.

**Tree Tips**

A guide to current bibliographies, indexes, abstracts, and other sources of value for newspapers is in Ancestry's *The Source*.

Some state libraries with extensive newspaper collections have compiled special lists by county and by town for those available. Look for those in your library's reference section.

# Checking for an Index

A surprising number of nineteenth-century newspapers have been indexed in recent years. Not usually every name, but certain subjects and the principal names are indexed. Often the items indexed were primarily those involving births, marriages, and deaths. Determine whether there is an index for the newspapers in your area of search. Try entering the name of that newspaper in your computer's browser and see what comes up. For example, I entered at random "Reading Pennsylvania newspaper" to see if anything would come up for Reading, Pennsylvania. I quickly found the *Reading Eagle*. A variety of articles were available online, including obituaries, some anniversaries with charming photos, and others. The newspapers on the Web are often searchable for a variety of topics. Give it a try.

Even if an index has not been published for the newspaper, a local group may have created an unpublished manuscript or card index available at their library or genealogical society.

After you determine which newspapers were published in the area and whether they are indexed, you need to identify which repository has the newspapers and whether you can borrow the microfilmed issues on interlibrary loan. Ask your reference librarian for assistance.

# Reading Every Word?

Nineteenth-century newspapers are difficult to read; often all the local items are combined into one long continuous column. It is hard to immediately locate the item you seek, unless you are fortunate enough to be working with a newspaper that headed its columns "Births," "Marriages," or "Deaths." There is a shortcut to finding notices when indexes are lacking. Determine the name of the community in which your family lived. That leads you to the local columns. Community columns included diverse items all mingled together. Residents who took trips, visitors from out of town, who was ill, deaths, social events—all were listed one after the other without break. The community notices can be particularly valuable when listing visiting relatives from out of town or noting the trips residents made to other localities to visit their kin.

# Topics to Target

There is so much that can be of assistance in genealogy, regardless of whether they are nineteenth- or twentieth-century newspapers. You may find these:

- ◆ Obituaries and death listings
- ◆ The family thank-you after a funeral
- ◆ Birth announcements

**Tree Tips**

When you are trying to get information from a county in which the courthouse burned, the newspaper can help fill some gaping holes.

- Marriages and anniversaries
- Church news of members (particularly births, marriages, and deaths)
- Sales of property
- Legal summons and citations
- Estate notices
- "Left my bed and board"
- Went west
- Advertisements
- Unclaimed mail at the post office
- Letters to the editor
- Visiting family and community events

# He Died on the Fifteenth of June

Notices of death vary greatly, whether in current newspapers or those published 200 years ago. There may be only a brief mention in a column of deaths (usually called "Death Listings"). There might also be a full obituary including age and place of residence, a summary of the deceased's life, career, church affiliation, lodge membership, and much more. Always, without exception, these should be sought. The name of the parents, where the deceased was born (providing the prior location of the family), when born, when and where died, and the places the deceased had lived—all might appear. This can serve as a pointer to other localities to search marriages of the deceased and the names of survivors—brothers, sisters, children, and others connected to the family may appear. The church where the funeral was held and the cemetery lead you to even more potential sources. Occupation, professional career, war service, special skills (weaving, making quilts), town offices held, and other such gems may help round out the details of your ancestor's life.

## Checking Several Papers

Do not limit yourself to one newspaper. Determine which newspapers were in the area and examine them all. In the weekly publications, check at least three to four weeks after the date of death. Examine daily issues for at least a week later.

Occasionally, the notice was not published for a significant time beyond the date of death. It is impractical, on a routine basis, to examine the newspapers for an extended period, but if it is important to your search and you have not been able to locate the notice, take the time. And if the person died in a new location, check the old location, too. News often drifted back several weeks later to the original hometown, resulting in a notice published on the death of one of their own.

After you have located the notice, do not stop. Look at the next two or three issues. In its rush to publish, the newspaper might at first have scanty details and enlarge upon them the following day or two. I have found this to be true often enough to warrant the search for at least a few days beyond. If the newspaper is a weekly, check the issue for the following week. In the issue of 6 December 1905 of the *St. Lawrence Republican*, a Nicholville, New York, newspaper, the obituary starts: "Hiram M. Rose whose death was mentioned *in last week's issue* …" (italics added). The subsequent notice tells that he was born in Vermont, came to New York as a boy, and gave his various residences during his life as well as where his mother and father died. It includes his three marriages, the year and to whom, and the children born of each. If you had stopped with the first notice, you would have missed this.

If the deceased died on 4 August 1871, do not assume that the newspaper of the same date would be too early. If you start searching with the following day, you may miss the notice. The newspapers were more flexible than present-day newspapers in their ability to add last-minute items, or that issue may have been late going to press.

Even a brief notice, such as the one that appeared in the *New York Herald* of Saturday June 26, 1852, can provide gems. The death of William E. Rose was reported, "after a short but severe illness," aged 27 years, 1 month, and 7 days. Relatives and friends of the family and members of Hook and Ladder Company No. 1 were invited to the funeral to take place from his late residence at 33 Forsythe Street." This provides an age at death from which a birth can be calculated, a residence address so city directories can be checked for others of the surname at that address, possible land records if he owned the residence, and even the occupation, which can lead to union or guild records in connection with his work.

## Other Unexpected Rewards in Obituaries

An immense value of obituaries is locating relatives who moved elsewhere. The list of survivors can include the brother who went west and the uncle who still lives in Boston. Others who traveled a distance (and might be related) may also be listed.

When you find the notice, try to get a photocopy (or a microprint if it is on micro-film). Note the date of the issue, full name of the newspaper, and the page and col-umn of the notice.

## Urban Versus Small-Town Newspapers

Normally the small-town newspaper was more expansive in its notices than the larger urban newspapers. Tight-knit communities wanted details. They knew the family intimately and could provide interesting bits of data. The sheer volume of people in populated areas mandated that only selected obituar-ies could be included: usually prominent individuals or long-time residents. This holds true today. It can be especially important to check for death listings in a city newspaper, because they publish so few full obituaries.

**Tree Tips**

Many newspapers charge a fee for a listing; therefore, death listings are not complete even in present times.

## The Family Thanks You

In some areas, it was, and still is, popular for the family to publish a card of thanks during the month following the funeral. Watch for these. A pair of examples are shown below.

These figures from early newspapers show two cards of thanks from the same family; one notice was published after the death of the father and the other after the death of the mother. Note the discrepancies in the lists. Some differences might be explained by marriages, but others are clear errors in one or the other list. Research will deter-mine which names are correct. Such discrepancies are common and emphasize the necessity for gathering as many records as possible on the same individual.

**CARD OF THANKS**

To those who have ministered unto our husband and father, J. M. Rose, and did all that loving hands could do, and to those who spoke of our aching hearts through the silent language of beautiful floral offerings, we turn with thankful hearts. May God of All comfort and bless you.

Mrs. J. M. Rose and Irl,
Mrs. Thirza Barr,
Mrs. Emma Wicke
Mrs. Kannie Fields,
Otis Rose,
C. H. Rose,
R. L. Rose,
Ira Rose,
Harve Rose,
John Rose.

*The family's thank-you after the father's death.*

**CARD OF THANKS**

We sincerely wish to express our thanks and appreciation to our many friends and neighbors for their kindness and sympathy to us in the sudden death of our mother.

Mrs. B. E. Wicker, Mrs. J. L. Gields, Mrs. J. R. Barr, R. L. Rose, Ira Rose, H. A. Rose, O. R. Rose, C. H. Rose, John V. Rose, Irl Rose, Ora E. James.

*The family's thank-you when the mother died.*

The family may have published a notice to mark the anniversary of the death of their family member. Typically, these are brief "In Memoriam" types of notices. They are often signed, providing names of living relatives.

# A Baby Was Born!

Some of the nineteenth-century newspapers published a special column of birth notices or mentioned them in community columns, although they were not prevalent. Columns became more popular in the early and mid-twentieth century. They were brief: "A daughter Mary was born to John and Martha Smith of Smith Twp." Such a notice might provide you with the first name of the mother if you didn't know it (and sometimes even her maiden name), the township, or other small bits of information you did not have.

# Wedding Vows

Marriage notices were—and still are—popular newspaper fodder. First, perhaps news of the engagement was published, often with photos. Next, the couple may appear in a column of wedding licenses issued. This column usually lists the name of the intended bride and groom, their ages, and perhaps other significant details. After the wedding, there may be an article with a full description of the event and, again, a photo.

The language and details or the editorial commentary in earlier newspapers was much more intimate than we see now. In a description of the wedding of one young woman, the newspaper reports, "It was intended that the father would give the bride away, but at the last moment he faltered, as it was more than he could do."

Silver and golden wedding announcements generate news. If you have the marriage date, add 25 or 50 years, determine where they may have been living, and check the newspaper. You may be rewarded with a photo and names and residences of close family members. There may even be a bonus: a wonderful description of the attire, the presents received, details of the original wedding, and relatives who came from afar to share the occasion.

# Christenings and More

If you can identify the religion of the family, watch for church columns. The baptisms, confirmations, and other church news may provide you with another source of information on your family. Perhaps your grandfather was an elder, or Grandma taught Sunday school.

# Love Gone Awry

When a couple separated, the husband sometimes published a notice to absolve himself of legal responsibility for the wife's bills. We think of this as a more modern legal maneuver, but it actually was used very early. When Ezekiel Rose and his wife separated, he published a notice: "Whereas Mary Rose, the wife of me the subscriber, has left my bed and board, without any just cause, I therefore caution all persons trusting or in any manner dealing with her on my account, as I will not be answerable for any debt she may contract, or any dealing she may make, after this date." It was signed by Ezekiel Rose in Hampshire County, March 15, 1794, and published in the *Potowmac Guardian and Berkeley Advertiser* of Martinsburg, [West] Virginia, now preserved in the collection of The American Antiquarian Society. Without this notice, you might assume when reading the will he made in 1818, omitting any provision for a wife, that he was a widower, though she actually survived him by 10 years.

In the late nineteenth century, in a moment of poetic inspiration, one husband submitted the following notice to *The Standard* of Jackson County, Ohio: "Mr. W. S. Williams of Illinois, announces that his wife, Ann Eliza, having left his bed and board without cause, he will not be responsible for any debts she may contract."

"Ann Eliza, Ann Eliza,

Once I loved but now despise her,

And So I no longer prize her,

I will go and advertise her,

For although I'm not a miser,

I won't pay for what she buys her."

# Sale of Property

These notices can be charming. And explicit. The executor of an estate is perhaps advertising the deceased's property, or the sheriff is selling a tract at public auction because of debt or taxes due.

In the following figure, the land commonly known as T. Rose's Old Place was advertised for sale in the *Maryland Herald* of Hagerstown, Maryland, on 3 March 1819. The description includes details that are just about impossible to find in other sources.

In a different matter, a lengthy advertisement was published in the issue of 17 September 1817 of the *Adams Centinel* in Adams County, Pennsylvania. Being sold was the following:

> *Valuable Grist or Paper Mill Seat or any other kind of Water Works with 18 feet of head and fall, situated on Conowago Creek, in Franklin & Menallen townships, Adams county, three quarters mile from John Arendts Tavern, on the Road leading from Pine Grove to Gettysburg, with a LOT of 12 acres of land whereof 7 are excellent timothy*

*meadow clear—the remainder is well covered with Timber. The improvements are a
new two-story log dwellinghouse, with a back shed to it … for terms of sale, apply to the
Subscriber living on the Premises.*

It was signed by John Mackley. The precise description in the advertisement enabled
the family to locate the piece of land.

Advertisement of land for
sale.

> THE subscriber offers for sale that
> well known Public Stand, commonly
> called T. Rose's Old Place, situated on
> the Potomac.   The Cumberland Turn-
> pike runs through the land nearly a mile,
> and passes immediately by the buildings.
>   This is one of the best scites for a
> Tavern between Cumberland and Ha-
> gers-town, being forty one miles from
> the former and twenty-two from the lat-
> ter place, and four from Hancock-town.
> There are about 40 acres of Potomac
> bottom, 12 acres of which are excel-
> lent meadow, and about 60 acres of
> upland, part cleared, the remainder
> in wood-land.  The improvements are
> but indifferent.  There is a tolerable
> good spring on the premises, and a run
> passing through, convenient to the im-
> provements.  It is presumed any per-
> sons wishing to purchase such property,
> will come and view it and judge for them-
> selves.  It will be divided to suit pur-
> chasers if required.  The terms of sale
> will be, one half in hand; the other half
> in three annual payments.

# Legal Notices: The Fine Print

Among newspaper items are the legal notices, those items usually in small print. They
include items directed by law to be published to notify possible interested people of
the action. Those items have often been omitted among modern indexes, which is
unfortunate. They can provide valuable leads in your quest.

## You Are Hereby Summoned ...

When a defendant in a suit or heirs of a decedent cannot be located, the law normally grants permission to publish the summons or citation to give notice to the parties involved. It may be published in more than one newspaper as directed by the court. Stop to examine these. You will readily see their value.

# Other Miscellaneous Notices

During the gold rush to the west and other surges of expansion, the newspapers were packed with bulletins such as "John Smith, George Martin, and Gregory Morton left last Tuesday to join the train at Huntsville traveling west." Or, "Josiah Martin finished outfitting his team and wagon and left yesterday." The Civil War also generated many items about home-town boys who left for service, or news when they wrote home.

**Tree Tips**

In many areas, paper was scarce during the war years. The local newspaper may have suspended publication for the duration.

# Those Charming Advertisements

Was your ancestor a tailor? A pharmacist? Owned a stable? Look for advertisements. They are charming. The doctor extols the cures reported from the latest herbal won-der; the tailor confidently announces that there is no workmanship that matches his own. Always make photocopies when you find advertisements placed by your ances-tors. They add interest when you assemble the story of their lives, and the copies will add eye appeal when you illustrate your written account. (Remember, though, to con-sider copyright. Note the year of publication and determine if the copyright has run out by going to www.copyright.gov/circs/circ1.html and reading about the duration of copyright. If it has not, get permission.)

# A Letter Is Waiting For ...

Letters sent by anxious relatives, or others, often went unclaimed at the post office. The recipient was either unaware that the letter had been sent, or the person had moved away. The newspaper periodically published the lists; it might be the only proof that your ancestor was supposed to be in the area. In other instances, a worried relative might have written a letter to the editor of the newspaper and inquired about "my brother who I have not heard from in over five years … have your readers heard of him … please have him write to …."

# Ethnic and Religious Newspapers

If you cannot find notices, in spite of an exhaustive search of the English language newspapers, the information you seek may be in an ethnic newspaper. Was the family German, and living in a large city? The item may be there. "But I don't read German," you may say. Doesn't matter. Watch for the name; you'll recognize it. If you find a notice, copy it and seek the assistance of a professor or student of the language at the local college or university. You can also seek assistance from an ethnic genealogical society to find others who can translate the notice for you. Some websites that offer translations can help, though personal experience with them has shown that these are not truly accurate. One that you can try is http://babelfish. altavista.com/babelfish/tr. It will at least give you a sense of what the article says, but supplement it with a true translation by someone knowledgeable.

# Can the Internet Help?

You have a good chance of being in luck, at least with some of your ancestors. Many organizations are digitizing newspapers and posting the images. Some are searchable on every word. When the complete images are unavailable, there may at least be indexes, often prepared by volunteers. Some of the websites offering newspaper notices are subscription sites such as Ancestry.com. And increasingly, libraries and genealogical societies are making large databases of newspapers available to their patrons and members. Go to www.godfrey.org for a number of newspapers. Or access ProQuest's database of *The New York Times* 1851-1998 through your membership at organizations such as the New York Genealogical and Biographical Society at www.newyorkfamilyhistory.org. Others offering free archived newspaper access to members include the New England Historic Genealogical Society at www. newenglandancestors.org. There are many others. Start your newspaper search with www.cyndislist.com but also experiment with your Internet browser, inserting the county, state, and the word "newspaper." See what comes up.

To locate the website of many current newspapers, try www.usnpl.com. Once there, click on the state of your choice, and peruse the links to the various websites of those of that state. Some of the current newspapers have archived past issues, though usually they are of a more recent time period.

# Flavor the Times

Use newspapers routinely during your search. They offer a rare opportunity to understand the times in which your family lived. Soak up a flavor of the area: the bake sales, local pageants, and sports-event winners. A strong feeling for the people and an understanding of the community atmosphere that influenced the lives of your family will be yours after reading those pages.

## The Least You Need to Know

- Newspapers differ widely.
- There's much more than obituaries to help in your search.
- Many newspapers have been indexed by general subjects.
- There are many published inventories to guide you to the locations of newspapers.
- It's hard to match newspapers for a flavor of the bygone era in which your ancestors lived.
- Some newspapers have been digitized and are available online.

# Chapter 17

# Did Great-Grandpa Carry a Rifle?

## In This Chapter

- Determining whether your ancestor served in the military
- Using Compiled Military-Service Record files
- The value of pension files
- Bounty land awards to soldiers
- The world of WWI and WWII draft records

Knowing that an ancestor served his country instills in us a sense of pride. The diary saying that our fifth great-grandfather served with Custer causes us to rush to the history books for an account of those Indian skirmishes. A newspaper account that another relation received a medal for his heroism at Gettysburg propels us to every website on that famous battle. These men who fought for our country helped shape our history. But, how often can we really prove their service? Learn which company they served in and what battles they fought. Descriptive records are there for the finding.

# Didn't Know He Served?

My husband's great-great-grandfather was born about 1788 and did not marry until 1819. Though he was about 25 and single when the War of 1812 erupted, no family tradition had indicated his service. Pursuing the possibility that he may have served, based only on age and the fact that he was unmarried, I contacted the National Archives. Completing the form they provided with my limited information on his age and places of residence, I requested a *bounty land* application file. Imagine the thrill a few weeks later when a packet arrived with copies of papers signed by this ancestor, giving all the details of his service! His widow's documents in the same file gave information about their marriage, his death, and many interesting sidelights. This success so many years ago convinced me to always seek military files. You, too, will be more than a bit excited when you realize the extent of the records that exist if your ancestor was a veteran. Compiled service files, pensions, bounty land papers, hospital rolls, draft registrations, and many others await your discovery.

**Genie Jargon** _____

**Bounty land** is public land awarded by the colonial and later federal government, under certain conditions, to veterans for their service in the military. Soldiers were promised this land either as an inducement to join the service, to extend their enlistment, or as a reward for having served.

# The Treasure of the National Archives (NARA)

For military records before World War I, there is no greater repository than the National Archives and Records Administration, often referred to as NARA. With its principal facility in downtown Washington, D.C. (known as Archives I), and the facility in College Park, Maryland (known as Archives II), this repository offers many documents, microfilm, and maps that can assist the researcher. Many (but not all) of the National Archives records on earlier wars have been microfilmed. These and records of all Archives branches can be accessed at www.archives.gov.

Study the catalog titled *Military Service Records: A Select Catalog of National Archives Microfilm Publications*, (called hereafter the *Catalog*), widely available in libraries and at all National Archives branches. Thousands of rolls of microfilm are listed. Some are indexes. Others are service records, unit histories, post returns, pensions, and more.

This catalog is also available online at www.archives.gov/publications, click on "Online Publications," and once there click on "Military Service Catalog." You'll use this catalog often, so bookmark it. Better yet, invest a small amount to buy a copy from the Archives—you'll use it often.

Photocopies of original files can be ordered through National Archives forms. Use NATF-85 obtainable through Archives I or any of its branches or order the form at www.archives. gov/contact/inquire_form.html. There is an easier way. The pension files and the compiled military files (as well as a few others that are listed) can be ordered and paid for online at the Archives' website. Go to an unfortunately long URL: www.archives.gov/research_room/obtain_copies/ reproductions_overview.html. Establish a password at the ordering page and then proceed to the order form using the links. If the Archives does not locate the file you order, there will be no charge.

**Tree Tips**

Though the National Archives in Washington, D.C. has all the available microfilm, the Archives branches have only selected series. If the rolls you want are not available at an Archives branch, try other major repositories, the commercial microfilm rental vendors, or a Family History Center.

The National Archives *Catalog* lists only the records on microfilm. Others, still in their original form (referred to as textual records) can be viewed in person in Washington, D.C., or photocopies can be ordered by mail.

Let's focus on the Revolutionary War (1776–1783) as a start, then bounty land, then the Civil War (1861–1865), and finally, some twentieth-century records. Valuable genie gems in these await your discovery.

# The Revolutionary War

Calculate the estimated age of your ancestor during the Revolutionary War. Don't consider 16 and 17 too young, especially when they misrepresented their age. Promises by the government to give land (in addition to pay) induced even older men to try to enlist.

## The Compiled Military Service Record

Fires destroyed most of the records of the American Army and Navy in the custody of the War Department in 1800 and 1814. In a project begun in 1894, abstracts were made from documents purchased by the War Department from a variety of sources. Individual packets were created for each soldier, and the abstracted records inserted. Muster rolls, pay rolls, rank rolls, returns, hospital records, prison records, and others were examined. Information was extracted to bring together all the records relating to an individual soldier.

A typical Compiled Military Service Record, as it is known, gives the rank, military unit, date of entry into service, and whether discharged or separated by desertion, death, or other reasons. It may show age, place of birth, and residence at the time of enlistment. There is no guarantee that all of this information will be in an individual's packet, but normally they contain at least some of these bits. These compiled records are arranged by the war or the period of service, and thereunder by state (or some other designation), then by military unit, and last, alphabetically by the name of the soldier. Those for the Revolutionary War not only have a microfilmed index, but the complete original files also have been microfilmed. Using them requires only that you find a repository with both sets of microfilm or borrow the films.

---

### Lineage Lessons

Indexes to Compiled Military Service Records are available not only for the Revolutionary War, but also for the War of 1812, various Indian wars and disturbances, the Mexican War, the Civil War, up through the Spanish-American War, the Philippine Insurrection, and the Boxer Rebellion. Though the indexes have been microfilmed, most of the actual files have not and are only available for in-person viewing at the National Archives or by ordering photocopies.

---

## Let's Try It Hands-On

Go to a National Archives branch or to a library that has the National Archives microfilm. Look in the *Catalog* previously mentioned for the listings of the "Compiled Military Service Records of the Revolutionary War." The Catalog lists micropublication M860 with 58 rolls by number, and indicates the range of surnames on each roll.

As shown in the following figure, it is easy to ascertain which roll has the index for the surname you seek. Upon accessing the correct roll, find the soldier's name, and copy all the information shown for him. With that you will be able to find his file. Return again to the Catalog; it will point you to a second micropublication, M881, the *Compiled Service Records of Soldiers Who Served in the American Army During the Revolutionary War*. Your file is on one of the latter 1,096 rolls.

| Roll | Description |
|------|-------------|
| 1 | A–Ange |
| 2 | Angi–Ballan |
| 3 | Ballar–Bearne |
| 4 | Bearnh–Biso |
| 5 | Biss–Box |
| 6 | Boy–Brown, Joh |
| 7 | Brown, Jon–Bur |
| 8 | Bus–Cartel |
| 9 | Carter–Chp |

*Example of roll listings on micropublication M860 by surname.*

Let's practice. Searching for John Carter, go to Roll 9 of M860, as seen in the above figure. Find his name in the index on that roll. Copy all the information: regiment, company, everything. Now return to the same microfilm Catalog; note that these records are available on M881, which contain the files. As seen in the following figure, the rolls in M881 are arranged by state, thereunder by regiment, and so on, and last by surname. Find the listed roll that matches the data shown by the index for the soldier. If John Carter served in Delaware in the 2nd Regiment of New Castle County, Militia (determined from the index), his record would be on Roll 380 of M881. Now you can find the Compiled Military Service Record file. It may consist of only one card or a number of cards.

| Delaware: | |
|-----------|--|
| 380 | 1st Battalion (New Castle County) |
| | 2d Battalion, Militia |
| | 2d Regiment, Militia |
| | 2d Regiment (New Castle County), Militia |
| | A–G |
| 381 | H–W |
| | 7th Battalion, Militia |
| | Hall's Regiment |
| 382 | A–Br |
| 383 | Bu–C |

*Roll listings of micropublication M881, which contains the actual files.*

A few of the rolls in micropublication M881 for the state of Delaware are shown here to illustrate how the rolls are listed. Match the information you found on your ancestor's indexed entry to determine the roll you need.

# Now His Pension File

Don't be too disappointed if the Compiled Military Service Record is brief. At least you can now document that your ancestor did serve. There are a multitude of additional records. One of the richest for genealogical information and interest are the soldiers' pension files containing facts we value—birth date and birthplace, marriages, and other similarly helpful details. After you discover that your ancestor served in the Revolution, the pension file indexes will reveal whether he or his heirs ever applied for a pension.

The Act of 1818, based on financial need, is the first major pension act for which the application papers are preserved. It was quickly followed by an act in 1820 tightening the requirements. As the government became more lenient, restrictions were lessened. In 1832, a general act awarded pensions based solely on six months or more of service. In 1836, widows received benefits. (Up to that time, generally only the widows of officers were eligible.) For more on the various pension acts passed by our government, see Christine Rose's *Military Pension Acts 1776–1858*.

The complete pension file for each soldier has been filmed. Micropublication M804 of the National Archives consists of 2,670 rolls of alphabetically arranged records titled *Revolutionary War Pension and Bounty Land Warrant Application Files, 1800–1906*. (The dates shown are correct; applications were made by heirs as late as 1906.)

## Lineage Lessons

In spite of the ease in using the alphabetized micropublication M804, you may find it handy to consult the *Index of Revolutionary War Pension Applications in the National Archives* in book form if microfilm is not readily available. After you determine from it that your ancestor has a file, you can then search for a repository with the microfilm.

Micropublication M804 reproduces every paper available in each pension file. Each soldier's file contains two groups: the "selected papers" (those papers that the National Archives considered the most important and which they used to use to fill mail orders), and the remainder of the file, marked as "nonselected." Examine every paper in your ancestor's file. The nonselected papers often include additional *affidavits* and forms; they might also include letters from descendants around the 1920s and 1930s, when many (wishing to apply to lineage societies) sought information on their ancestors. These letters can lead to descendants. Though the Archives used to provide only the "selected" papers for their minimum file, now they offer the complete file for a flat fee. Go to www.archives.gov for current pricing. If you have access to the microfilm, you can copy the papers yourself and read them at your leisure.

**Genie Jargon** _____

An **affidavit** is a written declaration made under oath before a notary public or another authorized official.

In another micropublication, M805, the Archives again reproduced the Revolutionary pension files, but in this one only the "selected" portion of the files were filmed. This shorter series was purchased by many libraries that could not afford the more extensive M804 series or didn't have space to store those voluminous rolls. If you find your ancestor on M805, make it a point to reexamine the file in its entirety when you can access M804.

Besides the availability on microfilm, the contents of the selected papers on M805 is also available on a CD-ROM "Revolutionary War Pension and Bounty Land Warrant Index," available from Heritage Quest. If you locate the name of your soldier on this index, a CD-ROM corresponding to the roll number is available though this company. A listing of all the rolls of M805 are at www2.heritagequest.com/qsearch/sr.asp?s=M805.

## Now in Print

Another resource for your search of the Revolutionary War pension files is Virgil D. White's *Genealogical Abstracts of Revolutionary War Pension Files*. The abstracts are in three volumes, with an every-name index in a fourth volume. These abstracts do not include every paper in the files and are not a substitute for examining the complete file. Nonetheless, they are invaluable in helping to determine if your ancestor did indeed serve.

**Tree Tips** _____

The publication by Virgil D. White is particularly useful because these published abstracts are indexed in their entirety. Your ancestor may have made an affidavit in the application file of another soldier. You would not find that affidavit without this index because only the applicants' names are included in the previously mentioned *Index of Revolutionary War Pensions*.

## Why Check Further?

Why bother to proceed to the pension file, if you already know from the Compiled Military Service File that your ancestor served? In short, because you will learn a lot more from the pension file. You will experience a connection to your ancestors as you read the words they spoke in detailing the battles in which they were engaged and the resultant disabilities and hardships.

You will read about some sad situations, such as that of the widow Rebecca Rose, who at the age of 91 was found in the poorhouse, blind, "nearly naked, entirely helpless," defrauded by two unscrupulous men who filed her pension for her and gave her little of the funds. A man of conscience in the county came to her aid, demanding federal government assistance for this aged widow.

James Rose, the husband of Rebecca, a Virginian, had his share of difficulties, too. He tells that he was at Mill Creek when "the picket guard came in great haste, scared nearly to death," bringing a report that thousands of British were coming, just on the other side of Mill Creek Island. "Col. Mazzard having no horses at that time to manage the cannon, commanded the army to hasten to Mill Creek, and draw with them three of the cannons. This soldier [Rose] was one of the number that managed the cannon in the stead of horses, and produced a rupture in his body of which he never has and never will recover by his great exertions in drawing …." Later, he was discharged, and returned to King George County. He left his discharge at the home of a friend and, on a borrowed horse, went to see his relatives in King William County. On the way he was taken up as a deserter "by a company of drunkards" and retained in custody three days before he could get his discharge, "which he procured by giving a man a regimental coat to take the horse back and bring the discharge."

James' troubles weren't over; all are recited in the voluminous file. Fortunately for the unlucky James, his service was substantiated, and later a special Act was passed by Congress on his behalf. Similar stories abound. The files are fascinating and give you a rare opportunity to know your ancestors.

Here is a bonus: your ancestor may be one of those soldiers who either tore out the pages from the family Bible and offered them in support of the statements, or had the Bible entries extracted and notarized. Those papers may be your only proof of dates and relationships in the family.

The compiled military service record file and the pension file you find are not the only records available for Revolutionary War service. There are many others, but these will get you started.

# The Inducement of Bounty Land

Bounty land was awarded by the federal government either as an inducement to serve or as an inducement to remain longer in service. Later it was a reward for service. Government legislation authorized bounty land (that is, a free right to government land) in 1776, and in a series of subsequent acts the land and requirements were defined.

The bounty land warrants for the Revolutionary War could be sold by the soldier. Because it was many years before there was a tract of federal land designated where the soldier could exchange the federal warrant for land on which he could settle, most soldiers were induced to sell their warrants (usually to speculators), and few actually located on the land. This defeated the government's hope that those veterans would settle on the frontier and help protect it. Learning from what happened in this earlier war, during the War of 1812 the federal government imposed restrictions on the disposition of the warrant. The soldier could not sell or assign the warrant, though it could be inherited if he died. This was not changed until 1852 when new federal legislation allowed any unused warrants to be sold.

Many early bounty land application files were destroyed in War Department fires in 1800 and 1814. Any papers remaining were combined with the Revolutionary War pensions and microfilmed in M804, previously described. Bounty land warrant files for the War of 1812, under early acts of 1811–1816, were microfilmed on M848 of the National Archives on 14 rolls, titled "War of 1812 Military Bounty Land Warrants, 1815–1858." The dates refer to the period within which the applications were made. The indexes are on the first roll of this series.

The bulk of the bounty land application files have not been microfilmed, and there is no available index. They are arranged alphabetically by the name of the soldier in thousands of legal-size manila files. These files are packed with items of importance genealogically: marriages, Bible records, death records, and many more. This mass of files resulted from more lenient acts passed from 1847–1855 that reduced the required length of service for eligibility and instituted other changes.

If you ascertain that you had an ancestor who served in the War of 1812, Indian Wars before 1855, or the Mexican War (or any service 1790–1855), fill out a National Archives Form NATF-85, and mark the box on that form for bounty land file. The Archives will search for a record when it receives your request. Keep in mind that the last act granting bounty land was passed in 1855; applicants who filed later were doing so for service prior to the passage of this final 1855 act, before the Civil War.

**Tree Tips**

Though the early bounty land application files for the Revolutionary War were destroyed, information from warrant registers and other related items will be found scattered throughout a number of repositories and states.

# The War Between the States

The Civil War tore families apart. Brother fought against brother. Families were divided, and many never did heal their differences. Feelings run deep to this day. Be aware of this as you query your family about their Civil War connections. Be sensitive. In one file, a Tennessean, who was faced with a decision of whether to stay with the Union or join the Confederacy, moved to Arkansas to join a Union force there. His wife, whose family was staunchly of southern sympathies, refused to accompany him. Under these circumstances, often the soldier later took a new wife in his chosen state—in this case without benefit of a divorce from the former wife, who still refused to live with him. The files are full of sad tales. Don't be surprised at what you may find. Remember the times in which these families lived.

It also is not unusual to find records of the same soldier serving on both sides. The 19-year-old who went into town to run some errands for his family was spotted by southern (or northern) recruiters and forced to enter the service. At his first opportunity, he deserted and joined the opposing side, where his sympathies lay. If your ancestor was from a border state such as Tennessee, Kentucky, Arkansas, or Missouri, you may find dual records for him.

> **Lineage Lessons**
>
> Don't assume that your ancestor's record showing "deserted" means that he was a "coward." There were many reasons for desertion: loyalty to the other side, going home for a few days because of sickness in the family and then returning, and more. He may even have been improperly listed as a deserter when he fell into the hands of the opposing army.

## He Wore Gray

Start your search for the Confederate soldier with National Archives micropublication M253, *Consolidated Index to Compiled Service Records of the Confederate Soldiers*. Consisting of 535 rolls, this is arranged alphabetically by surname. When you locate the surname in the index, take down all the listed information.

Next, return to the Catalog. Look for the micropublication number for the Confederate Compiled Service Records of the state from which your ancestor served. The state rolls are arranged by regiment, unit, and so on, and last by surname. It should be fairly easy to determine the correct roll. You can then view on the microfilm the entire file for your Confederate ancestor.

## The Confederate Pension Records

In the years after the war, a number of states granted pensions to veterans of the Confederacy. These were not federal pensions and are not in the National Archives. These pensions were granted by the states to the Confederate soldiers who resided in their states at the time of their pension application. A soldier who served from Louisiana, but who lived later in Texas, filed for his pension from Texas. Some states have published indexes to their Confederate pensions. Typically, the indexes are available at the state archives or state historical society of the states granting the pension. Those same repositories usually hold the originals as well, so you can order a photo-copy.

**Tree Tips**

Some states have microfilmed their Confederate pension application files. The state repository can advise you. Be sure to check their indexes for the widow's name, too; she may be the applicant. Or there may be two files: one for the soldier and a later one for the widow.

## He Wore Blue

There is no consolidated index to the Compiled Military Service Record files for those who served with the Union. Indexes exist state by state only. In the Catalog, look for the state from which your ancestor served; next look for your ancestor's name in that state's list for the proper film number. Copy all information shown for your ancestor—unit, regiment, or anything else, exactly as it appears. That will lead you to either his original record (still in textual form) or to a series of microfilm that contains the file. If you do not find your ancestor but feel sure that he served, then check the surrounding states.

After you have located your ancestor and copied the information from the index, determine through the Catalog if the actual files have been microfilmed. Some of the Union service record files have been filmed, but others (depending upon the state from which the man served) are only available in their original form. You will have to view any unfilmed file personally, by ordering it online or by mail as previously described. Follow the Archives' instructions for submission of the form. If you order the file online, you can arrange for payment at the same time. For the fee schedule, go to www.archives.gov/research/order/fees.html.

# If He Got a Pension

The chances are good that if he lived long enough, your Union Civil War ancestor applied for a federal pension. Five acts between 1862 and 1907 provided pensions based on Union service. The earlier acts provided for those who were disabled or killed. A widow, children, or a parent who could prove that an unmarried son contributed significantly to his or her support may have applied soon after the death of a soldier in service.

To locate a Union pension file, consult National Archives micropublication T288, *General Index to Pension Files, 1881–1934*. This index includes service for the Civil War and, in some instances, earlier war service by a Civil War veteran. Other entries in the same film series relate to service in the Spanish-American War, the Philippine Insurrection, the Boxer Rebellion, and those who enlisted in the regular Army, Navy, and Marines before World War I. The index is arranged by surname, and then by state from which the soldier served. Be sure to take down all the information: You will need this whether ordering the file by mail or viewing it in person at the National Archives.

**Tree Tips**

When using the index, if you don't find the soldier under the name you expect, try variations. Benjamin Franklin Jackson may be listed as Benjamin, Benjamin Franklin, B. F., Frank, or Franklin. If he was known by his middle name, the names or initials may be reversed, such as Franklin B. or F. B.

To order the pension file, use the same procedure as described for ordering Revolutionary War pension files. You can do it by mail on Form NATF-85, or online.

Some of the Civil War Union pension files are in the custody of the Veterans Administration. If that is the case, the National Archives will respond to your request by sending you the appropriate VA office address to which you must write.

Though you can get a Civil War Pension file with only a few pages for a smaller fee, don't take that route. Get the full file, using the fee schedule already mentioned. Otherwise you are likely to miss important information. The Civil War pension files are routinely 40, 50, 100 pages, or even more. If you get the shorter version, you save some money but may miss crucial clues. Perhaps other researchers of the family will chip in for the cost. The files are not copyrighted, so after you have them, they can be photocopied and distributed to those relatives who may have helped finance the cost.

# The Twentieth-Century Conflicts

What if your research hasn't taken you back far enough to benefit from the wonderful records of the Revolutionary and Civil Wars? Don't despair. World Wars I and II, the Korean War, the Vietnam War—all generated records of interest to genealogists. As the memories of battles fade and participants die, the records become available, some even online.

## WWI Draft Registration

In 1917–1918 about 24 million men completed draft registration cards. This included aliens, who were not subject to induction, but were required to register. This created a vast database of men born between 1873 and 1900.

**Tree Tips**

If your immigrant ancestor was born between 1873 and 1900 and was in the United States in 1917–1918, he had to register for the draft even though he was not required to serve. Draft cards can be an important source of information on your immigrant ancestor.

These records are immensely helpful to genealogists, providing all sorts of personal data. Birth date, birthplace, whether a citizen, dependents, occupation, martial status, father's birthplace, this and more might appear depending upon which draft call was answered. To see what you might glean from these records, go to www.ancestry.com/save/charts/WWI.htm for blank draft forms of the following calls for registration:

- 5 June 1917: All men between ages 21 and 31

- 5 June 1918: Men who had reached age 21 after 5 June 1917, supplemental registration 24 August 1918 for those reaching age 21 after 5 June 1918

- 12 September 1918: Men ages 18 through 21 and 31 through 45

The original records are housed at the National Archives-Southeast Region, Georgia. Microfilms are available through the Family History Library, and Ancestry.com is in the process of placing the images online. For an extended description of the WWI Draft with links to explanatory articles, go to www.ancestry.com/search and then click on "WWI Draft Registration Cards" under the Military heading.

## Personnel Records

The National Archives in Washington, D.C. does not house personnel records of World War I and later. These are at the National Personnel Records Center, 9700 Page Blvd., St. Louis, Missouri 63132. If you are considered next of kin of a deceased veteran (father, mother, spouse, sibling, child), you can request a file on the special online form provided at www.archives.gov/veterans/eveutrecs. You'll see the large "Request Military Files" link at the bottom of the page. If you are not the veteran or next of kin, on that same website page click instead on "Standard Form 180" to order records. Read the statements at the Archives' website relating to privacy issues, and what can be ordered under the Freedom of Information Act. Experiment with the various links for other pertinent information.

A devastating fire in 1973 destroyed many records, but contrary to popular belief, not all of them were lost. About 80 percent of the personnel records of those discharged from the U.S. Army 1 November 1912 to 1 January 1960 survive. About 75 percent of U.S. Coast Guard personnel discharged 25 September 1947 to 1 January 1964 (whose names fell alphabetically after James E. Hubbard) are extant. The U.S. Navy and U.S. Marine Corps records are intact.

## Searching for Details

Start your twentieth-century search for a relative's records by going to one of the following National Archives Web pages. Each has several links. Explore.

> World War I:
> www.archives.gov/research/military/ww1.html
>
> World War II:
> www.archives.gov/research/ww2/index.html
>
> Korean War:
> www.archives.gov/research/korean-war/index.html
>
> Vietnam War:
> www.archives.gov/research/vietnam-war/index.html

Also check www.cyndislist.com for listings under military records. There are general sites listed, and others specifically listed by war.

# Other Ways to Locate Evidence of Military Service

Your ancestor's gravesite may have a flag or marker indicating service, as might his tombstone. His obituary or death record could mention service. For the Civil War, the discharge might be recorded in the courthouse. The 1910 census, which includes a column for Civil War service, could list him; the 1890 special federal Civil War census (discussed in Chapter 11) could also list him. In later wars, the separation papers might be recorded in lieu of the discharge. County histories are another source, often including rosters of those who served from the county. Lineage society records, many published, will also assist.

Virgil D. White, mentioned previously for his abstracts of Revolutionary War pension files, has also published a series of indexes for pension files of other wars, and a variety of other military records. Look for these, too, at your library. And don't overlook state records: the Adjutant General's office, the state library, and special state projects, such as graves registration for soldiers or biographical sketches of all known soldiers of the state. Sources for military service are endless.

# There's More?

This introduction to the military files of the National Archives acquaints you with some basic records created in the establishment and preservation of the United States. There are hundreds more files and records available: enlistment papers, Quartermaster records, headstone applications, post returns, applications for military academies, and much more. The Catalog will give you an idea of the number of records available. However, remember that the Catalog lists only the microfilm, which is a small part of the vast records created by military service. The suggested books will lead you to a multitude of additional sources.

There is a fascination with the history of the wars and those who served. You will find information surprisingly abundant once you have started your search. Don't skip these records "because I already know he served." Details—physical description, age, occupation—these and much more are yours for taking the time to understand these amazingly informative records. For the actual records of your ancestor's service, the National Archives is the best resource, whether the records are textural, filmed, or electronic. But the Web shines at its best when providing historical background and images. You will find photographs of ships, planes, battlegrounds, uniforms, medals, national cemeteries, interactive maps, photos of servicemen, battle details, and even the memoirs of those who served.

## The Least You Need to Know

◆ Always, without fail, seek military records for your ancestors.

◆ The National Archives has thousands of rolls of filmed military records and thousands of unfilmed files, manuscripts, and records books.

◆ Military records can be as brief as the period of service or comprehensive enough to give you three generations of ancestors.

◆ Such diverse items as physical description, marriages, deaths, Bible records, and others may be found in military records.

# Part 5

# Making Sense of It All

You're going to collect a whole lot of records before you get through. You'll be cramming files into closets and under beds unless you learn to keep control of the "paper mountains" from the beginning. In this section, you'll learn how to keep everything organized before it gets out of hand. You'll record your information with citations and effective numbering systems so that it will make sense to you and to others.

You'll learn to make the records "talk" to you so that your ancestors will come alive. They'll no longer be just names in dusty records, but real people with personalities. You'll use the Web and many other resources to begin your understanding of the times in which they lived. You'll become aware of conflicting records and how to make judgments to resolve those conflicts.

# Order Out of Chaos

## In This Chapter

- ◆ Using binders effectively
- ◆ Establishing an expandable filing system either on or off the computer
- ◆ Using the computer for maximum benefit

It won't be long before you discover one of the major problems of genealogy: the amount of paper generated by your research. If you work on several lines, as most researchers do, you will quickly become confused. "Where are the notes from Aunt Mattie's interview?" you'll exclaim in despair.

The charts and family sheets that will help record what you find are discussed in Chapter 4. However, knowing how to use the charts and family sheets is not enough to keep you from being flattened under a mound of paper. You don't want to throw away anything important. "What do I do?" you lament.

If you are new to genealogy, establish a good filing system right away and use your computer (if you have one) to facilitate storing and searching. You have an advantage; you can prevent the massive paper problem before it engulfs you in a sea of paper. If you have been into genealogy for a while and already are swimming in letters and documents, allocate some time to getting your files onto your computer and disks. Not only will you be able to breathe again, but it will also help ensure that your collection is not later thrown out because of sheer size.

# Filing the Charts and Sheets

When I first started in genealogy I made no attempt to keep pedigree charts together. There were only a few, and there was no problem. But it didn't take long before I was hunting all the time. Where is the Thompson chart? The Burney chart? A three-ring binder proved to be the answer. The Pedigree Charts (see Chapter 4) can be stored in a binder numerically, starting with yourself as number 1 on chart 1. You will see that each pedigree chart is assigned a number. As you leave one chart and start another, the new chart is also numbered.

After filing the pedigree charts, create a series of binders to file the family group sheets you have accumulated. Assign one binder per surname. If the sheets overflow that binder, continue into a second binder, still maintaining the filing system by family name. If you are tracing the family of John Jordan, who married Martha Adams, you would create a binder for the family group sheets of the Jordan family and another for the the Adams family.

# Filing Systems

Using binders for your pedigree charts and family sheets is a start, although you will accumulate considerable additional paper. You want a simple system, easily expanded as your search progresses. Create a set of file folders. Use either standard 8½" × 11", or legal-size 8½" × 14" folders. Legal size may seem the most desirable, since many document photocopies will be legal size. However, legal-size filing cabinets are wider than standard size. That difference in width can be significant if you eventually need two or three filing cabinets. Legal size is also more expensive. It may be best to stick with standard size and just fold the legal documents you need to file.

Now set up a system for filing the "papers"—all those letters, photocopies of censuses, documents, biographies, and so on that you have been systematically gathering.

Consider creating files by various categories:

◆ Family name

   ◆ State

      ◆ County

   ◆ Subject

   ◆ Correspondence

If you do not have enough papers in the file to create subfiles (shown in the following figure), then don't. Generate new files only as the need arises.

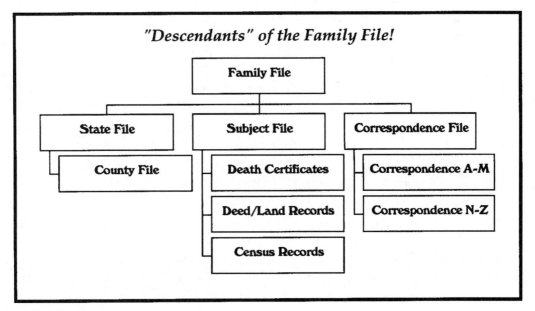

*Flow chart of files.*

When you start your search, set up family files for each of the surnames you are tracing. In each of these files, insert letters that you write regarding that surname and any documents you find involving that name: the deed, the marriage record, the Bible record. Anything that involves that family will go into that family file.

## They Called Tennessee Home ... and North Carolina ... and ...

If you get deeply involved in one surname, you will find that one file will not be sufficient for handling all the paper. It will not be adequate to simply create a second family file for the same surname. Then you would have to search two family files for the record you want, and later three, and then four. Resist the temptation to start that second file; instead, establish some specialized subfiles, starting with state files.

Suppose you are working on the Martins. This family has become a focal point. The major part of your energy is devoted to them. As is typical of many early families, they lived in several states, defying your erroneous belief that your ancestors were not mobile. Your file is overflowing with censuses of Tennessee, deeds and tax lists from North Carolina, and a raft of documents from Virginia. Now is the time to set up state files. For each state in which you have perhaps 10 or more items for the Martin family, create a state file. Label it as "Martin–Virginia" "Martin–Ohio," or "Martin–North Carolina." Also create a "Martin– Miscellaneous State File." Anything that does not fit into the first three will go into the "Miscellaneous State File." When you accumulate sufficient records on another state, perhaps Pennsylvania, then create another state file with that title. (At that time you will remove the Pennsylvania records from the Miscellaneous State File, and insert them into the new Martin–Pennsylvania file.)

> **Tree Tips**
>
> Consider using color-coded file labels or colored file folders, assigning a different color to each family name or each type of file or even each state. Perhaps all Pennsylvania files would be pink, and all vital records files would be blue, etc.

When creating the state files, do not label them solely as "Virginia" or "Ohio." Later you may need to establish state files for records of another surname, and it will be confusing. Always include the surname on the label, such as "Martin–Virginia." Be sure the surname is first, followed by the state. The folders will be filed alphabetically. In order for all of your Martin files to be properly filed together, the file name should begin with the word "Martin," followed by a one- or two-word description of the file.

## County Files

As the search progresses, even the state file may not be sufficient. If it gets too full, it will be unwieldy. You have a state file for "Martin–Ohio" but you find that your family lived in Pickaway County, Ohio, for a long time. They left so many records in Pickaway County that they take up half your "Martin–Ohio" file. Now is the time to create a subfile called "Martin–Ohio–Pickaway County" Move all the items in the

Martin–Ohio file that relate to Pickaway County into this new file. Now when you want to examine the deed to the land in Pickaway County or verify that you have a copy of the estate papers filed in that county, you know immediately where to look.

Remember, when creating the new file for the Pickaway County, Ohio, records of the Martin family, it will be labeled as "Martin–Ohio–Pickaway County" to preserve an alphabetical filing system that draws all the Martin files together. Files should always be labeled with the broadest classification first, followed by each of the subject subdivisions in order. If you are breaking files down by 1. surname, 2. state, and 3. county, then the file label should be so marked.

## Document Files

When you get several of a particular type of document on the surname, you can create a subfile for those specific documents, such as "Martin–Death Certificates." This time you won't do it by geographic location; all of the Martin death certificates will go into this document file. On the family group sheet that you maintain on the family, note that the information came from the death certificate. When you want to re-examine the certificate of John Martin, you will know exactly where to find it. Similarly, if you have a number of newspaper items—obits, marriage notices, published legal notices, etc., then create a special "Martin–Newspaper items" file.

**Tree Tips**

It will help if you file the certificates in your special death records file alphabetically by given name for easy retrieval. Not enough death certificates to have a file by itself? Name it instead "Martin–Vital Records" and include birth, marriage, and death records in the file.

## Correspondence Files

At first, you may file correspondence relating to a particular surname in your basic family file, mentioned earlier in this chapter. But if you do considerable research on the family, you'll have correspondence mixed in with your other notes and papers. It is usually best to reserve the family file for research papers: the published biography, the manuscript written by your grandfather 40 years ago, and others. If so, then you need a way to handle the filing of correspondence. Create a set of correspondence files. At first you will need only one for the surname: "Martin–Correspondence." As the file gets larger, you can separate it into two files, "Martin–Correspondence A–M" for all your correspondents with surnames A through M who have written to you on the Martin family, and "Martin–Correspondence N–Z" for the rest. You can break it down even further as needed, such as A–C, D–G, and so on. (If you have a great deal of correspondence with one individual, you may want another file devoted just to correspondence with that individual. Label it "Martin–Correspondence of Steve Stark.")

# Correspondence Cards

In addition to the correspondence files, you need an easy and effective index. One way to keep track of your correspondence, no matter which family it involves, is to keep a master correspondence card or log.

The card shown in the next figure can either be a standard 4" × 6" card, or a log on the computer. It will include the name and address of your correspondent, phone numbers (home and office), fax number, and e-mail address. Also include the name of the spouse if known. If a correspondent moves or changes telephone numbers and the phone is listed under the spouse's name, you may need it to obtain the new number. Leave room on the card for comments, which should include the specific branch of the family that the correspondent is tracing.

The very last line should be "SEE FILE." This is one of the most important items on the index card. Here you enter the name of the family file in which you filed their correspondence. If Mary Adams is tracing the Martin family and you filed her correspondence in the "Martin–Correspondence" file, then insert that in the SEE FILE space, showing "See Martin Correspondence file." The correspondence card will enable you to quickly note where the correspondence is located. If you establish this index of correspondence cards early in your search, you will avoid many frustrations in trying to remember which file holds Mary Adams' letters and e-mails.

If you use a computer, you can easily establish a correspondence log similar to the card shown in the figure. Investigate the options. A spreadsheet or personal information management software such as Outlook or TreePad could be used. You can even set one up using your word-processing program. If using the latter, insert the correspondent's name alphabetically. The advantage of having the information on your computer is that you can use the program's find command or the sort command, depending upon the program you are using, to locate those who are tracing specific branches of the family. All those tracing the "John and Mary (Smith) Jordan" branch can be quickly found.

**Tree Tips**

Don't be discouraged if you don't have a computer. Standard 4" × 6" cards will do for your correspondence index. Use a standard format to type or print the information onto the card, and maintain the cards alphabetically by the name of the correspondent.

```
┌──────────────────────────────────────────────────────────────────┐
│                    CORRESPONDENCE CARD                             │
│   Name _____        │
│   Address _____        │
│   City and State _____ Zip _____        │
│   Spouse _____        │
│   Family Traced _____        │
│   County Traced _____        │
│   Phone _____ Work Phone _____        │
│   Fax _____ email _____        │
│   Comments _____        │
│                                                                    │
│   SEE FILE: _____ Updated: _____        │
│                                                                    │
└──────────────────────────────────────────────────────────────────┘
```

*Sample of a correspondence card.*

# Using Computers to Cut Down on Paper

At first you'll keep every scrap of paper. You photocopy a marriage record from a book and photocopy the title page; now you have two pieces of paper in the file. Multiply this many times over, and you'll be overflowing with paper unless you find a way to reduce the stream. The problem is not limited to providing the space needed to store all the paper. Consider that some day others will use the records. Unless your files are condensed sufficiently, others will not want to store them. Even repositories will be reluctant to accept them if they are in complete disorder or too voluminous.

## The Computer Becomes the Filing Cabinet

File on the computer in the same way you file in file drawers. Set up some computer files by family name, state, county, subject, and correspondence, just as suggested for your paper notes. As you have time, take some of your paper notes, copy them to the computer, proofread them carefully, and then discard the paper copies. There may be certain copies you want to keep, but make your selections carefully. Always keep the following:

◆ Copies of Bible records

◆ Family notes (written in the hand of an ancestor)

◆ Photocopies of original documents

◆ Birth, Marriage, and Death certificates

◆ Obituaries and other newspaper notices

Keep the items that will not be easily replaced, or that you might need to prove your documentation in the future. Items you can discard (after entering the data onto your computer) are items from published books and notes that can be replaced if necessary. If you transfer a marriage record from a book onto your computer and include the full bibliographic citation, you can find the book easily again, should you need to. Always be sure to proofread what you have entered before discarding the paperwork.

**Tree Tips**

A good rule of thumb is to transfer to disk all items from books that can be easily accessed again. If the book is rare, or the copy is from an original (or it is lengthy), keep it. If the item is more than a paragraph or so, consider scanning it to your computer. Scanning can be a tremendous time-saver.

## Naming the Computer Files

As you establish computer files and name them, be sure to keep some sort of master index to all your genealogy file names. You should be able to consult this master list to see what files you have established. When naming your computer files, use some designation for each family, and start each file name with that designation. For example, in the following, each of the Martin files starts with the name "Martin:"

*INDEX TO GENEALOGY FILES*

File Name

Martin: Alabama

Martin: Alabama, Limestone Co.

Martin: Bible Records

Martin: Correspondence A-M

Martin: Correspondence N-Z

Martin: Vital Records

You may wish to name your files in some other descriptive fashion. Anything will do, as long as you keep an index to them. You won't always remember what they are named. It is best to create a different subdirectory on the computer for each family. You might name a directory (folder) MARTIN FAMILY and then create all the Martin subdirectories under it.

## Correspondence Computerized

At first you save every letter and a copy of every response. That works until you suddenly realize that you have 10 thick files of correspondence. To go back and try to reduce the paper is time consuming. Start now, in the beginning, to establish some firm rules for saving those exchanges by mail and e-mail.

There are many ways to store your computer files. The one that works for me is to create correspondence files in the same manner as you would if using file folders. If you start one for correspondence A–M, it will hold the letters and responses to all correspondence with anyone of the surname A through M. If storing the summary on the computer, however, take a few minutes after you answer the letter to transfer the main points to the computer file. For example, you received a letter from Sandra Williams, in which she sent some information on the Martin family, and asked for assistance. Examining the letter, you might summarize it on the computer as shown in the following figure.

---

WILLIAMS, Sandra, 1111 NoWhere Street, Anywhere, U.S.A. 12345. Wrote April 17 1997; says that great-great-grandmother was Agatha Roberts who married Jonathan Martin on 3 April 1863 in Montgomery Co., Va. She thinks Jonathan was son of Roger Martin listed in tax records of the county in 1855 but is uncertain. This couple had: Jeffry b. ca 1866, Martha b. ca 1868, Mary b. ca 1870 (m. John Webster), and Joseph b. ca 1875. They are in 1870 Montgomery Co. census (she doesn't give citation. Wants to know if I have further info.) Wrote to her April 20, 1997: told her I am tracing a Joseph Martin who was born 4 April 1874 in Virginia by his tombstone in Hamilton Co., Ohio. I don't know if he is the same person, but I note that my Joseph named a son Roger Martin. Asked her for the listing she has in 1870, and sent her the 1860–70–80 census of my Joseph Martin. Suggested that we check deed records.

See MARTIN File.

Updated: July 20, 2005

Now you can discard the three-page letter she sent and your two-page response. You have recorded the essential details. I like to make a printout of the synopsis and place it in my correspondence file. You may decide to keep only the summary on the computer, and avoid the paper filing. If the correspondent writes again, add comments to the synopsis. The last notation at the bottom of the figure tells you when you last updated the contents of this summary.

**Tree Tips**

If you started your genealogical pursuits by keeping all correspondence, set aside at least a half hour a day to transfer some of your material to the computer. It will go slowly, but doing it daily, in a small-enough dose not to get too boring, will enable you to complete it. You will be encouraged to continue as you see the empty space in your filing cabinet grow, and usability of the data increase.

You now have the notes in handy form on the computer and you can search them with your program's "search" or "find" feature. When someone writes three years from now inquiring about a Roger Martin, you can open your file of correspondence summaries, enter his name for a search, and presto! In a few seconds you have identified all correspondents with whom you exchanged data on him. Condensing your correspondents' letters onto the computer will only take a few minutes if you do it at the time the mail comes in or goes out. And another important thing is, it will make your collection easily usable by others who come after you. Otherwise they may throw up their hands and toss everything out.

**Tree Tips**

If you have the capability of "burning" a CD-ROM or a DVD, once or twice a year make a "Save This" disk of all the files you wish your family to save. This is in addition to the daily or weekly backup you routinely make of your computer files for your own use. This extra "Save" file is those specific files that you want your family to retain. This special "Family Save" version will only contain those folders you consider important for your family to retain. Put some thought into what is important for your family to keep for the future generations. You will avert the disaster of having your years of research destroyed because no one knew what to save.

## Mail Files

If you want to keep a full copy of every letter you write to others on the computer, you can set up a "genealogy mail" file. Title it "Mail Genealogy 2005." Each year start a new file, but retain the old. In this mail file you will put a copy of your letter, simply adding it at the end so that it is actually in chronological order. "But how will I find anything?" you ask. Easy. Want to find the letter to Jonathan Latimer that you wrote in 2005 inquiring about his great-grandfather? Go to your "Genealogy Mail 2005" computer folder, use the "find" or "search" feature, and enter "Latimer." It will quickly surface. You want to find the letter you wrote inquiring about the Oak Lawn Cemetery, but you don't remember to whom you wrote? Enter "Oak Lawn," hit "find," and there it is. Imagine what you would have gone through sorting paper letters by hand, trying to uncover it.

I do not store letterheads with my copy of the letters. I have several letterheads set up as templates on the computer—business, personal, spouse and I, mine alone, etc. I start by writing the letter on the appropriate letterhead, and print the letter. Then I cut and paste the letter (not the letterhead) into the end of my mail folder, leaving the letterhead intact and ready for my next letter. If for any reason I need another copy of that letter in the future (which isn't often), I can simply "find" it in my mail folder, copy it and paste it onto my letterhead, and print it out again. You may however prefer to save the entire letter, including the letterhead, in spite of the additional computer storage space.

# The Commercial Products

The filing system suggested in this chapter enables you to easily expand your system with a minimum of cost. However, you may prefer to use one of the commercial products designed to help you store your records in binders or on the computer. Examine the genealogical periodicals for advertisements. One popular program is Clooz, an electronic filing cabinet designed for genealogical records. It doesn't just record the results of your search, it is also a database for systematically organizing and storing all the clues you find. For more information, go to the website at www.clooz.com and determine whether it is right for you.

No matter what system you use, establish it now. Staying organized from the beginning will allow you more time to spend on what you enjoy most: the search for those elusive ancestors.

## The Least You Need to Know

◆ Creating specific files for "paper" makes for easy retrieval.

◆ Correspondence index cards enable you to readily find letters and e-mails by directing you to the file in which they are stored.

◆ Condensing correspondence onto the computer has several long-range benefits.

◆ Burning a CD-ROM or DVD periodically with the specific genealogy files that you want your family to retain will help ensure that your years of research are not lost.

# Chapter 19

# Doing It Right

## In This Chapter

- Why citations are necessary
- Numbering systems to organize the compilation
- Approximating dates to assist in planning the search

You located crucial dates and locations of your family. It wasn't easy. You had to do an exhaustive search to find the information. Now you enter into your compilation: "John Washington Jackson was born 10 April 1857, in St. Louis, St. Louis County, Missouri, and died 5 July 1935 in Springfield, Greene County, Missouri." You look it over, and wonder if you missed something. Indeed you did—the citation is missing! On which record did you base the birth date, and on which did you base the birthplace as St. Louis? It is important to let others know on what the facts are based. They can't judge their weight as evidence without knowing their basis.

Published genealogies in the past commonly lacked almost any citations. Present-day standards require a *citation* for every fact. It is easy to underestimate the importance of the citation. You may need a source again, too. You suddenly realize that items you copied from a book of abstracts appear to have a child missing. Did you just omit it when you copied it? You want to recheck. With the source citation, you could quickly relocate it through the library catalog. Learn the correct procedures for citing when you first start your search, and use them diligently. Later you won't be constantly frustrated as you try to find important records again.

# Getting Help with Citing

There are books to help you learn how to cite properly. One of the best and most detailed is *The Chicago Manual of Style*. Look also for the excellent guidebook by Elizabeth Shown Mills. Titled *Evidence! Citation and Analysis for the Family Historian*, it illustrates, simply but effectively, the manner in which almost every type of source encountered by genealogists should be cited. This includes books, magazine articles, journals, microfilm, manuscripts, CD-ROMs, websites, and others.

If you keep in mind that the purpose of the citation is to enable the reader to readily find the same source, it will be easier to remember which items should be included. Basically, the citation for a book must include the complete title of the book, the full name of the author, the city and state where it was published, the name of the publisher, the year published, and the edition (1st ed., 2nd ed. revised, reprint, and so on). Citations for articles, microfilm, CD-ROMs, and other sources have specific rules on what to include so that the source can be accessed again. None of the components should be omitted.

Also cite personal documents, such as letters and photographs. The citation for the letter that Aunt Martha wrote to Cousin Jim in 1910 giving the family history should at least include the letter's date, to whom addressed, by whom, and in whose possession the original letter now resides. If referring to an oral interview, give the date, who was interviewed, by whom, and where. Add also whether it is based on a tape recording, a video, or handwritten notes. For Bibles, besides the date of publication, note whether your information is from the original Bible, a photocopy, a handwritten transcription, or a typed copy, etc. This will assist in evaluating whether errors may have crept in while copying or transcribing. (For fuller examples and illustrations, refer to the mentioned manuals.)

You may think, "But I am only doing this for fun." Your diligent search of your ancestors, if not properly cited, could someday puzzle and even mislead descendants who will wonder upon what the statements were based. Your record may be correct, but they won't know unless they know where you got your information.

Undocumented data is an immense problem for genealogists. In the past, there was little effort to include citations. Today there is increased interest in restudying earlier records to add details, and to thoroughly document compilations to correct prior errors and omissions. This applies not only to dates, but also to locations, parentage, and other important details.

**Tree Tips**

Some researchers photocopy the title page of the book to prepare the citation. Though this appears to be helpful, it adds expense and adds "paper" to your files. Learn early the correct citation techniques, and write the details on the photocopy. Check also the reverse of the title pages of books; some of the needed information for citing may be there.

## Family Group Sheets Are Convenient, But ...

Family group sheets, those forms leaving room for the names and statistics of an individual family, are popular because they are a convenient form of entering data. However, seldom do the forms have sufficient room to enter the sources. Computer programs now available usually handle the problem by allowing text notes to be included. But those prepared in earlier times, without the benefit of a computer, encouraged the researchers to enter dates and locations without documentation. Genealogists who did attempt documentation normally wrote on the back of the form, which was often omitted when photocopying it for others.

**Tree Tips**

The necessity of adding citations is not a reflection on your ability. You may use a record that appears correct when you locate it; another record you didn't even know about may later be found that is in conflict with it. Knowing the source of each statement will help in judging the merits of each.

# Putting It at the Bottom or at the End?

If you are using a standard word processor for your compilation, you can add your citations in one of three ways:

♦ In-text citation

♦ Footnotes

♦ Endnotes

**Tree Tips**

Whenever examining a family sheet sent by others, note whether it is fully cited. If not, use it only for clues. The information may be correct, but you will have to systematically check each bit of information before accepting it.

The in-text citation adds the information immediately following the fact: "Mary Morgan was born 3 April 1846 [*Family Bible, adding the full citation here*]. She died 8 March 1895 [*Death Certificate: adding the full citation here*]." As you can see, the text is considerably broken up with each of the citations. This method has fallen into disfavor because of the choppiness. The two favored systems are either to footnote or to insert endnotes at the end of the chapter or compilation.

Because many word-processing programs can handle footnotes, they are easy to implement. A superscript number is added to the statement in the body, which keys it to the footnote that holds the citation. The advantage of footnotes is that the citation remains on the same page as the text to which it refers.

In endnotes, you use the superscript number and key it to a citation or notation either at the end of the chapter or the end of the compilation.

Use whichever of the three mentioned systems of citation placement that suits you; the important thing is that the citation be there, keyed directly to the fact it is citing. It is not enough just to add a list of "Sources" to the end of the compilation. The person using the data must know specifically which source goes with each fact.

# Keeping Track by Numbers

When you start using published genealogies in the library, you will be stumped many times by complicated numbering systems. When faced with a massive listing of descendants in a family, compilers often devise their own system to keep track. Later they

decide to print it for the family. Being fully
familiar with their own style, they resist
any thought of transferring it to a uni-
formly accepted system. The increased use
of computers seems to have encouraged
many to create their own, forcing the
reader to devote considerable time to understanding a complicated or offbeat system.

An excellent publication by Joan Ferris Curran, Madilyn Crane, and Dr. John H.
Wray, *Numbering Your Genealogy: Basic Systems, Complex Families and International Kin*
will assist you in understanding the numbering systems that are widely accepted by
genealogists.

## Descending Genealogies

The two most widely used and recommended systems are the Register System (developed by the New England Historic Genealogical Society for their NEHGS *Register*),
and the NGSQ Numbering System (formerly known as Modified Register System)
used by the *National Genealogical Society Quarterly*. They are applied to descending
genealogies. The NEHGS system normally starts with the immigrant, but if the
immigrant's identity is not yet known, it can start from the earliest-known ancestor of
the family. He or she is assigned an Arabic numeral 1. The children of number 1 are
all given Roman numerals in order of birth. In the Register System, those for whom
there is sufficient information to carry forward include the next Arabic numeral in
front of the Roman numeral, alerting the reader that more will be found in the section corresponding to that Arabic number.

In the following figure, there is no need to carry child "i." to her own section; nothing further is known about her to warrant carrying her forward in the compilation.
Mary, child "iii." died young (d.y.) and is also not carried forward. More information
is known about Jonathan, so he received the next Arabic numeral 2, notifying the
reader that there is something further on him in section 2. More details are also
known for Ezekiel, so he received the next Arabic numeral, 3. Those Arabic numerals
will precede the sections in which further details on Jonathan and Ezekiel are
presented.

*The NEHGS Register system of numbering.*

---

1.  John[1] Smith was born 3 April 1788, etc. [include here rest of information on him, events of life, marriage, documents, etc.]

    Children; surname SMITH:

        i.   Mercy b. 5 Apr. 1808, Richmond, Va., further unknown

    2.  ii.  Jonathan b. 18 Mar. 1810, Richmond, Va.

        iii.  Mary b. 3 Aug. 1813, Richmond, Va., d.y. 4 May 1814

    3.  iv.  Ezekiel b. 22 Dec. 1816, Alexandria, Va.

2.  Jonathan[2] Smith (John[1]) was born 18 March 1810, Richmond, Virginia, etc.

3.  Ezekiel[2] Smith (John[1]) was born 22 December 1816, Alexandria, Virginia, etc.

---

**Tree Tips**

If you are using a computer, use a somewhat larger typeface for the numbers that precede the sections, and insert them in bold face as illustrated in the preceding figure. This larger, bold type will help distinguish section numbers preceding a specific section from the reference numbers preceding the Roman numerals in the children's listing.

Note that generational numbers are also included. John[1] Smith indicates that he is either the immigrant, or the first identified progenitor in this family. The children who are carried forward are also shown with a generational number in superscript, followed by a "runner" showing their line back to the earliest-known progenitor. Let's say that you have researched Abraham Smith of the fifth generation. He is carried forward to his own section. The generational runner would be something like this: Abraham[5] Smith (George[4], William[3], Jonathan[2], John[1]). It is easy to distinguish these generational numbers from the overall numbering of the compilation. They can also be distinguished from any citation numbers you may insert, as the superscript generational numbers are inserted after the first name of the individual, whereas superscript numbers for citations follow the surname. Thus, John[2] Smith is referring to John Smith of the second generation. John Smith[2] would indicate a citation reference.

## NGSQ System

The NGSQ System is based on the Register system, but assigns an Arabic numeral to *each* child. The "+" mark in front of the Arabic numeral designates whether the child is carried forward.

As seen in the figure below, the "+" readily identifies the sections that hold further details when carried forward. Those sections that are carried forward are preceded by the Arabic numeral assigned to that individual (in larger, bold typeface if using a computer).

*The NGSQ System.*

1. John[1] Smith was born 3 April 1788, etc.

   Known children of John Smith and wife Mary Martin were as follows:

   2.   i. Mercy b. 5 Apr. 1808, Richmond, Va., further unknown

   +   3.   ii. Jonathan b. 18 Mar. 1810, Richmond, Va.

   4.   iii. Mary b. 3 Aug. 1813, Alexandria, Va., d.y. 4 May 1814

   +   5.   iv. Ezekiel b. 22 Dec. 1816, Alexandria, Va.

3. Jonathan[2] Smith (John[1]) was born 18 March 1810, Richmond, Virginia, etc.

5. Ezekiel[2] Smith (John[1]) was born 22 December 1816, Alexandria, Virginia, etc.

Each of these systems has devotees. Those using the NEHGS Register System find it simple and "clean" in appearance, but most will admit that it has a disadvantage. When the compiler must add newly found information on a child whose data was previously unknown, creating a new section to carry forward that child's data requires complete renumbering.

Those who prefer the NGSQ System like the advantage of having an Arabic numeral already assigned to each of the children. If more information is located on that child, it is simple to insert a plus sign before the Arabic numeral, and insert the section in its proper place. (Even those using the NGSQ System have to renumber if they discover that the couple had more or fewer children than was originally known when the compilation was first numbered.)

## Before They Came

Because the immigrant is numbered with an Arabic 1, you will wonder how to "number" the generations before the immigrant's arrival. You are tracing a family from England and have information on earlier generations. These are handled by assigning the closest pre-American generation as A, the next as B, and so on. If the father of immigrant John Jackson was George Jackson, and his grandfather was William Jackson, this numbering system will show John[1] Jackson (George[A], William[B]). This immediately conveys that John is the immigrant, his father is George, and his grandfather is William.

The NEHGS Register System and the NGSQ System lay out the family generation by generation. The systems are easy and will become second-nature to you. Further details and illustrations can be studied in *Numbering Your Genealogy* previously mentioned in this chapter. See also *The BCG Genealogical Standards Manual* for treatment of numbering.

# Approximating Dates

If an exact date is not known, then whenever possible estimate the dates rather than leaving them entirely blank. In this section, we discuss a few of the many ways in which this can be accomplished.

## By Date of Will

If John Morgan made his will on 17 April 1853, and on 15 July 1853 the will was presented in court for probate, you know that John Morgan died between 17 April 1853 and 15 July 1853. It's best not to show "died 1853," but specifically that he "died between 17 April 1853 (date of will) and 15 July 1853 (date will proved)." Be as precise as you can in presenting the information if you have the records to do so. It will prevent confusion when someone finds an entry that John Morgan sold a piece of land on 12 February 1853. If you had only entered the date as "ca. 1853" (about 1853) they might have been puzzled, but if you entered the death as being between the date of the will and the date it was proved (as above noted), those using your records will realize that he was living until at least 17 April.

## Rule of Thumb

Studies of countless families living in the seventeenth and eighteenth centuries (and earlier) have determined that a good rule of thumb is that children were born two years apart. When you examine the lists of children of your earlier relatives, you may find gaps, but often that can be accounted for because of the death of a child. You know that the couple married in 1816, their first child Amy was born in 1818, Timothy was born in 1822, and Jonathan, the youngest, was born in 1824. When you discover a child Joseph, you can estimate that he may have been born ca. 1820. Do not state it as absolute fact, but include "ca." (*circa*, about) to indicate that it is an approximated date.

Similarly, if you know the marriage date and don't have the birth dates of any of the children, you can approximate their births based on the marriage date. If John Taylor was married in 1838, and had three sons and a younger daughter, you can estimate that the sons were born ca. 1840, 1842, 1844, and the daughter ca. 1846, two years apart.

You can also use several census records to provide an approximated date. If the age of John is 15 in the 1850 census, 22 in the 1860 census, and 37 in the 1870 census, you can approximate that he was born ca. 1833–1838.

**Tree Tips**

You not only used the rule of thumb in the example given, but combined that with the fact that Jonathan was the youngest, and the couple married in 1816. It is often possible to glean clues on the approximate date from several related records.

## Choosing Their Own Guardian

Minors had guardians appointed by the court if they had any property due to them. Most states allowed those minors, upon reaching the age of 14, to choose their own guardians. If your ancestor is noted in court records as making that choice, you can estimate that he or she was between the age of 14 and 21. (By the latter age, a guardian would not be necessary if the person was deemed competent.)

## Of Age to Marry?

You will find records of those who misrepresented age to get a marriage license; nonetheless, the marriage license can be a gauge for determining age. If the couple applied for the license without the consent of a parent or guardian, assume that they were of age unless other records prove otherwise. The legal age varied by location and time period, but usually the groom had to be 21 and the bride, 18. (The legal age was lower in some areas, especially for the bride.)

**Tree Tips**

As you progress in your genealogical pursuits, you will turn to the laws to determine the legal age for certain matters, to best evaluate the ages involved. Remember that states differed and laws changed.

## Why Bother with Approximate Dates?

The purpose of establishing an approximate date rather than leaving it blank is to better determine the records that can be examined. If you know only that your ancestor William Carr was born in Tennessee, then you have nothing on which to determine a course of action. If you know that he was born ca. 1791 in Tennessee, you see that by age he could have served in the War of 1812 and you can investigate the possibility of military service. Or, knowing he was born ca. 1791, you can examine the 1820 census of Tennessee to see if he was listed as head of a household, because he was about 29 at the time of that census. Other ideas will come to you, too, after that date is estimated.

# The Little Children

Always include in your compilations the little children who were stillborn or who died before maturity. They, too, were important in the overall genealogy. They may carry a name that is significant—perhaps named after the mother, grandmother, or other family member. That name may be the clue that triggers a breakthrough. Their ages are important; they can explain gaps in the family groupings. Their burials are important; they may lead to family plots. Lacking any other reason, those children were precious to their families. If you don't remember them, no one will. Even their causes of death can explain a mystery; if the child died of cholera, you may understand why three of the family members disappeared from the records that year.

Genealogy should be fun. And it is. Developing sound techniques does not diminish that fun—it adds to it. Taking the time to do things right, from the beginning, will save you many headaches later. It will also preserve your information in such a way that you will be proud to share the results with others. You will know that you have produced a family history documented to the best of your ability, and that it will be easily understood by those who read it.

## The Least You Need to Know

◆ Citations are important; they enable others to locate the sources you used.

◆ Knowing the source helps in evaluating the trustworthiness of the information.

◆ Numbering systems should be standard.

◆ Approximating dates will assist in pointing you in the right direction for the search.

# Chapter 20

# Gaining Historical Perspective

## In This Chapter

- ◆ Gathering more than the bare facts
- ◆ Analyzing and interpreting the documents
- ◆ Interviewing the oldest relatives
- ◆ The Life Story: a practical example

You've been gathering the bare facts about your ancestors: their names, their dates, their locations. So far, so good. But, at this point, they are just shadowy figures. Who were these people whose genes you share? You can connect with them and make them come alive, if only on the pages of your family history. How can you know what life was like for them? Make the records talk to you. Add historical background and visualization so that your ancestors become more real. You enhance your family history by looking at records in more depth, scouring historical material for its relevance to your ancestors, and gathering stories and artifacts from relatives.

# Taking a Fresh Look at What You've Found

By analyzing the records, you will find the information to flesh out your ancestors. You dutifully wrote down (preserving all spelling, of course!) the items listed in the inventory taken when your ancestor's estate was probated, and you filed it away. Take it out and look at it again. What does it say to you? Even the arrangement of the inventory can give you clues. Think about how you inventory your possessions for insurance purposes. You start in one room and progress through the house. That is the way most inventories are taken. Stand in the doorway with the appraiser of Elias Drollinger's possessions and look around the room with him. (Note the spelling and capitalization is as it was in the original.)

| | |
|---|---|
| two beds and bedsteads | tea canister |
| four sheets four pillows six blanketts | pitcher set |
| two double coverlets | red plates |
| one Bureau and stand | one saw |
| table | two trunks |
| chest | looking glass |
| two sets bed curtains | one wash tub |
| stove | wash board |
| one set chairs | sugar tub |
| rocking chair | lard tub |
| little oven | one flat Iron |
| one set silver teaspoons | one par hand irons |
| one set silver tablespoons | one bible and 10 Books |
| molases can | one cow |
| sugar bowl | |

The possessions in the preceding list, meager by our standards, probably describe a house with two rooms. One room had two beds complete with bedding and curtains for privacy. The other room was the all-purpose kitchen, family-, dining-, living-, laundry-room. The looking glass hangs on a nail over the washtub that was also used for bathing. Picture the saw, leaning against the wall, perhaps next to the stove, and the table set with red plates and silver spoons. Where are the books and Bible? (And who got the Bible with the family records, you might wonder.) Someone in the family was literate, hence the books. Outside is one cow, probably kept for milk, cream, and butter. No implements suggest an occupation. Was the individual elderly and perhaps retired?

**Tree Tips**

Use your imagination to bring your ancestors to life. Just be careful not to blur the line between nonfiction and fiction. You are not writing a novel.

# Expanding Your Research

Look for records that give you data to work with. Comparing the New York state censuses of 1855 and 1875, you can learn a great deal about your farming ancestor. For example, suppose that in 1855, an enumerator in Onondaga County mentioned that yields were down one half to one third because of drought and wind, yet your ancestor's crop yields were much better than those of the neighboring farmers. From that you know that either he was a better farmer or he had better land. You learn that he harvested 100 pounds of honey; he probably kept bees to pollinate the fruit trees, because he also had 100 bushels of apples and 20 gallons of cider. In 1875, his crop land allocations were quite different. By this time, he was 75 years old, so it is conceivable that he was slowing down. Yet 15 years later a newspaper article remarks that at 90 he is the oldest native-born resident of the county and "is an excellent farmer, though nearly blind." These small details enhance the picture you're developing.

Does the deed you found tell what great-grandmother paid for her house? When she sold it did she make money on it? Use one of the inflation calculators such as www.westegg.com/inflation to relate those amounts to today's monetary values. What do newspaper ads from your ancestor's time tell you it cost him to purchase necessities he couldn't grow or make? What was he taxed on? The minutia of your ancestor's life is what makes her more than just a name on a pedigree chart. Would you want less for yourself?

# Court Records Tell Many Secrets

Your ancestors' court appearances give you more insight. They appear in court for "unlawful gaming" or because a speculator wants to foreclose on their land. They want water rights, or they are evicting a tenant. There may be statements in their own words.

Divorce records can be quite telling. He accuses her of infidelity; she accuses him of drinking too much and hitting her. After the divorce is granted, they continue to appear in court, wrangling over their young daughter. The mother says that the father does not meet the little girl's train; the father says that the mother doesn't send her dressed warmly enough. Reading this, you understand a little more about the bitterness in the family and how the family became estranged.

# Treasuring Your Ancestors' Enemies!

Disputes create records and provide glimpses of your ancestor that you might not otherwise have. You never know what you'll find. In an 1805 Bourbon County, Kentucky, deed book, Peter Sap releases Thomas Glass from further liability for having cut or bitten off the top part of his ear in "an affray."

You may find something similar to my own discovery: Great-Grandpa's Civil War pension was challenged by a disgruntled townsman who wrote his congressman, saying, "after coming home they all say he been an auctioneer, if a man is very deaf it does seem to me that a deaf man would make a very poor auctioneer." As a result of this complaint, there was an investigation, including a physical examination that showed the old man to be quite frail, and testimony from numerous townsfolk about Great-Grandpa's fine character. Your ancestor's enemies can be just as important as their friends in generating records for you to find!

**Tree Tips**

Deed books often contain more than land records. They may include the record of an adoption, an apprenticeship, or a livestock brand. Perhaps a bill of sale for "one yoke of oxen, one red and one brindle color, I call one Bill, the other John."

# Unexpected Finds

There is much to be said for examining the original records even if you have seen them on film, but especially so if you have only seen the abstracts. Perhaps the record has a notation that the abstracter didn't include. In Wabash County, Indiana, Marriage Book 6, there are three handwritten notes pasted on the inside front cover.

The notes were written to the County Clerk by three fathers telling him not to issue marriage licenses to their children. My favorite appears in the following:

---

Wabash County, Ind. Jan. 11, 1867

Bro. E. Hackleman Dear Sir do not issue a marriage license to Marshall Murray & Mary E. Shortridge without a certificate from me. Mary is underage & I am not being treated as respectfully as could be desired if everything goes off right I will give them a certificate.
Respectfully    L. Shortridge [signed]

---

You may be lucky enough to find a record that is annotated and gives you totally unexpected information: the census taker who marks a name with an asterisk and at the bottom of the page writes "died of drink," or the assessor who adds comments beside the names on his list: "bankrupt," "left for Kansas," or, my favorite, "not dead, but asleep."

By scrolling to the end of the Sevier County, Utah, 1870, census roll, I found this notation: "The foregoing number of houses were abandoned by the Whites during the late Indian War of 1865–'6–'7." If your ancestors were in this area then, this could well be relevant to their lives, and you'll want to follow up by reading about the events that took place there.

# Looking Beyond the Records

Follow every opportunity to learn about the times of your ancestors. All over the United States there are towns and museums creating living-history celebrations. Colonial Williamsburg in Virginia, Sturbridge Village and Plimouth Village in Massachusetts, Skagway in Alaska, and Columbia in California, are some of the larger ones, but there are many small projects, also. For now, attending these is the only kind of time travel we can know. If your ancestor was a blacksmith, visit the recreated blacksmith's shop. Observing the activity will make you realize how much physical strength your ancestor had to possess to pursue this occupation. Visit the kitchen garden where your ancestor grew things for the table and the medicine cabinet. Families had to be self-reliant, and mothers learned the benefits of many herbs for treating illnesses.

Board the full-scale ships' replicas and consider how you would survive an ocean crossing. Visit a colonial farm, a plantation, or a Victorian home. The Wild West really was wild. Look for reenactments of gunfights and train robberies. Tour a coal mine or a gold mine.

Libraries, museums, and historical sites continue to digitize their collections. The millions of documents, photographs, films, and recordings online can distract you for hours. The Library of Congress's online archive, known as the American Memory (www.memory.loc.gov/ammem), astounds with its breadth. The mere thought of searching for something specific to your ancestors or to their experiences is dizzying. But the searches are well worth the effort. An obituary states Frederick Harkrider was a U.S. guager [*sic*]. Learning that a guager was a revenuer, specifically, a fed who measured or "gauged" the whiskey for tax assessment, I searched the American Memory for more information. The sheet-music collection includes an 1883 ditty "The Wine Guager," by B. W. Foster, that opens with

> "A wine guager down in its vault so cold,
>
> Thus sang to himself a song.
>
> 'Oh what care I for place or gold,
>
> 'Tis wine makes me happy and strong.'"

That definitely adds color and perspective to the family history.

**Genie Jargon** _____

**Sic** means "thus" or "in this manner," and is usually italicized and enclosed in square brackets to indicate a misspelling, an unusual spelling, or to otherwise call attention to something that could be perceived as an error.

# Tornado Watch

Weather is a factor in our everyday lives, but it loomed even larger in the lives of our ancestors. Their crops were dependent on the rain. They learned how to prepare for the usual occurrences of harsh winters and blistering summers. It was the unusual that dealt them severe setbacks: the tornado, the hailstorm, or the flood. Families in precarious financial situations were pushed over the edge by bad weather. This can affect your research and may explain why families pulled up stakes and left an area.

Reading about the weather can help you interpret the records or support a family tradition. The family says Fred drowned in the creek in 1892; no obituary or death record has been found. A local newspaper from that week tells of heavy rains and flash floods in the creeks, which lends some credence to the story.

# Being a Student of Local and Family History

As you try to complete the pictures of your ancestors' lives, steep yourself in the history of the period and locality. There may be clues there. Reading about the coal-mine disaster or the opening of the canal, you may finally understand why your family left the area. The newspaper article in the weekly paper extolling the virtues of Nebraska may explain why they left the fertile land of central Illinois and headed west.

Our ancestors were passionate about their religion, and religious upheaval was not uncommon. Arguments over doctrine among the parishioners often caused a dissident group to start another place of worship—down the road, in another county, or in another state.

Letters or diaries that pertain to your ancestors' experiences give you insight. Seek them in books, manuscript collections, and online at university and state libraries or at sites such as www.eyewitnesstohistory.com.

> **Pedigree Pitfalls**
>
> Be sure that historical events are relevant to your ancestors before including them in your narrative. The lives of famous people probably touched your ancestors no more than they do yours. But, legislative action, such as the Homestead Act, or events, such as the Gold Rush, may well be important.

## Illustrating Your Story

Don't be satisfied with just portrait photographs of your ancestors themselves. Collect photographs and maps of the local area. The National Archives in Washington, D.C. has millions of still photographs with an incredible range of topics. There are photographs of military units, photographs documenting the terrible conditions in the Dust Bowl, and photographs of federal projects. The grandeur of national parks and the bleakness of tenements are preserved. On a less sweeping scale, local museums and historical societies tell the stories of their counties. It is there that you'll find the picture of Grandpa self-confidently astride his horse and Grandma posing with the students she taught in the one-room school.

Visit online photographic collections such as www.photoswest.org, a part of the Western History Collection at the Denver Public Library.

If you know the ship your ancestor came on, look for a picture of it or a similar ship. Maritime museums are a good source for sketches and photographs of old ships. Check www.theshipslist.com, which has not only illustrations of ships, but also descriptions of their voyages, travelers' diaries, and other resources.

Historical maps and atlases will help you locate the exact spot of the farm. The atlases may have drawings of local sights, such as the livery stable in the following figure. The caption under the sketch says, "The only first class livery in Morris. Ladies & gent's driving horses a specialty. Particular attention paid to funerals. Good accommodations for farmers." Your ancestors in Grundy County may have patronized this place, but even if they didn't, it was probably a part of the scenery of their everyday life.

*Livery stable sketched in Atlas of Grundy County and the State of Illinois, (Chicago: Warners & Beers, 1874).*

# Closer to Home

In addition to analyzing the records and reading history books, contact all the relatives you can find. Ask them to look in their attics, basements, and filing cabinets to see if they have some long-forgotten piece of family history. Carefully examine jewelry and pin-back buttons with letters or symbols that indicate membership in a fraternal organization. For help in identifying the organization, go to www.exonumia.com/art/society.htm for a comprehensive list of secret societies and fraternal orders.

This particular part of your genealogy research depends a great deal on serendipitous finds. From a family you only recently learned existed, you may receive a copy of a letter such as this one written on December 15, 1875, in Bear Grove, Iowa, from Alice Dunn to her cousin Lis Harcourt [spelling as in the original]:

---

Dear cousin I received your most welcome letter yesterday and was very glad to hear from you once more. It found us all well. I was at church when I got it. Our father got it from the office and brought it to church and gave it to me …

Well you said you expected my school was out. So it is but I have taken another one but for a longer term than that one. I have taken one for life this time. How is that for high. You know we promised to tell each other when we were going to get married. Well I wrote you a letter and told you to answer it right away and I would tell you something but I guess you did not get the letter from the tone of your letter. I was married on the 18th of November 1875 at home at seven 7 o'clock in the evening and also Willson was married the same day at twelve in the morning. He married a lady by the name of Miss Nora Mason and my name is Mrs. Parsons. I guess you know the rest of his name. I wish you could have been there. We had a real nice time. There was about 30 at the wedding. I will send you a piece of my wedding dresss and tell you how I made it. Well I trimmed the front breadth in knife pleatings and sheared ruffing and the rest of the skirt on down and put it on in box plaiting and put a mould over each plait and made it to trail and looped the skirt. The back bredth were just one yard and three quarters long. I got it in Desmoines city and my hat is white velvet trimmed in drab rep ribbon and drab plume and veil. My veil is one yard and a half long. Come over and see me. I am keeping house now. I live just one mile from fathers. I am going to look for you in one year from now and I want you to be sure and come. I expect it will be your weding tour. Be shure and write me when it is and I will come and then you can come on home with me and we will have some buckwheat cakes and beef juice and

*continues*

---

*continued*

dried turkey and boiled frog and old rooster and row potatoes boiled [?] and stewed cake and fried biscuit and stewed onions and baked beets and roasted turnips and other things to numerous to mention. I will send you our picture as soon as we get some taken but do not wait for them but send your picture without delay. John and Willson are going to start for Marion Co this state next week and me and Ed are going to go with them and visit so no more at this time.

Please answer soon. Give my love to all enquiring friends and keep a portion for yourself. From your cousin Alice.

Here is a wonderful glimpse of life. The new bride excitedly telling her cousin about her wedding dress, and detailing the feast they will have when the cousin visits. Notice, also, the genealogical information. Alice gives her husband's name and her brother's as well as that of his bride, and the date of both weddings, and mentions locations.

# The Art of the Interview

You want to conduct interviews with everyone still living who knew your relatives and remembers the stories that were handed down. Do not delay. Deaths and illnesses may put their recollections and insights forever beyond your reach. Glean all you can from still-living family members and their associates. Seek out the stories of their youth.

You want a general feel for the events and traditions of the family, and you want to know about the individuals. So your questions should be designed with that in mind. You have to be more explicit than "Tell me about yourself and tell me about the family and friends."

**Tree Tips**

Always have a list of interview questions, starting with the things you want most to know. But, be flexible, ready to go in a new direction as the reminiscing progresses. Make the interview a pleasant conversation, not an interrogation.

The "things" of our ancestors are catalysts for stories. When family treasures are handed down, they are accompanied by tidbits such as "Mama always made potato salad in this bowl," or "My mother won these pearls at the raffle at St. Joseph's, and she wasn't even Catholic." Often the quilts are made from pieces of clothing the family wore. (If the stories are from a time beyond the memory of anyone living, be careful in accepting them as completely accurate. The story probably has a kernel of truth, but may have been altered from years of telling.)

Appendix B has suggestions for interview questions. For more help in devising your list of questions, go to www.cyndislist.com and scroll to "Oral History & Interviews." You'll find websites that discuss the art of oral interviews, guides for interviewing, tips, and tools for oral interviews.

We can't know our parents as vigorous young adults the way their contemporaries did, but we can learn about them by interviewing their friends. You will be amazed at the stories their friends share—the time your mother borrowed the dishes to impress your father's wealthy aunt who was coming to dinner and then forgot to serve the rolls; how your father grew beautiful flowers, but he showed his practical side by planting the daffodils marching along the garden border rather than flamboyantly scattering the bulbs.

**Tree Tips** _____

Older people often feel self-conscious talking into a tape recorder. Make it unobtrusive so that they forget it's there. I had great success in taking my mother 2,000 miles to the town where she grew up. As we drove slowly around, the tape recorder on the dash recorded her excited recounting of past events and people.

# Putting It into Practice

Let's take an example of how you might direct your research to build on the facts you've accumulated, using the previous suggestions of contact with relatives, interpretation of records, and reading historical background.

Anson Parmilee Stone, born 9 January 1815 in Oneida County, New York, married 14 October 1835 in Vernon, New York, to Cornelia Adams, daughter of Isaac Ward Adams and Eunice Webster. She was born in Vernon on 5 May 1812, and was a distant cousin of the Presidents Adams. Her grandfather Abraham Webster was brother of Noah Webster, the lexicographer. Anson died 14 March 1852 in Ft. Atkinson, Jefferson County, Wisconsin, and is buried there at the Lake View Cemetery. Cornelia died 16 February 1882 in Ft. Atkinson, and is buried with him. They had five children, the three oldest born in New York in 1837, 1839, and 1842, and the two youngest born in Ft. Atkinson, Wisconsin, in 1845 and 1850.

The preceding contains the facts. But we want to know more. One of the first items that might interest us is the trip from New York to Wisconsin sometime between 1842 and 1845 (based on ages of children.) What took them there? How did they travel?

## Contacting and Interviewing Living Relatives

Following the suggested pattern of research, interviews were conducted with all the grandchildren who were living when this research was undertaken in the 1960s. They were exhaustively interviewed about their recollections, and each scoured his or her own collection of family material. A handwritten paper was found in Anson's son Marsena's hand, stating that "Father went ahead out west, to grow up with the country, and he bought a farm, 200 acres, one half mile from Ft. Atkinson and built a small house and a large barn, split rails and fenced in the farm ...." Anson sent word to his wife Cornelia to bring the family, and in 1844, according to the same writer, they joined him, making the trip from New York to Milwaukee. Said Marsena, "[Father] sent for Mother, Emory, Newton and little me, we followed up on a sailing scooner across the lakes. Newt told me when I had grown up that we had a terrible squally time crossing the lakes and I squalled so loud and long that he and Em put their heads together to throw me over board, but Mother never gave them a chance. Theres no one that walks on earth like a mother ...."

Use the events in the lives of your ancestors to trigger a search for interesting side-lights. The event mentioned in Marsena's letter led to a study of travel via the Great Lakes. Cornelia and her children took part in the great sailing era that had begun about 1834. The three boys, ages seven, five, and two, were no doubt enthralled with the billowing sails of the schooners crowding the Great Lakes, whereas Cornelia was preoccupied with trying to keep them from falling overboard.

There was no Internet research in the 1960s, but today you could add to your knowledge by examining sites returned from an online search for "Great Lakes schooners."

# Checking Records for More Details

The events of Anson and Cornelia's lives were chronicled through the records. Census listings were examined; They showed that Anson was a farmer. County records were searched for his estate record. His will revealed that he was in "a very infirm state of health" when he made it in 1852. He left his wife Cornelia in control until the oldest child became 21. He added that she was to treat each in a manner as "nearly equal as possible" but "always giving those that are the most needy and unfortunate the preference." He desired that his estate be sold and the family maintained from the funds. He specified that funds were to be for support and education.

His obituary confirmed his parentage and his birth, and his age at death as 37. It added that at age 14 he joined the Methodist Episcopal Church, and served as class leader and steward most of the time until his death. He died of pulmonary consumption (tuberculosis).

# Beginning to Know and Understand

Now we start to understand this family and the lives they led. We sense the struggle of the family: moving from New York to Wisconsin and then having the father die before reaching 40; the young mother, nursing her sick, contagious husband, then left alone to raise five children and keep the farm going. Researching the land sales, we find that Cornelia sold the farm in pieces for their maintenance, following Anson's instructions. She kept some of the land, and, in 1860, was listed as a farm widow. In 1880, although no longer on the farm, Cornelia was still in Ft. Atkinson, living with her school-teacher daughter.

To continue the story of the family's life, the lives of the children were followed, too. The son Marsena served in the Civil War, opening a new study area for details to add to his life story. The children began marrying, and some moved to Illinois, Missouri, and, ultimately, California, when the transcontinental train was connected. (The historical events surrounding the completion of the train route also provided fascinating details.) Another son became a doctor and went to Montana, while a third became a dentist and headed to Alaska. Cornelia had done well, seeing that they were educated. The family continued to make its way, and then adventure and the Far West beckoned the children, just as it had their parents.

# Writing the Story

Writing your family history is more than a mere rearrangement of the family group sheet into a narrative paragraph, but you need not be a professional writer to complete the picture. If you have difficulty, write brief sections with the goal of piecing it all together. Try writing it as a letter to some other family member.

**Tree Tips** _____

Many books can give you ideas of how to craft the stories you're telling. One of the best is Lawrence Gouldrup's *Writing the Family Narrative*. He includes an annotated bibliography of books written about families. The books he lists are examples of various approaches.

Never think that your writing must be polished and of publishing caliber to be worthwhile. Think of how excited you are to find *anything* written by your ancestors. What your reader wants are the details that perhaps only you can supply. A bonus of writing about your ancestors is that you will quickly see what you are missing and what events you want to investigate.

Your ancestors were ordinary people, making choices good and bad, raising wayward teenagers, caring for elderly parents. These stories are about them: real people coping with real problems and successes. They are as much a thread in the fabric of history as the important personages in the history books.

## The Least You Need to Know

- ◆ Genealogy is more than a family group sheet.

- ◆ Reconstruct your ancestors' lives by interpreting their records.

- ◆ Look for records that amplify and expand the dry statistics you've accumulated.

- ◆ Use the vast resources of the Internet to find enhancements for the life stories you are writing.

- ◆ Read historical fiction and nonfiction about the people, places, and events of your ancestors' times.

- ◆ Interview your elderly relatives now.

# **21**

# Resolving Discrepancies

## In This Chapter

- ◆ What to do when the data conflicts
- ◆ Creative thinking to find data
- ◆ Customs that impact your research
- ◆ How the calendar change affects your research
- ◆ Understanding evidence

As your research progresses, you might begin to notice that your information doesn't agree. Dates don't seem to work out correctly, or you seem to have two children in the family with the same names. You can't find someone you are sure was in a certain place. "What's happening here?" you may wonder.

To solve these mysteries and others, you need strategies to deal with conflicting data and lack of information.

## When the Information Doesn't Agree

The census says Great-Grandpa was 9 in 1870, but the 1900 census says he was born in 1860. His tombstone says he was born 4 April 1861. The Bible record in his father's pension file has 7 April 1861. Which is correct?

First, recheck your notes and sources to be sure you didn't make a mistake. Then, analyze the information you have collected. Evaluate the sources from which you collected the information. Ask these questions and apply the answers to your problem:

- Was the information from a published source or from an original document?

- If from a published source, what do you know about its reliability?

- Who supplied the information? Was there anything to be gained or lost by giving false information?

- Was the document created at the time of the event?

- Have you misinterpreted something because you are unfamiliar with a custom, an abbreviation, or the use of certain words?

**Tree Tips**

An abstract is only as good as the abstracter. Whenever possible, confirm the information by looking at the original documents.

Published sources with unsubstantiated data, and this includes the Internet, cannot be counted on to provide you with accurate information. The facts in them must always be corroborated with other sources. Even reliable published sources can have errors. There are many steps to publication, and at any point mistakes can be made, particularly in dates.

Who supplied the information? It is unwise to depend solely on the information given to the census taker. You don't know who answered the questions. Was it the head of the household? A child? A neighbor? Maybe the census taker thought he knew the answers, so he didn't bother to ask. Maybe Grandma shaved a few years off her age not wanting Grandpa to know she was older than he thought, or she didn't want her neighbor, the census taker, to know how old she really was. Human nature hasn't changed over the years; mistakes, both honest and deliberate, are made.

The accuracy of the date on the tombstone depends on the knowledge of the informant and the skill of the stone cutter. The Bible record, if made near the time of the event by someone who was an eyewitness, is probably the most accurate of the records in the preceding conflict among the dates on the tombstone, census, and Bible record.

When the family seems to have had two or more children with the same name, consider the possibility that one child died and a subsequent child was given the same name (a common custom). Or that the family was German and used the same first name for all the boys, distinguishing them by giving them a different second, or middle, name.

Perhaps you have read an abbreviation as Jas. and assumed that was James, when actually the abbreviation was Jos. for Joseph. Or you couldn't figure out why the place of birth for so many people was "do." When you learn that "do" was an abbreviation used for "ditto," you go back to the record and find the actual birth place that was dittoed.

# Don't Get Counted Out

You are certain that your family was in the county at the time the census was taken, but you cannot find them. What could be the reason?

- Have you tried all the variant spellings?

- Do you have the right county in the right state? Many states have counties with the same name. Do you need to look in the parent county? County boundaries change.

- If you're working with Soundex, did you code the name correctly? Were the Soundex cards filmed out of order? This is a more common occurrence than you would expect. Check throughout the microfilm roll to see if the cards have been slipped into the wrong sequence.

- Are you looking at the right roll of microfilm? It is surprisingly easy to pull the wrong film out of the drawer.

- Are you in the right place on the film? There may be more than one county on the film, and if the family you're looking for is in Hardin County and you didn't scroll through Hancock, but started looking at the first county on the roll, you're in the wrong place.

- Do you have the right page? Often, more than one page number is on the sheet, and it may be difficult to figure out whether the index referred to the typed number, the small handwritten number, the large handwritten number, or the stamped number. Try them all.

- Did you check the end of the county enumeration? Occasionally, the census pages stuck together as they were filmed, but the mistake was caught in time to film the missed pages at the end of the county.

It is possible that you have done everything correctly and still can't find the family. Before you give up, consider that the indexer may have made a mistake. Names are misinterpreted and sometimes alphabetized incorrectly, or are omitted. Some censuses have been indexed by several organizations; check to see if another index to the same census includes your missing ancestor. If you are using a subscription service on the

Internet, try searching on just the first name (if it's not too common) plus the name of the county. Then study those whose last names may have been misinterpretations of the one you seek.

If, after all this, your ancestor remains elusive, there is one more avenue. Go through the county's census pages one by one, looking at every name. This is definitely tedious work, but if you have exhausted all the other possibilities, this may be the only way to find the listing, if it exists. It is best to attempt this method when you are rested and fresh, and to stop when you realize your scanning of the pages has become a blur. Note where you stopped checking, and start there another time. Continue this process until you have examined the entire county.

## Maybe They Were Missed

Keep in mind that your ancestor may not have been enumerated. Many people, especially those on the frontier, were suspicious of the government. They were conveniently not home when the census taker stopped by. Or, if living with another family, your ancestor may have skedaddled out the back door when the census taker walked in the front door. Or the census taker, tired, cold, and wet after traipsing from farm to farm for several hours on his final route, decided not to visit the family living two more miles down the road. Or, having visited the homestead once and finding no one there, he didn't return. Your ancestors may have been in transit when the census was taken at their old residence, and arrived at their new location after the census was finished there.

## Maybe They Were Listed Twice

You found two listings so similar that it makes you wonder if you've found the same family, or the same individual, twice in the same census year. Perhaps you have. The census taker was instructed to enumerate everyone living in the household on the official census day, and he had several weeks (in some census years as long as nine months) to get to every household in his district. It appears that sometimes the census taker enumerated everyone in the household on his visitation day rather than on the census day as set by Congress.

**Tree Tips**

In some counties you may find two or more listings with only slightly different data for the same family. In some census years, the enumerators were paid by the number of families they visited. This system led to some abuse.

# The Data Doesn't Conflict; There Isn't any Data!

Your ancestor just seems to appear in town with his wife and children, and you have no idea from whence he came. Start looking at the records created by his neighbors. Families did not move alone. They came with their friends and relatives. They came because of discord in their old church or because they wanted more land or new opportunities.

Remember how difficult overland travel was through uncleared lands and over the mountains. Might they have come to the area by water from another area or through a natural mountain pass? Could they have crossed an ice-frozen lake in the winter to get to a new territory? Do their deeds tell you where they lived prior to now? Or perhaps county histories detail a migration of an ethnic or religious group from another county.

If you can't find a burial where you expect it, one of several things may have happened. Elderly parents may have moved closer to their children in another county. Widows and widowers, who moved to be near sons or daughters, may have died in the new county but were shipped back to the original home to be buried next to a spouse. Pioneers died en route to new homes and were often buried in unmarked graves along the way. In the twentieth century, cremations became more acceptable with remains scattered rather than buried.

Coaxing information about our female ancestors from the records can be especially frustrating. The general advice is to examine the records of the men in her life—her husband, brothers, brothers-in-law, and her father. An exhaustive search through basic records available in print, on the Internet, and onsite is essential.

# Everything Is Relative

When the United States was primarily a rural society, the marriage pool for young men and women consisted of their neighbors within walking or horseback distance. Young men and women married the other young men and women they grew up with and saw at church and family gatherings. "Older men" of 25 waited for the beautiful 14-year-old to reach marriageable age. Because the marriage pool was so limited, first cousins married in areas where the law permitted. (This custom of the past is no longer allowed.)

**Tree Tips**

If you can't find the maiden name of your great-grandfather's wife, look for families with female children in his immediate neighborhood to see if you can find some approximate candidates. Look for more records of those families to see if they will lead you to the right young woman.

Families became intertwined when a brother and sister married a sister and brother from the same family, or when two sisters of one family married two brothers of another. These situations made their offspring "double cousins."

Many women died in childbirth, leaving a widower with several young children and perhaps a tiny infant to raise. He was eager to marry again, if only to have help with the children, and sometimes married a sister of his dead wife. Aunt Rachel became a stepmother to her nieces and nephews.

# Happy New Year—25 March

When the glossy new calendars start arriving in December, it probably doesn't occur to you that New Year's Day was not always 1 January. Furthermore, it may not be obvious how this can affect your genealogical research.

Calendars were developed to make sense of the natural cycle of time: days and years from the solar cycle, months from the lunar cycle. It took some experimentation before folks got it to the current system. There are many calendars, but for right now, we need be concerned only with the *Julian* and *Gregorian* calendars.

The Julian calendar resulted from Julius Caesar's reformation of the system to conform more closely to the seasons. The Gregorian calendar was Pope Gregory XIII's solution for the gradual problem that had developed with the Julian calendar: over time the calendar was 10 days off the natural solar cycle. To compensate, the Gregorian calendar dropped 10 days from October in 1582. And to keep this problem of extra days from reoccurring, one day was added to February in every year divisible by 4.

**Genie Jargon**

**Double dating** is the practice of giving dates, from 1 January, through February, to 25 March before 1752, two dates to represent the old and the new calendar, for example 23 January 1749/50. This may alternately be shown as 23 January 1749 O.S. (old style) or 23 January 1750 N.S. (new style).

The Gregorian calendar was adopted by different nations at different times. It was generally adopted by Britain and her colonies in 1752. The day added to the calendar every four years (leap year) meant that the calendar was now 11 days out of sync with the solar cycle. To take care of this, the system was adjusted so that the leap day is dropped from every century mark not divisible by 4. Instead of dropping 10 days in October, the British dropped 11 days in September and changed the New Year from 25 March to 1 January. Why do you need to be aware of this interesting bit of trivia? The calendar change makes dates in the months of January, February, and up to 25 March, prior to 1752, subject to *double dating*.

George Washington's birthday, 11 February 1731, under the old calendar became 22 February 1732 under the new calendar, and would be expressed as 22 February 1731/32. This doesn't actually change the date of his birth, merely the way it is expressed. In 1731, February was almost the end of the year because 1732 began on 25 March. After the year 1752 there are two things to contend with: the dropping of 11 days, and the change of the beginning of the year from 25 March to 1 January.

The calendar change affects your research because it is sometimes hard to determine whether the dates are meant to be old style or new style. You may think that the change was not significant enough to make a difference in your research, but it does. If you find records that indicate Abraham was born on 27 March 1741 and his younger sister Ruth was born on 23 March 1741, you may think there is something wrong. In reality, it is likely correct, because 23 March of 1741 in the old style calendar followed 27 March 1741 by about 12 months.

The change in calendar can also explain the seemingly erroneous court item that shows the will was dated 3 December 1740, and proved in court 1 January 1740. "That can't be," you think. But it can, and was, because 1 January 1740 followed 3 December 1740 (expressed as 1 January 1740/41). Once you understand this, you need to show it in your records, or others will think you have erred. The best way to show it is this: the will was dated 3 December 1740, proved in court 1 January 1740/41. Be sure to use a slash and not a dash; it is the slash that clarifies you are referring to the double dates caused by calendar changes.

Don't just convert the date with no explanation. If you do prefer to express it in new style (N.S.), show it as "1 January 1741 N.S." so that others understand under which calendar the date is given. For more on calendar history see www.infoplease.com/ipa/A0002061.html#A0880641.

**Tree Tips** _____

Though the difference of 11 days can explain some records (he died on the third of the month but was not buried until the thirteenth), genealogists should not convert dates to account for the 11-day difference unless the old style date would cause confusion. If it does, change it, but indicate that the date has been conformed to the new style calendar. Or leave it as is and explain the seeming discrepancy.

It is important to interpret carefully when faced with dates that were shown in months. This prevalent Quaker custom was also used by some others. A date of "30 9ber 1741" (or "30 9 mo 1741") is 30 November 1741, based on the calendar of the time in which the first month was March and the ninth month was November. It is best, in extracting records that are expressed in months, to write them in your abstract as shown in the original record. If you want to show it also as it would be under the present calendar, add that in brackets. For example, John Betts was born, according to the Quaker Monthly Meeting record, 30 9ber 1741 [30 November 1741 N.S.].

# Rushing to Conclusions

Other things besides conflicting or missing data and new dating systems can throw off your research. Pay attention to the clues. If you find William and Mary on the 1860 census with three children, and on the 1870 census you find William and Polly with five children, don't assume that Mary and Polly are one and the same, even though you know that Polly is a nickname for Mary. They may indeed be the same woman, but analyze the record. Is the woman on the 1870 census approximately 10 years older than on the 1860 census? Are their birthplaces the same? Are the children's ages consistent with one marriage, or is there a gap between numbers three and four, or four and five? If the older children are teenagers and the younger is a three-year-old, there might have been two marriages.

The will you find for James makes bequests to "my wife" and "my children," all named. Don't assume that the named wife is the mother of these children. She may be the mother of all of them, some of them, or none of them, but this wording does not tell you.

How about the census record? You found your ancestor John Matson listed as age 30, and with him is Mary, 28, and children George, 5, Martha, 3, and Sally, 1. You write in your records, "John Matson was born ca. 1820, married Mary—born ca. 1822, and had children George, born ca. 1845; Martha, born ca. 1847; and Sally, born ca. 1849." What's wrong? You have just assumed that Mary was his wife! It is likely that she was indeed his wife, but the 1850 census does not include relationship. If further examination of the family records proves to be perplexing, consider the possibility that his wife died. Perhaps a relative (most likely a sister) came to help out with the small children until he remarried, and it was she who was living with him in 1850. (It is even possible that the head of the household is not the father of the named children. They could be nieces and nephews; if not, they are probably related in some other manner. Keep this possibility in mind if the census doesn't match other known records of the family.)

**Tree Tips**

Does finding a record with the title "Colonel" immediately send you searching for the military record of his appointment? Pause and consider; is this colonel a southern plantation owner or a man of some substance in the town? If so, Colonel may be an honorary title of respect. He may have had some military or militia experience, but may not have attained the military rank of colonel.

You find two men with the same name, except one is designated Senior, one Junior. Don't assume that they are father and son. Junior and senior might have been used to distinguish individuals in the community with the same name. They may be father and son, but it is just as likely that they are cousins, uncle and nephew, or totally unrelated. The only thing you know for sure is one is older and one younger. Additionally, when "Senior" dies, "Junior" may be promoted to Senior, further confusing us as we try to determine the correct line. If a man with the same name came into the area who was older than the original inhabitant, the town might designate the original resident as John Smith I, and call the new resident John Smith II.

You discover a will in which John refers to his "now wife." It could mean that he was married previously. But, it usually means nothing more than designating his wife at the time of the will, rather than a woman he might marry after the will was signed if he were to divorce or become a widower.

# Theories of Relativity

Sooner or later, usually sooner, you are going to find records that suggest there are two people with the same name in the same place, only one of whom is your ancestor. How to sort them out?

One method is to write each thing you have found on a 3" × 5" card or in a table in a word-processing or database computer program. Then sort the cards or data to connect the events with each other, watching for inconsistencies and contradictions. Remember that you are not researching a name, but a person. Look for associates, occupations, church affiliations, anything that will develop identities for the people you found who happen to have the same name. Look at their neighbors.

*Deed:* Thomas Dunn in 1822 sold 100 acres in Decatur County, Indiana. Land adjoins that of Robert Johnson and William Ballard.

*Census:* Thomas Dunn, farmer, 1850 census in Decatur County, Indiana, age 30, wife Elizabeth, children James and Elizabeth.

*Military:* Thomas Dunn served in War of 1812.

*Will in probate file:* Thomas Dunn's will, dated 20 July 1852, probated 1852; bequests to wife Sarah, son James, daughter Elizabeth; witnesses to will were Robert Johnson, William Ballard. Admitted to probate in December, 1853.

Begin to build a mini-biography for these men. The Thomas Dunn who sold land in 1822 cannot be the Thomas Dunn age 30 on the 1850 census because he would have been two years old in 1822. (To sell at age two, it would have had to be through a guardian.) The Thomas Dunn age 30 on the 1850 census can't be the Thomas Dunn who served in the War of 1812 because he wasn't born yet, but the Thomas Dunn who sold land may have been the same one who served in the War of 1812. The Thomas Dunn whose will was probated in 1852 may be the same man who sold land because the witnesses to his will owned land adjoining the land he sold in 1822. Who are the neighbors of the Thomas Dunn on the 1850 census? Are there any Johnsons or Ballards?

Your problem may be more difficult than this, but the approach is the same. Sort out what you have, and make the connections.

# Based on the Evidence...

In the preceding example, the *evidence* is the deed, the military record, the census record, and the will. They are all useful in proving or disproving that there are two Thomas Dunns.

**Genie Jargon**

**Evidence** is the information offered as proof of a fact relating to a lineage or relationship.

You will often be faced with three or four records of a specific event, all differing. The Bible shows that Hattie was born 3 February 1851. Her tombstone shows date of birth as 3 February 1852. Her death certificate, filed in 1915, gives her birth as 3 February 1852. Which to pick? Do you decide that since two records showed 3 February 1852, that is the correct date?

Consider three questions: *WHO* gave the information; *WHY* did they give it; and *WHEN* did they give it? The answers will assist in determining which is the most likely date.

It is not unusual to see the death record, obituary, and tombstone all showing the same date, even if the date is incorrect. It is likely that the same person supplied the information for all three. If that person had the date wrong, all three records will be in error. Fall back on *WHO*. Was it someone who was in a position to have the correct information? Or was it a daughter who never knew that her mother fudged her date of birth all those years?

Consider the Bible. *WHEN* was the Bible published? If the title page on the Bible was 1848, and the family entries start with the marriage of the parents in 1849, followed in the same handwriting by the births of the children, it seems likely that the couple acquired the Bible when they were married and subsequently added births as the children were born. Because that was done close to the time of the event (answering the *WHEN* question) and by someone in a position to have the correct information, it would appear to be correct.

We then ask *WHY*. In this case, there doesn't appear to be any reason why the Bible date might be purposely entered incorrectly. (On the contrary, if a record was being provided to establish a pension, or social security, and did not jibe with other records, you might consider the *WHY* important.)

# Reaching a Sound Conclusion

There are basically three ways to build a case in genealogy. You can build it with pieces of direct evidence, pieces of indirect evidence (sometimes referred to as circumstantial evidence), or a combination of both. When the records conflict, each piece of evidence must be weighed and evaluated for authenticity, applying the criteria of *WHO* created the record, *WHEN* it was created, and *WHY* it was created. Additional factors are weighed, such as whether it is an original source or a derivative source. All information must also be examined with an understanding of the time period in which it was created because customs and laws changed. For the case to stand, you must do a thorough study, and the evidence gleaned from the accumulated information must correlate. Learning to evaluate evidence is essential for arriving at sound conclusions to link your generations of ancestors.

## The Least You Need to Know

◆ When the data conflicts, weigh the evidence.

◆ Write mini-biographies to sort out individuals with the same name.

◆ Don't read more into the records than is there.

# Part 6

## Expanding Your Horizon

Now you're really hooked, and are starting to look at all the things you'd like to have: books, magazines, equipment. There are even national conferences, regional seminars, institutes, and courses. Where to spend your money!?

You'll also learn a bit about sources that won't be your first line of attack, but you'll need as you dig deeper. Records on orphans, the naturalization process—these and much more await your discovery. And we'll introduce you to the sizzlin' new tool for genealogists—the DNA tests.

Finally, with some strategies for success and some words of caution, you are well on the road to many happy years of climbing your family tree!

# Chapter 22

# Spending Your Money Wisely

## In This Chapter

- ◆ Analyzing your needs
- ◆ Allocating your expenditures
- ◆ Gradually acquiring references

Your genealogical education is a life-long process. Everything you learn leads to areas where you need to delve more deeply. Much of what you want to know is available without cost through public libraries, but there are also many educational opportunities for which there is a charge. You start wondering how you can afford to acquire all the knowledge and resources you need. Don't despair; there are many values for your money.

Just as you apportion your money for the necessities of life, budget for your interests. Consider these five areas:

- ◆ Education, classes, and basic reference materials
- ◆ Memberships and subscriptions
- ◆ Services
- ◆ Resources including books, computer software, and Internet access
- ◆ Luxuries such as the books you constantly consult at the library, and CD-ROMs that save you time

# Readin', Writin', and 'Rithmetic

Seek every opportunity to attend classes and lectures on genealogy. Become familiar with the names of outstanding genealogists, and look for opportunities to hear them lecture. Read their published articles.

In addition to the seminars sponsored by your local genealogical society, there are regional and national seminars and conferences. Attending the conferences will give you new ideas for solving your problems, help you hone your skills, introduce you to new materials, and connect you with others who share your enthusiasm for genealogy.

> **Tree Tips**
>
> Regional conferences are not on a regular schedule. Watch for announcements of them in your region. The dates and locations are published in the genealogical magazines and sometimes posted on the bulletin boards of libraries. You can also find them in the online calendar at the FGS site www.fgs.org.

The National Genealogical Society (NGS) at www.ngsgenealogy.org and the Federation of Genealogical Societies (FGS) at www.fgs.org each sponsor a national conference in a different location every year. The NGS conference usually takes place in May or June, while FGS is in August or September. These conferences run for three or four days, and feature five or six simultaneous presentations by top genealogists and lecturers every hour. The topics are wide-ranging: military files, land records, problem solving, ethnic research, newspapers, courthouse research, and methodology, to name a few.

Presentations on DNA, digital cameras, and scanners integrate technological advances with genealogy.

Your conference registration includes a syllabus, a thick volume with material submitted by the lecturers. The material ranges from a few paragraphs to a detailed outline of the lecture, including bibliographies, maps, special instructions, and more.

> **Tree Tips**
>
> The syllabi are good references for future research. As you tackle a new problem, see if there were any lectures pertaining to it, and study the bibliographies. They can give you ideas on information sources. Even if you have not attended a conference, you might find the syllabus helpful. Occasionally, sponsoring organizations have syllabi from past conferences for sale through their offices.

## Networking

Networking is a vital part of the national conferences. In talking to your table mates at lunch or relaxing during a break, you may find that you share a common research problem or possibly even an ancestor. Many attendees have made connections from such contacts.

## Exhibits

National conferences draw hundreds of attendees. In addition to the lectures, one of the attractions is the exhibit area where vendors sell everything from rare books to T-shirts with genealogical messages. You'll find genealogical supplies such as charts alongside materials for preservation such as acid-free paper. Books (new and used) and maps are big sellers. The major genealogical book publishers stock booths with their new releases along with a selection of older titles. Computer programs are popular, as are CD-ROMs. Some vendors specialize in photo restoration. Large genealogical societies sponsor booths, recruiting members and selling publications. National and local research libraries and archives are well represented.

## Hands-On

At both the regional and national conferences, there are hands-on workshops that enable you to develop and practice skills important to your research. Workshops on land platting are usually oversubscribed. This skill can be crucial to solving genealogical problems of many kinds. Practical experience under the guidance of knowledgeable, patient instructors makes the techniques easier to acquire.

Occasionally, there are workshops devoted to abstracting and handwriting, as well as workshops on how to complete successful lineage society applications. In the latter, the emphasis is on the types of evidence needed to establish your line, and suggested sources for finding that evidence.

Computer workshops concentrate on specific genealogy programs, explaining many of their features, or on general topics, such as learning to use the Internet for genealogical research.

## Institutes

For a week of saturation in genealogy, attend one of the various genealogical institutes. Rather than a series of unrelated lectures, the institutes usually offer one or more tracks of related subjects. For instance, at the Institute of Genealogy and Historical Research at Samford University, Birmingham, Alabama (www.samford.edu/schools/ighr), there may be tracks for introductory genealogy, intermediate and advanced methodology, records of the South, military records, genealogical writing, and others. Some tracks are offered yearly; specialty tracks are available periodically.

**Tree Tips**

Brigham Young University also has a four-year college curriculum culminating in a bachelor's degree in Family History. This requires class attendance on campus at Provo, Utah. Details are at http://familyhistory.byu.edu/majors.asp.

The National Institute of Genealogical Research (NIGR), Washington, D.C. (www.rootsweb.com/~natgenin) takes place at the National Archives and concentrates on genealogical materials available in the National Archives. Other institutes are held in Illinois and Utah. Some genealogists return to these institutes year after year, taking advantage of the variety of courses offered each time.

## Staying Independent

In-depth lessons that you can do at your own pace are the attraction of home study courses. You miss the interaction of classroom instruction, but home study may fit better into your time and budget. The National Genealogical Society has the accredited and highly rated NGS American Genealogy: A Home Study Course. Completing the lessons gives you a good grounding in how to find and record your sources, maintain your records, and evaluate your evidence. To register or learn more, go to www.ngsgenealogy.org/eduhsc.cfm. Brigham Young University offers a distant learning certificate in Family History (genealogy). Information is online at http://ce.byu.edu/is/site/courses/index.cfm.

# Being a Joiner

Allocate part of your genealogy budget to society memberships and subscriptions. You will usually benefit from belonging to at least three organizations: one local, one state or regional, and one national. As you become aware of more areas where your ancestors lived, consider joining societies there. The newsletters and journals you receive as part of your membership dues are a part of the continuing education process that is so essential to successful genealogy. To locate societies, check the Society Hall Directory developed by FGS and Ancestry.com at www.familyhistory.com/societyhall/search.asp. You are sure to find several of interest to you among the over 500 listed.

Consider subscribing to some of the pre-mier genealogical journals that publish the results of scholarly work. Even if the information presented has nothing to do with the surnames you are researching, the methodology used is important and may eventually help you solve a problem. Genealogists often develop an interest in obscure records or subjects; the articles they write about those interests may lead you to new sources. Journal articles can alert you to newly published abstracts or compiled genealogies.

**Tree Tips**

Don't overlook the footnotes or bibliographies accompanying journal articles. They are rich sources of new ideas for your research.

An important part of all journals is the book-review section with its evaluations of recent publications. The books may pertain to a specific region, a family, general ref-erence, related topics, or other area of interest. Reading the reviews may suggest books that would be useful in your research—and some to avoid.

In addition to the scholarly journals, there are popular publications with articles of general interest. They often include question-and-answer columns on different topics, such as ethnic research, computers, or a particular geographic location. Other period-icals focus on one subject, such as computers or Irish genealogy.

# Are You Being Served?

Genealogists use many fee-based services that are quite reasonable but add up to sub-stantial amounts over time. Budget for photocopying, postage, loans of books or films through interlibrary loan or rental companies, and, if you have a computer, an Internet provider.

Occasionally, you may need professional help with a stubborn problem. The *Directory of Professional Genealogists*, published by the Association of Professional Genealogists, is online at www.apgen.org; and the *Certification Roster*, published by the Board for Certification of Genealogists, can be seen at www.bcgcertification.org. Lists of accredited genealogists for specific geographic areas can be obtained at www.icapgen.org, the site of the International Commission for the Accreditation of Professional Genealogists.

It may be more economical and efficient to hire a researcher than to travel to a distant area where you are unfamiliar with the resources. In some counties, the officials are too busy with the daily work of the county to engage in research, so they provide a list of researchers. Many archives and libraries also maintain rosters of researchers. Lists such as these usually are merely for the convenience of inquirers and are not meant as endorsements of the researchers' skills.

Before hiring genealogical help, you should know what to expect. The Association of Professional Genealogists developed a brochure, *Why Hire a Professional Genealogist*. It has tips on how to find a professional, how to evaluate the credentials, and what to expect in the way of costs and results. Download it from www.apgen.org.

# Developing Your Home Support System

Add to the references and resources you keep handy at home. Tapes, books, catalogs, computer programs, Internet subscriptions, and CD-ROMs can all advance your research from the comfort of home.

Most national conference lectures, and some regional ones, are taped on cassette and then converted to CD-ROMs, which you can purchase. Although you miss the visual parts of the lectures, the CDs are nonetheless useful aids for your education. Peruse the online catalog at Heritage Books (www.HeritageBooks.com) and order CDs relevant to your particular interest.

## Adding to Your Library

Build your collection little by little. Start with some basic guidebooks, and as you progress in your research, add to your collection. You may find that there is one book you regularly consult at the library; consider investing in a copy for your own bookshelves. When you find a geographic area where you are doing a great deal of research, you will probably want to purchase books about that area—not just genealogical books, but also histories.

If you find that you have an interest in a special ethnic group, look for books in that field. There are numerous books on many aspects of Jewish genealogy, as well as on Italian, German, Russian, Scottish, and so on. One way to learn about these is by attending lectures, or studying the bibliographies in conference syllabi or those in journal articles. If your library has the selected book or can get it for you through interlibrary loan, review it there; consider purchasing the book if you think you will use it often.

## Bookstores

There are several large booksellers that specialize in genealogical materials. Their owners and managers are genealogists who understand the needs of the field. Some specialize in books that are not generally thought of as genealogy books, but are aids to your understanding the laws, customs, and conditions that influenced your ancestors' behavior.

Don't overlook the major societies and archives. Many of them publish historical books and finding aids for their collections. North Carolina Archives, National Archives, New England Historic Genealogical Society, National Genealogical Society, and Illinois State Genealogical Society are only a few with publications.

Booksellers, and many societies and archives, advertise in genealogical publications. Look for them and send for their catalogs or reach them through their Internet addresses. Check http://rootsweb.com/~vagenweb/books.htm for links to genealogy bookstores. Online bookstores, search services such as AbeBooks (www.abebooks.com), or eBay can be good sources for rare or special-interest books.

**Tree Tips**

Don't concentrate on genealogical offerings only. Social histories that deal with particular geographical areas or periods of time can be quite useful, especially when you start writing narratives about your ancestors. You may learn stories about your ancestors while reading the history of an area.

## Feeding Your Computer More Software

Numerous programs have been developed by genealogists for genealogists to help in record keeping and research. Among the most widely used genealogy database programs are Family Tree Maker, Personal Ancestral File (PAF), Reunion, The Master Genealogist, and RootsMagic. Complementary programs that enhance the database programs are always in development. Look for them on the websites of the programs as well as in the periodical *Genealogical Computing*.

Mapping programs are useful for converting a legal description of land to a graphic representation. DeedMapper enables you to plat the land.

## Using Your Computer to the Utmost

When inspiration strikes in the middle of the night, your subscriptions to online sites permit you to confirm, refute, or enhance your ideas on the spot. Definitely allot some of your genealogy funds to subscriptions including census records. When deciding on a subscription service for access to census records, also weigh the value to you of the services of other collections such as historical newspapers, British records, French-Canadian records, and others of that ilk.

Before Internet research became commonplace, much information was published on CD-ROMs. They take advantage of one of the things that computers do best—quickly searching through mountains of information. As with any publication, however, be wary. Many CD-ROM compilations are incomplete or have errors, just as many printed indexes do, and many of them are out-of-date. Still useful, though, are CD-ROMs with the fully digitized, every-word searchable, scholarly journals from their inception up to the present as well as long-out-of-print books.

# Budgeting for Genealogical Luxuries

All these resources can move into the luxury category as genealogy takes hold of your life. You find you want to attend all the conferences and institutes and load up on memberships, subscriptions, books, tapes, and computer programs. You'll covet the latest multivolume indexes available on CD-ROM. You'll buy into the reasoning that a copier and even a microfilm reader will save you time and money.

If you don't have a computer, you'll want one. If you have a computer, you'll want multimedia, a scanner, a digital camera, a PDA, and more … and more. If you have a laptop, you'll hear the siren song of travel accessories: tiny mice, travel keyboards, miniaturized surge protectors, security cables—the list lengthens.

Surely you'll be tempted to take a genealogy cruise. Imagine enjoying a vacation in the Caribbean or Alaska or Mexico with all that implies, as well as attending onboard lectures presented by prominent genealogists. Exchanging ideas with other attendees in a social setting can supercharge your research, but the price can be somewhat steep.

Before you go on a spending spree, study your budget. Be an informed consumer, first buying the essentials that will help you become a skilled researcher. Ask yourself, "Will this purchase add to my genealogical skills and knowledge?" "Will it help me trace my ancestors?" Later, you can contemplate the purchase of the "big ticket" items.

## The Least You Need to Know

- Budget for your genealogical necessities and luxuries.
- Make taking classes and acquiring books your priority.
- Always ask yourself if the purchase will contribute to your genealogical knowledge.

# Chapter 23

# DNA—Why the Hype?

## In This Chapter

- ◆ Why Y-DNA tests are the best for genealogy
- ◆ Who is eligible for testing
- ◆ What can be expected from participating in a project
- ◆ How it all came about

Do you get frustrated when trying to figure out who is who? I've dreamed of having a séance—just to call upon some of those long-departed relatives and ask, "Hey Grandpa, who was your dad?" "Was your mother a Cassidy or a Morgan?" What a dream. Maybe séances aren't practical, but DNA is. It's not going to specifically identify our progenitors, but it can oftentimes point us to the right trail.

## G&G—Genetics and Genealogy

DNA testing for genealogical purposes is a fairly recent technological advancement, which can provide a means of breaking through "brick walls." It also provides a level of scientific certainty of connections to family groups within a surname.

DNA has been used to identify people for many years in forensics, but tests for genealogical purposes were not publicly available until 2000. Advances have been made at a very rapid pace since then, though limitations still exist.

# The Popular Y-DNA Testing

What is known as *Y-DNA test* is the major *DNA* application for genealogy at present.

Because this type of DNA is passed from father to son, it is ideally suited for single surname studies. Since late 2000, hundreds of such family projects have been established. For best results, it is best to go through one of these projects. They will have all the test results from studies conducted on the surname you are researching. And, their cost is less than doing it on an individual basis.

## You Gotta Be a Male

Y-DNA tests can only be done on males, as it is performed on DNA from the single Y chromosome, only present in males. This is the sex-determining chromosome. If you have it, you are a male. If you don't have it, you are a female. This DNA is passed on directly from father to son for many generations unchanged, as there is no input from any female parent along the line. This means that every male direct descendant of any man living many years ago will have an extremely similar Y-DNA pattern, called a *haplotype*. Aside from possibly connecting ancestry through haplotypes, test results will indicate a *haplogroup*. Tests consist of a certain number of *markers*; at least 25 are recommended—more of this later.

**Genie Jargon**

The **Y-DNA Test** is based on the Y chromosome, only present in males, passed from father to son. **DNA** is short for deoxyribonucleic acid—the genetic material of cells.

**Genie Jargon**

A **haplotype,** also called a DNA profile, is a set of certain values for genetic markers inherited as a unit. **Haplogroups** are similarly patterned and related descendant haplotypes that share a common ancestor and that suggest the geographic origins. Haplotypes and haplogroups can assist in defining the ethnic origins. **Markers** are specific positions on the DNA ladder that can be easily identified and measured.

# Are They Discriminating Against Females?

No, no discrimination. It's just a "fact of life" that females do not carry the Y chromosome. However, females (and males not descended from the surname in a continuous father-to-son descent) can still benefit by helping to sponsor tests for relatives that fit the requirement.

---

### Lineage Lessons

Eligible males must be from an unbroken male direct line. That is, if the DNA project is for descendants of the Atkinson family, the only males eligible are those who had a father named Atkinson, a grandfather named Atkinson, a great-grandfather named Atkinson, and so forth. If the male had a great-grandfather named George Atkinson whose daughter Martha married George Mallory, and that couple had a son named Victor Mallory, Victor is not eligible to test for the Atkinson project. This is in spite of the fact that he is a male and a direct descendant of an Atkinson. It must be an unbroken male descent from the surname.

---

When you hear that the male being tested must "bear the surname," keep in mind there could be unusual circumstances that create exceptions. In one early New York City Rose marriage, there was a divorce in the 1820s and the wife resumed her maiden name of Smith. The younger children took that name and remain Smith to this day. Some of these males who had a direct line from their Rose ancestor would in this case be eligible for the Rose testing project, in spite of their Smith surname. Another exception would occur in adoptions. In spite of the adoptee carrying the surname of his adoptive father, he would only be eligible for testing in the surname project of his biological father. There could be other reasons for a name change; the important factor is that the line be an unbroken direct male line through the surname.

For example, Aldert Roosa was born in Holland, sailed to America in 1660, and settled in Ulster County, New York. He had several children, including four sons. All of his male descendants (those still carrying the surname, or those who changed the spelling to Rose or Rosa) will have an almost identical and distinct Y-DNA pattern. Additionally, all such descendants of Aldert's brothers and male cousins will also be very similar, even if their names are yet unknown. Thus, if two males named Roosa/Rose are tested, one with a proven line back to Aldert and the other whose line was unknown at the time of testing, and they turn out to have very similar markers, they can now be easily determined to be from this Roosa family. This has exciting implications. If Aldert Roosa, for instance, had a brother who remained in Holland,

**Tree Tips** _____

A minimum number of 25 markers should be tested for reliable results. This level is generally conclusive, providing a good degree of proof of relationship. Ten- or twelve-marker tests, available at lower cost, can often establish that people *are not* related, but cannot confirm that they *are*.

and a descendant of that brother tested and matched with a descendant of Aldert who came to the colonies, these branches could now reunite. The American branch would finally know of some of their relatives in Holland and could learn more about their heritage from those who stayed in that area. Those who had remained in Holland would have discovered through the test what may have been a "lost" branch of their family in the United States. Some believe that the origin of this particular Roosa family is in England or Scotland before going to Holland. Going a step further, the possibility exists that a male from England or Scotland may test and match the Holland male, or the American male, reuniting yet another branch and perhaps providing clues to the earlier origin. The possibilities are awesome, as the family Y-DNA projects expand and add tests from a variety of countries.

In confirming a line to a particular ancestor, it is necessary that at least one male line be well documented. Then, other tests that match the markers of that line are "proved" to be from the same ancestor.

# Chipping in to Help

Females, and males who no longer carry the surname they are researching, can still participate in a DNA study by helping to finance a test for a male relative who is eligible. Results of a test from one known male relative of the surname effectively applies to all known relatives equally. It is in the best interests of all descendants to sponsor one or two tests from the family, preferably from different male sons of the progenitor.

To establish ties to an early family, it is only necessary to compare results of living individuals. Any two samples descended through different sons of any early progenitor can establish the DNA profile, or haplotype, of that ancestor. There is no need to obtain bones from the past!

# What Started All This Fuss?

DNA was first identified in the 1950s. Over the following 20 years it became clear to scientists that this carried the blueprint for all life on Earth.

By the 1980s it had been established that DNA could be used very effectively for identification purposes, leading to widespread use in the fields of forensics and criminology. Only very small samples were needed, with sources varying from a body to traces left by a body, in what is referred to as "genetic fingerprints." DNA paternal testing soon followed, effectively proving paternity far past the limits of earlier blood tests. A major achievement occurred in the early 1990s, with the exhumation and identification by DNA testing of the remains of members of the royal Romanoff family of Russia.

First public attention was brought to potential use of DNA as a genealogical tool in the late 1990s. Of special significance were efforts to determine if Thomas Jefferson was the father of some or all of slave Sally Hemmings' children.

A genetics study at the University of Arizona led to the formation of the firm Family Tree DNA in early 2000. A study by Dr. Brian Sykes of Oxford about the same time led to the formation of Oxford Ancestors. These companies were the first to offer commercial testing services to the public. Although a major turning point, these early tests were on a small number of markers, and thus somewhat limited in scope. However, this changed as tests were expanded to more markers. Testing of DNA from the Y chromosome (Y-DNA) became clearly the most advantageous for genealogical purposes, and surname projects became very common, providing the lion's share of testing. By 2002, Y-DNA testing quickly expanded to 21 and then 25 markers, creating a much higher degree of certainty than previously possible. Other firms also began testing; 37- and 42-marker tests became available in 2004.

# Taking the Plunge

Testing is best done through individual surname projects whenever possible. Surname administrators carry databases of all tests done to date under their surname project and have many tools available to them to compare results. They usually have close ties with family associations and researchers with expertise in the particular family. This is extremely important, as DNA results only become meaningful when coupled with traditional genealogical research. Another advantage is that participants in group projects are often offered substantial discounts by the testing facility.

Each surname project is generally operated by the administrator using a single testing facility. Lists of group projects can be found on the Internet at www.familytreedna. com/surname.asp or http://worldfamilies.net/search.php.

## Be Sure You Understand!

Before being tested, it is important to understand the tests offered, and what information can be expected from the results. In addition to what is briefly described in this chapter, the major companies providing services have extensive websites, including tutorials and other aids:

- ◆ Family Tree DNA (Houston, Texas): www.familytreedna.com

- ◆ DNA Heritage (Dorset, Eng & Rochester, New York): www.dnaheritage.com

- ◆ Relative Genetics (Salt Lake, Utah): www.relativegenetics.com

- ◆ Oxford Ancestors (London, England): www.oxfordancestors.com

In addition to these, an excellent tutorial on DNA prepared by Charles F. Kerchner, Jr., can be found online at www.kerchner.com.

The limitations should be strongly considered to reduce false expectations. No meaningful match can be guaranteed from any test. However, if any people who are directly paternally related to you have been tested, and you are sure of your relationship to the person tested, the results will help you, too. Project administrators are generally helpful in this task of matching the various tests and explaining the results.

## What's in the Kit?

DNA can be obtained from any portion of the body, with little exception, and all results would be theoretically identical. One exception is hair, which contains only mtDNA (see later). The preferred choice at one time was to test from blood, but this has since been replaced by a *buccal swab*, or, in some cases, a mouth wash.

**Genie Jargon**

A **buccal swab** refers to a specimen taken from inside the cheek or the mouth cavity.

To order a test kit, go to the website of the company providing the surname project of your choice and contact the surname project's administrator. Specify which test you wish to take. If the kit is to be sent to a relative and billed to you, that can be arranged.

Also provide the project administrator with the identity of the earliest proven male ancestor in your line, and some basic information about him such as dates and locations. (This will assist the administrator in grouping your results with others.) The administrator will order the kit sent to you from the lab; then you'll return it to that lab. The test kits are identical regardless of the test being performed. Generally they contain two swabs, two miniature vials of preservative, complete instructions, a waiver form (which must be signed), and a return-mailer envelope. The sample is obtained by simply brushing the inside of the cheek with the swabs. The tips of the swabs are then ejected into the vials. Payment is made with the return of the kit, unless otherwise arranged.

## On Pins and Needles

You'll be excited and impatient awaiting the results. Will you finally know to which family you belong? The ethnic background? Will you find relatives? Results of the test are usually available about four to six weeks after the return of the kit. At that time, basic numeric results and information are sent directly from the testing company to the participant by e-mail. These are also supplied to the project administrator, who compares the results with all others of the surname. The administrator should then report to you any matches or similarities found, together with relationships of earliest-known male ancestors. You also usually receive the e-mail addresses of those whom you match, so you can share information toward your common goals. And in the future you will be notified of any new matches.

# Looking Into a Crystal Ball

All DNA samples from current tests can be and often are routinely saved for an extended period (up to 25 years—see the testing company's literature), in case further tests are desired on the sample. Better tests are being developed constantly, and this enables you to take advantage of them simply by ordering an upgrade without taking another sample.

Various kits are also available to take and save samples for future tests. These special kits, available at a minimal cost, can often be stored along with your family history. Inquire about this at dnatestingbiz/DNA%20Archving/dnabanking.html. (Note carefully the spelling and symbols in the foregoing URL, especially the spelling of "Archving" or you won't find the page!)

# Okay, Let's Get Serious—What Is DNA?

If you don't want the technical stuff, skip these paragraphs! But most of you will want to know a bit of what it's all about.

DNA is short for deoxyribonucleic acid. This molecule carries the genetic code for all organisms, and provides the capacity of recreating them from single cells, to and through the procreation process.

The human body is made up of a tremendous number of cells. Although many cells have specific applications, virtually all cells of the body contain virtually exact copies of the original chromosomes in its nucleus and in the mitochondria surrounding it. Reproduction of cells goes on throughout life continuously.

The egg is, in essence, a cell itself with a nucleus containing only half of 23 chromosome pairs.

On conception, the sperm penetrates right into this nucleus, fertilizing, or supplying, the other half of each of these pairs. These pairs all combine by spiraling around each other, and exchanging small portions throughout. The only exception is the "sex" pair, of which everyone obtains either an X or Y from the father and an X from the mother, which team up as XX in female children, and XY in males.

**Tree Tips** _____

Want further explanation of loci, genome, and other terms? Try your own dictionary, or go to an online genetic dictionary such as www.ornl.gov/sci/ techresources/Human_Genome/ publicat/primer2001/glossary.s html. See also the glossary in Megan Smolenyak and Ann Turner's *Trace Your Roots with DNA*, or Charles Kerchner's genetic dictionary available for ordering at www. geneticgenealogydictionary.com.

The single cell formed from egg and sperm then starts reproducing itself, forming the body together with all its integral parts.

The strands of DNA making up the chromosomes are in the general shape of a helix or twisted ladder.

In a DNA test, the markers tested are at specific "loci" or locations in the DNA, known by DYS numbers. The number listed at each locus is actually the number of short tandem repeats (STRs) at that location, analogous to the distance between steps on the ladder. These STRs are repeated neucleotide sequences, which form little more than spacing, as between the rungs. They are tandem in that they are repeated on both sides of the ladder.

# Different Types of DNA

There are three types of DNA potentially of interest to genealogists, though the Y-DNA testing we discussed earlier in this chapter is the most prevalent and useful.

## Autosomal DNA—A Hope for the Future

Autosomal DNA makes up the vast majority of DNA in the nucleus of the human cell. It is comprised of 22 of the 23 pairs of chromosomes, those which contain randomly mixed DNA from both parents. (The twenty-third pair combines one of the X and Y chromosomes from the male and one of the two X chromosomes from the female. This additional pair is not in the randomly mixed DNA from both parents.) Autosomal DNA contains almost the entire genome, or blueprint, for the body. Most of the genes, which result in various inherited traits, ranging from eye and hair color to disease susceptibilities, are found in autosomal DNA. This mix is approximately half from each parent in each generation, or one quarter from each of the four grandparents, one eighth from each of the eight great-grandparents, etc. As it is almost entirely randomly mixed, it is not yet possible to establish from which ancestor any specific portion is inherited.

A DNA Print Test was developed from this, and first offered in 2003, intended to provide approximate percentages of ethnic or racial mixtures. At this time, their accuracy remains in some doubt, although improvements are being made.

Applications of autosomal DNA for genealogy is minimal at this writing, but it is considered to have great potential. It provides the only means of crossing the gender barrier, but major advances will take considerable time.

## Mitochondrial DNA or mtDNA

Although this type of test can be done either on males or females, the results are restricted to the all-female direct line only, with no crossing of the gender barrier at any point in the past. Inherited only from the mother on conception, the mitochondria comes directly from the egg, outside of the nucleus, but within the cell wall. This DNA essentially serves as the power pack of the cell, obtaining nutrients, processing, and disposing of wastes in cooperation with blood.

Fairly slow mutation rates make mt-DNA good for anthropological research and very early origins, but not practical for strictly genealogical applications at the time of this writing. As the surname on the female side changes with each generation back, there is no means of connecting specific maternal ancestors in groups. Surname studies or groups can provide little assistance in applying them to your genealogical work, except to confirm that two females are related in some manner. However, if you do want such a test, it is often less expensive when ordered through existing family surname projects, as group discounts may apply.

# Medical Concerns

All companies involved in testing for genealogical purposes subscribe to very strict standards. Primary among these is that the tests performed are strictly for the purpose intended—genealogy!

As such, they are not useful for any other purposes. Anyone wishing to uncover medical information must go elsewhere, as this requires completely different tests. Any DNA samples kept by these companies are not shared in any way without the written consent of the person involved (or kin, if the tested person is deceased).

# Privacy Issues

In addition to confirming paternal relationships, it must be noted that DNA testing is very capable of disproving a father/son relationship. A test can easily establish that "brothers" are not truly brothers, or paternal "cousins" are not really cousins. They can also disprove family connections, effectively knocking down a very sizable portion of a family tree that was very painstakingly created. Be prepared. What is referred to as "nonpaternity events" is much more common than we might suppose. You must enter into DNA testing with an open mind, in the spirit of finding out what is really so, even if it means disregarding years of research on what you thought was your family. If you are not prepared for unexpected results, don't take the test.

**Tree Tips**

Nonpaternity events could be the result of illegitimacy, adoption, raising an orphaned child without benefit of a formal adoption, etc. The rate of such nonpaternity events is generally estimated at about 2 to 3 percent per generation.

If a DNA project covering the surname you are researching already exists, it is strongly recommended that you take part in it. This will avoid duplication, and ensure that all results from the surname are included in comparisons. If you proceed solely on your own, you will not have the benefit of the accumulated database of matches.

# Want To Start a Project?

If you have checked the websites of the major DNA-testing firms and do not find a surname project, start one! Go to the websites of the companies offering testing to see their requirements. Become knowledgeable on the subject. Read the excellent book by Megan Smolenyak and Ann Turner, *Trace Your Roots with DNA*. Also visit www.genetealogy.com for more on this subject.

Try starting a project with a particular goal in mind. Do you have a male line proven back to a particular progenitor that is well documented? Test an eligible male descendant from that line. When others match that test, you'll know they are the same family.

**Tree Tips**

The project administrator needs to keep track of all the results, and inform those who tested of the results and their possible meaning.

What will you get from the project? Here is a start:

- Hopefully you will either confirm relationships or stop going down the wrong path.

- You may be able to direct your research to a specific area or to a specific time period.

- You might establish your ancestor's region of origin so that you can pursue the search there.

- Your test may match someone with a variant spelling you had not considered.

## The Least You Need to Know

- Only males with an unbroken father-to-son descent can participate in Y-DNA testing.

- At least 25 markers are needed to sufficiently match results with other tests.

- Participating in a group project is normally less expensive and has the advantage of comparisons to a larger database of tests.

- DNA results are only truly meaningful when coupled with traditional genealogical research.

# Chapter 24

# Discovering Lesser-Used Sources

## In This Chapter

♦ County records not to be missed

♦ Federal records with genealogical information

♦ Hundreds more federal records

♦ Ethnic records

Previous chapters discussed the fundamental records for your research: federal population censuses, deeds, wills, estates, Revolutionary War records, Civil War records, and bounty land. Those alone will keep you busy for some time. As you gain experience, you'll learn to think in terms of, "What other records might tell me more?"

The records you'll need to solve your advanced research problems are often somewhat obscure. There are good reasons for some records to be used less often: many are unindexed, their genealogical value may not be well known, or they may not be filmed or digitized and, therefore, are not available unless you travel or hire a researcher. Nonetheless, being aware that certain records exist may eventually be your key to a seemingly impossible problem.

# County Records

Within the counties are numerous records with genealogical information besides the ones we've discussed. Chances are, some of them have been filmed, although each county has many more records still in their original form. Before you head out to the county to check on these records, check the Family History Library catalog online at www.familysearch.org or at your nearest Family History Center to see what has been filmed for your county of interest. Always remember, however, that errors can occur, and that a filmed series may be incomplete.

# Guardianships

Guardianship and orphan records are important to genealogists. They are usually found in the county probate court records. When a decedent left an estate that required administration or probate, and left minor children as heirs, the court appointed a guardian to act in the children's interests. Sometimes children in the same family had different guardians. The children may have been from different marriages, or there may have been so many children as to make it impractical for one person to care for them all. If you find a child selecting a guardian rather than the court assigning one, usually that child is over the age of 14 but under 21. Children older than 14 could legally make their own selection.

> **CAUTION**
>
> **Pedigree Pitfalls**
>
> If you see the word "infant" in guardianship or other records, do not assume that the child is a baby. In law, an infant is any minor under the age of majority, usually 21 for males and 18 for females.

When you find the record of a guardian having been appointed or selected, don't stop there. Guardians appear in court records regularly, reporting on income and expenses in administering the affairs of their charges, or perhaps protesting the management of a farm or business in which the charge has an interest. When the child came of age, a final accounting was submitted to the court. If that record survives, it might provide more information on your ancestor.

If a child inherited property from a deceased mother, the father (or someone else) may have been appointed as guardian for the child's interests. The records created by a child inheriting from a deceased mother's estate can provide you with the maiden name of the mother. Someone might have petitioned to be guardian for children "entitled to distributive shares of the estate of their grandmother Catherine Carter by reason of the death of their mother Elizabeth Shimmin." Now you have three generations—the children, their mother, their grandmother. And the petitioner is probably related, too.

## Orphans, Apprentices, and the Poor

Orphans were not always children without parents. Sometimes they were children with one parent who could not support them. As with the other poor, the county often accepted responsibility for them. Orphans were sometimes sent to institutions: workhouses, almshouses, poorhouses, or asylums. Look for county records of the poor; these records are seldom microfilmed. Records of the institutions under some form of governmental jurisdiction may be at the county or state level. The records of privately run orphanages can be difficult to locate; they may be in historical societies, university libraries, or private collections, or they may no longer exist.

Poor children were often sent out by their parents as apprentices to learn a trade. A father without the means to provide for all his children might designate in his will that one or more of the children should be apprenticed to a specific trade. The master who took on an apprentice was usually obligated to feed, clothe, and educate the child until a certain age, and perhaps required to give him a suit of clothes, a small sum of money, and a Bible when released.

## Acting on Behalf

*Powers of attorney* can contain marvelous genealogical information. Seek them out when you visit the courthouse. Though they are sometimes recorded in the deed books, often they are a separate set of books with their own index, or each book may be individually indexed.

**Genie Jargon**

A **power of attorney** is a legal document allowing someone else to act on an individual's behalf.

Powers of attorney were often given by individuals who were settling land transactions at some distance from their residences. The individual who inherited property in another state and wanted to sell it might not have been willing or able to travel to that state. The person often appointed someone to act on his or her behalf. The document appointing an agent, often a relative or close friend, might provide details of what was being sold.

In Kentucky, in 1807, Hugh Rose, "a native of Amherst Co., Virginia, now a surgeon in the 1st Regiment of Infantry," gave power of attorney to two individuals to convey property that was part of his father's estate, and "my Sister Paulina's Estate who died Intestate and without an heir, also my properties ... left by my grandfather Robert Rose, left to his sons, John, Hugh, Henry, Patrick and Charles ...."

The document was executed in New Orleans where Rose was stationed. Look at the details: his birthplace; his current residence and occupation; the location of the property; and the names of his grandfather, uncles, and sister. The information is important in and of itself, but it also offers many leads for continuing research.

## Taxing Matters

Tax records are important to genealogists. There were poll taxes, a tax on all free white males in a community over a specified age, and property taxes, both real and personal. Personal property tax records can document the existence of ancestors who owned no land. They verify that an individual was in a particular place at a particular time. If the person remained there, he should appear on the tax rolls year after year. Property tax rolls reflect the acquisition or divestiture of land. The tax information may guide you to more records. If an individual disappears from the tax rolls, you'll know that he reached an age (or condition, such as blindness or poverty) of exemption from tax, died, or left the area. Any one of those reasons is valuable to your research.

Tax records are best used not in isolation, but in a series. If you find your ancestor on a tax list, follow him year by year back to his first appearance and forward to the year he disappeared from the roll. There may be some gaps in the existing records, but try to follow your ancestor throughout the rolls. Occasionally, abstracts of tax records are published and indexed, but original tax records are not indexed.

## Waving the Flag—Vote!

If your ancestor participated in the political process, you may find voter registration records. These records may be in the county along with current registrations, or they may have been transferred to the state archives. Voter registration information varies from state to state but can include such vital information as birth date, marital status, residence, telephone number, citizenship data, and physical description. More current registration rolls have residence and telephone number, and may have party affiliation. Accessibility to voter registers depends upon the laws of the state in which you are researching. A few voter registrations are online; see "Voters, Poll Books, Electoral Records" at www.cyndislist.com.

# Swearing Allegiance

*Naturalization* records are often neglected as a source of information because they are difficult to locate. Continual tinkering with laws governing naturalization results in confusion as to the naturalization process, where the records are, and what they might contain. For many

**Genie Jargon**

Naturalization is the legal process for an individual of foreign birth to become a citizen.

years, any court, (federal, state, county, or local), could accept the declaration of intention to become a citizen and grant citizenship once the individual had fulfilled the requirements. Since 1906, naturalization proceedings have taken place in federal courts. Christina K. Schaefer's *Guide to Naturalization Records of the United States* is a county-by-county guide to available records and, though not complete, will help you locate these important records.

Because of continual changes in the law, no blanket statements covering naturalization apply to all situations. However, generally, the citizenship process began with the *declaration of intention*, or "*first paper*," in which the alien stated a desire to become a citizen and renounced allegiance to his native country. When the prevailing residency requirement was fulfilled, the alien went back to court, petitioned for citizenship, and took an oath of allegiance to the United States. The first paper was usually filed in a court near the alien's residence, although until 1906 any court of record could accept it. The petition and final certificate could be in a completely different state because the alien had moved. In some instances, the alien's wife and children automatically became naturalized when the  husband received his certificate.

Prior to 1906, when the Bureau of Immigration and Naturalization was established, there was no uniformity in naturalization records. After 1906, standard forms were developed, and the resulting records yielded important information and even photographs. Records pertaining to naturalizations after 1906 will be with the Bureau of Immigration and Naturalization Service and in the courts.

**Genie Jargon**

The **declaration of intention** or **first paper** is a sworn statement by an alien that he intends to become a citizen.

Information on microfilmed naturalization records is in the micropublication catalogs of the National Archives, as well as in *The Guide to Genealogical Records in the National Archives* and *The Archives: A Guide to the Field Branches of the National Archives.* Another helpful booklet is John J. Newman's, *American Naturalization Processes and Procedures 1790–1985.*

# The Settling of America

Among the many federal-land records are the homestead records. The Homestead Act of 1862 was instrumental in settling the West. Many of our ancestors submitted papers and fulfilled the requirements to claim the allotted 160 acres. Any citizen (or person who had filed papers to become a citizen) over the age of 21 could claim 160 acres of unoccupied, available federal land. The individual had to live on the land for five years while cultivating it and building a home. Women, as well as men, were homesteaders, so don't overlook your female ancestors.

**Tree Tips**

There were other acts, earlier and later, pertaining to acquisition by private individuals of federal land. There are case files for Cash Entry Sales, Preemption Sales, Timber Culture, Desert Land, and others, all in Record Group 49 at the National Archives in Washington, D.C. These records do not usually contain as much personal information but, nonetheless, are worthwhile.

The case files for the homestead lands vary, but nearly all have valuable genealogical information, such as the age and address of the person applying for the land, family members, descriptions of the land, house, crops, and testimony of witnesses. For a naturalized citizen, you'll find information about the immigration, such as date and port of arrival, and date and place of naturalization. Some files even have copies of discharge from Union service in the Civil War, because a subsequent act gave special privileges to those veterans.

Homestead files are in two series: one for completed land entries and one for canceled land entries. Both are useful. The completed land entry files are in the custody of the National Archives in Washington, D.C., in Record Group 49. The canceled land entry papers are scattered among a variety of repositories, but they can yield clues to why the requirements were not fulfilled.

For help in understanding and locating homestead and other land records, consult Ancestry's *The Source*, Greenwood's *Research Guide to American Genealogy*, and Wade Hone's *Land and Property Research in the United States.*

# Passport Records

Although passports were not required until World War I, (except for a brief period during the Civil War), many individuals obtained them as a little extra protection. This was especially true for male immigrants who were afraid of being conscripted into the military service in their country of origin if they journeyed there. Immigrants to the United States did return to the "Old Country" to visit relatives, marry, take a child to see his or her grandparents, or, perhaps, to bring a family to the United States. Later passport records are more complete, but you will usually get some personal information from older ones. Two micropublication series to check are the Register and Indexes for Passport Applications 1810–1906, M1371, and Passport Applications 1795–1905, M1371.

# The Mail Is Here

Most villages had a post office, even if it was only a tiny back room in the general store, and a local resident was employed as the postmaster. *The Records of Appointment of Postmasters, 1832–30 September 1971*, micropublication M841, is available at the National Archives and all field branches. For each post office, the registers contain the dates of establishment and discontinuance, and the names and dates of postmaster appointments. Earlier appointments are on *Records of Appointment of Postmasters, October 1789–1832*, micropublication M1131. Although there is usually no genealogical information in these records, the dates prove residence in a specific area, and knowing that an individual was a postmaster adds interest to the family history.

# Defending the Country

The military records discussed in Chapter 17 are just the tip of the iceberg. The National Archives contains many more. The National Archives catalog *Military Service Records: A Select Catalog of National Archives Microfilm Publications* will give you ideas of records to check. One series of particular interest is the *Registers of Enlistments in the United States Army, 1798–1914*, micropublication M233. The men listed there were in the Regular Army, and this series may be the only information you will find on their service. The information varies but may include time and place of enlistment, age at enlistment, place of birth, civilian occupation, physical description, and unit or regiment to which assigned. There is no index to these files, but they are arranged chronologically in each register (which spans a number of years) and then alphabetically by the first letter of the surname. If you suspect that your ancestor served in the Regular Army, check the films for the appropriate time period.

## On the High Seas

Immigrants usually arrived by ship, and may have come into any number of port cities: New York, Boston, Baltimore, Philadelphia, New Orleans, Key West, Mobile, Charleston, Savannah, New Bedford, New Haven, Providence, San Francisco, Galveston, Seattle, Port Townsend (Wash.), Gulfport, Pascagoula (Miss.), and others.

---

### Lineage Lessons

Indexed ships' passenger lists are increasingly available online. Thousands arriving in New York between 1892 and 1924 passed through Ellis Island. Volunteers of The Church of Jesus Christ Latter-day Saints indexed the National Archives' microfilms of New York passenger lists for that time period. The indexes are searchable on www. ellisisland.org. A more comprehensive search engine for these records, developed by Dr. Stephen P. Morse, is at www.jewishgen.org/databases/eidb; it offers better control of searches. Ancestry.com has indexes for passengers on ships from foreign ports to New York, 1851–1891. The indexes are accessible by subscription only, but many libraries subscribe and offer access to their patrons.

---

Passenger arrival lists were originally created for customs, and they contain less information than those created as a result of immigration laws beginning in 1882. Because so many of the passenger lists are not indexed, to use them you need to know the ship and or date of arrival, often the very information you seek. Nonetheless, it is worthwhile to learn about these records. Even the early customs lists are useful because they usually give age, occupation, country of origin, and place of intended settlement. You may find the whole family traveling together, and they may be accompanied by other relatives or friends. Be careful, however, of accepting the information on these lists without further confirmation. On a ship sailing from Liverpool in 1858, the country of origin for all the passengers is listed as Great Britain when, in fact, they were from many European countries.

Records amassed after passage of immigration laws are more useful. The immigrants were asked many questions, such as whether they had been in the United States before, and if they were going to join a relative (and if so, the relative's name, address, and relationship). Their answers were duly noted on the immigration passenger lists. Later, the lists included a physical description and the name and address of the nearest relative in the immigrant's home country.

Consult Michael Tepper's *American Passenger Arrival Records* or Greenwood's *Research in American Genealogy* for good discussions of passenger lists. Also helpful is John P. Colletta's *They Came in Ships*.

## More Taxes

Before there was a federal income tax, the federal government reached into your ancestors' pockets several times. The surviving tax lists contain little or no genealogical information, but they can give you a glimpse of the economic status of your ancestor. The first direct tax was a 1798 tax on real property and slaves. The National Archives has the Pennsylvania lists (*United States Direct Tax of 1798: Tax Lists for the State of Pennsylvania*, M372), which are organized in a complex geographic division. What a wonderful resource it is! For individuals on the lists, you'll find the size and construction material of their houses, the number of windows and lights in the houses, and how many stories they were. Acreages, outbuildings (such as a milk house or distillery), and other tantalizing facts are there. Sometimes the list gives adjoining landowners, enabling you to sort out men of the same name. The other surviving lists (Connecticut, Delaware, District of Columbia, Maine, Maryland, Massachusetts, New Hampshire, Rhode Island, Tennessee, and Vermont) are in various repositories and are well worth hunting for if you have ancestors in those areas at that time.

Easier to use are the Internal Revenue Assessment Lists for the Civil War Period. To pay for the Civil War, taxes were levied on various businesses and licenses. Carriages, yachts, billiard tables, and gold and silver plates were taxed as luxury items. In 1865, one of my collateral relatives was taxed $10 each for his licenses as a claims agent, insurance agent, real estate agent, and retail dealer. He was taxed $25 as a retail liquor dealer, and assessed $1.00 each for his carriage and two gold watches, and $4.00 for his piano. No genealogical information here, but you can get an idea of his economic status from the tax list. As with most records, it helps to read the background information on whatever taxes you are studying. An informative article is "Income Tax Records of the Civil War Years," by Cynthia G. Fox. Originally published in *Prologue*, it is online at www.archives.gov/publications/prologue/1986/winter/civil-war-tax-records.html.

# Still More Federal Records

The scope of federal records with genealogical information is mind-boggling. Just glancing through the *Guide to Genealogical Research in the National Archives* will start you thinking. Some of the records of the federal government will be useful to you only after you have done a great deal of research in other sources. Others can be used early in your search if you have access to them. This selected list (in no particular order) gives you an inkling of the kinds of records that might be useful at some point in your research:

- Bureau of Indian Affairs

- Bureau of Refugees, Freedmen, and Abandoned Lands

- Southern Claims Commission

- U.S. Marshals

- U.S. Coast Guard

- Seamen's Protection Certificates

- Department of the Interior

- U.S. Treasury

- Bankruptcy

- Birth, Death, and Marriages at U.S. Army Posts

- Diplomatic Records

- Records of the Continental Congress

- Veterans Homes

- Amnesty and Pardon Records

- Japanese Evacuations

Archival research is somewhat different from other kinds of research. Because of the vastness of the federal records, there are no overall indexes. Records are organized as they were when the originating federal agency used them. The biggest obstacle to using federal records is that many of them are not on microfilm. You will have to go to the National Archives or one of its branches, or hire a researcher to look at the records for you.

The Archives has published many useful guides to its records. There are micropublication catalogs, preliminary inventory lists created by the archivists, and the three-volume Robert B. Matchette et al., *Guide to Federal Records in the National Archives of the United States*. The *Guide* is available online at www.archives.gov/research/guide-fed-records. Check at www.archives.gov/research_room/genealogy for many pointers for using federal records.

# Ethnic Records

If your ancestor was part of a particular ethnic group, then your research will be enhanced by seeking special resources. Start with Ancestry's *The Source* to see if there is a chapter on your ethnic interest. Look for special topic books, such as Ryskamp's *Finding Your Hispanic Roots* or Carr's *Guide to Cuban Genealogical Research*. New books by ethnic specialists appear regularly; watch for ones applicable to your field. Search for the collections of religious denominations and periodicals devoted to various nationalities. Numerous federal government records exist that pertain to particular groups, especially Native Americans and African Americans.

Genealogists who specialize in ethnic groups, whether racial, national, religious, linguistic, or cultural, often lecture at national conferences. Many presentations have been taped, been converted to CD-ROMs, and are sold through Heritage Books, www.HeritageBooks.com, 1-800-876-6103.

# Potpourri of Other Records and Sources

You may have to be creative in your thinking to discover your ancestors in other records. Did someone work for the railroad? There are records. Maybe they came into the country through Canada or Mexico; find those border-crossing records. High schools and universities often have student evaluations more than 100 years old. Prisons, too, keep records and not just for the inmates; my third great-grandfather was a guard at an Illinois penitentiary and his file was extant in the 1980s even though he retired in 1883. Look for connections to fraternal organizations and not just for men. Women belonged to auxiliary groups of the Masons, International Order of Odd Fellows, and others. Grandmother may have belonged to Royal Neighbors of America, and their headquarters can tell you when she cashed in her insurance policy. Biographies exist for even less-famous politicians at the state and county level. Could your ancestor have been on an orphan train? Your ancestor may be mentioned in someone else's records. Physicians and storekeepers kept account books that can detail services rendered to your ancestor.

The minutia of your ancestors' lives differentiates them and makes them more than just a name on a pedigree chart. It's up to you to accumulate the minutiae wherever you find it.

# Being Alert for New Sources

It is beyond the scope of any book to give you in-depth coverage of every record available for genealogical research. Be on the lookout for new-to-you sources of information. Rich sources of genealogical information are everywhere, mostly in records not created with genealogy in mind. Weave Internet research into your overall plans, but do not depend on it to the exclusion of all other sources.

# "I Know a Shortcut ..."

Modern technology makes it possible and practical for companies to amass huge collections of unrelated data. Some companies claim that you can now find your ancestors with a few clicks of a computer mouse. We've heard ads for online sites promising to find your family in five minutes. In that raw data, you may find individuals with the same names as your ancestors but no proof that they are the individuals you are seeking. Good genealogy requires the researcher to go beyond indexes, beyond undocumented lists. There are some shortcuts in genealogy, but there are no shortcuts to proving that you have discovered *your* ancestors. Technology continues to provide new tools to cut your research time, but there is no substitute for the systematic, thorough research necessary to prove a line.

# Wrapping It All Up

Your enthusiasm builds as you discover the continuity of history told through the fascinating stories of your ancestors. Whether you research in a traditional library or the digital world, healthy skepticism is important when evaluating your finds. Remember most of all that tracing a family is fun. It strengthens family ties, reconnects lost branches, and forges new friendships. Enjoy the journey.

## The Least You Need to Know

- There are many sources beyond the basic ones for genealogy research.
- Lesser-used records can be in the county, state, National Archives repositories, or in private, public, or university libraries.
- Rich sources may not be on microfilm, but remain in their original form at the custodial repository.
- Read widely to learn about records that deliver the goods on your ancestors. Trust, but verify.

# Relative Resources

Following is a smattering of resources. You'll discover many more, but these will get you started.

*BCG Genealogical Standards Manual, The.* Washington, D.C. Board for Certification of Genealogists, 2000.

Bentley, Elizabeth Petty. *Directory of Family Associations.* 4th ed. Baltimore, Md.: Genealogical Publishing Company, 1998, or the 5th ed. available only on CD-ROM by the same publisher.

———. *The Genealogist's Address Book*, 4th ed. Baltimore, Md.: Genealogical Publishing Company, 1998. The 5th ed. is available only on CD-ROM, from the same publisher.

Berry, Ellen Thomas and David Allen Berry. *Our Quaker Ancestors: Finding Them in Quaker Records.* Baltimore, Md.: Genealogical Publishing Company, 1987.

*Black's Law Dictionary.* Rev. 8th ed. St. Paul, Minn.: West Publishing Company, 2004. The 4th edition covers more obsolete terms.

Bockstruck, Lloyd DeWitt. *Revolutionary War Bounty Land Grants: Awarded by State Governments.* Baltimore, Md.: Genealogical Publishing Company, 1996.

Burroughs, Tony. "The Original Soundex Instructions," *National Genealogical Society Quarterly* 89, no.4 (2001): pp. 287–98.

Carmack, Sharon DeBartolo. *A Genealogist's Guide to Discovering Your Female Ancestors.* Cincinnati, Ohio: Genealogical Publishing Company, 1998.

———. *Your Guide to Cemetery Research*, Cincinnati, Ohio: Betterway Books, 2002.

Carr, Peter E. *Guide to Cuban Genealogical Research*. Chicago, Ill.: Adams Press, 1991.

*Census of Pensioners for Revolutionary or Military Services Under the Act for Taking the Sixth Census.* Washington, D.C.: Blair and Rives, 1841. Reprint, Baltimore, Md.: Southern Book Co., 1954.

*Century of Population Growth: From the First Census of the United States to the Twelfth 1790–1900.* Washington, D.C., U.S. Government Printing Office, 1900; reprint, Orting, Wash.: Heritage Quest Press, 1989.

*Chicago Manual of Style, The*, 15th ed. Chicago and London: University of Chicago Press, 2003.

Colletta, John P., Ph.D. rev. 3rd ed. *They Came in Ships*. Salt Lake City, Utah: MyFamily.com, 2002.

Curran, Joan Ferris, CG, Madilyn Coen Crane, John H. Wray, Ph.D., CG. *Numbering Your Genealogy: Basic Systems, Complex Families and International Kin.* Arlington, Va.: National Genealogical Society, 1992.

Drake, Paul J.D. *What Did They Mean by That? A Dictionary of Historical Terms for Genealogists.* Bowie, Md.: Heritage Books, Inc., 1994.

Eichholz, Alice, Ph.D., CG, ed. *Ancestry's Red Book*, 3rd ed. Salt Lake City, Utah: MyFamily.com, Inc. 2004.

Filby, P. William. *A Bibliography of American County Histories.* Baltimore, Md.: Genealogical Publishing Company, 1987.

Gouldrup, Lawrence P., Ph.D. *Writing the Family Narrative*, Salt Lake City, Utah: Ancestry.com, 1998.

Greenwood, Val D. *The Researcher's Guide to American Genealogy*. 3rd ed. Baltimore, Md.: Genealogical Publishing Company, 2000.

Grundset, Eric. *American Genealogical Research at the DAR*. Washington, D.C: National Society Daughters of the American Revolution, 1997.

*Guide to Genealogical Research in the National Archives*. 3rd ed. Washington, D.C.: National Archives, 1982, Chapter 1, Census Records, pp. 13–48.

*Handy Book for Genealogists, The*. Logan, Utah: Everton Publishers, latest edition.

Hatcher, Patricia Law, CG. *Producing a Quality Family History*, Salt Lake City, Utah: Ancestry Inc., 1996.

Hinckley, Kathleen W. *Locating Lost Family Members & Friends: Modern Genealogical Research Techniques for Locating the People of Your Past and Present*. Cincinnati, Ohio: Betterway Books, 1999.

————. *Your Guide to the Federal Census*. Cinncinati, Ohio: Betterway Books, 2002.

*Index of Revolutionary War Pension Applications in the National Archives*. Bicentennial Edition. Rev. and enlarged Arlington, Va.: National Genealogical Society, 1976. [Originally compiled by Max E. Hoyt and others, and known as *Hoyt's Index*.]

Hone, E. Wade, *Land and Property Research in the United States*. Salt Lake City, Utah: Ancestry, 1997.

Ingalls, Kay Germain. "Cherchez la Femme! Looking for Female Ancestors." *National Genealogical Society Quarterly* 88, no. 3 (2000): pp. 165-178.

Kerchner, Charles F. Jr. *Genetic Genealogy DNA Testing Dictionary*. Emmaus, Pa.: Charles F. Kerchner, Jr., 2004.

Kirkham, E. Kay. *The Handwriting of American Records for A Period of 300 Years*. Logan, Utah: Everton Publishers, Inc., 1981.

Lainhart, Ann S. *State Census Records*. Baltimore, Md.: Genealogical Publishing Company, 1992.

Leary, Helen F.M. *North Carolina Research*, 2nd ed. Raleigh, NC: North Carolina Genealogical Society, 1996.

Matchette, Robert B., et al. *Guide to Federal Records in the National Archives of the United States*. Washington, D.C., National Archives and Records Administration, 1995. 3 vol.

Melynk, Marcia D. *Genealogist's Handbook for New England Research*, 4th ed. Boston, Mass.: New England Historic Genealogical Society, 1999.

Meyerink, Kory L., ed. *Printed Sources: A Guide to Published Genealogical Records*. Salt Lake City, Utah: Ancestry Incorporated, 1998.

Mills, Elizabeth Shown. *Evidence! Citation and Analysis for the Family Historian*. Baltimore, Md.: Genealogical Publishing Company, 1997.

———, ed. *Professional Genealogy: A Manual for Researchers, Writers, Editors, Lecturers, and Librarians*. Baltimore, Md.: Genealogical Publishing Company, 2001.

Mokotoff, Gary. "Soundexing and Genealogy," www.avotaynu.com/soundex.html.

Neagles, James C. *The Library of Congress: A Guide to Genealogical and Historical Research*. Salt Lake City, Utah: Ancestry, 1990.

———, *U.S. Military Records: A Guide to Federal and State Sources, Colonial America to the Present*. Salt Lake City, Utah: Ancestry Incorporated, 1994.

Newman, John J. *American Naturalization Processes and Procedures 1790–1985*. n.p.: Indiana Historical Society, 1985.

*PERSI (Periodical Source Index)*. Fort Wayne, Ind.: Allen County Library Foundation, 1986+.

Rose, Christine. *Courthouse Research for Family Historians: Your Guide to Genealogical Treasures*. San Jose, Calif.: CR Publications, 2004.

———. *Genealogical Proof Standard: Building a Solid Case*, 2nd ed. San Jose, Calif.: CR Publications, 2005.

———. *Military Pension Acts 1776–1858*. San Jose, Calif.: CR Publications, 2000.

———. *Nicknames Past and Present*, 4th ed. San Jose, Calif.: CR Publications, 2002.

*Revolutionary War Pension and Bounty Land Warrant Index*, CD-ROM. Heritage Quest, 668 West 900 North, P.O. Box 540670, North Salt Lake, UT 84054.

Rubincam, Milton. *Pitfalls in American Genealogy*. Salt Lake City, Utah: Ancestry Incorporated, 1987.

Ryskamp, George R. *Finding Your Hispanic Roots*. Baltimore, Md.: Genealogical Publishing Company, 1997.

Schaefer, Christina K. *Guide to Naturalization Records of the United States*. Baltimore, Md.: Genealogical Publishing Company, 1997.

Sperry, Kip. *Abbreviations and Acronyms*. Orem, Utah: Ancestry Publishing, 2000.

Smith, Juliana Szucs Smith. *Ancestry Family Historian's Address Book: Revised Second Edition, The*. Salt Lake City, Utah: Ancestry, 2003.

Smolenyak, Megan Smolenyak and Ann Turner. *Trace Your Roots with DNA, Using Genetic Tests to Explore Your Family Tree*. Emmaus, Pa.: Rodale Books, 2004.

Sturdevant, Katherine Scott. *Bringing Your Family History to Life Through Social History*, Cincinnati, Ohio: Betterway Books, 2000.

Szucs, Loretto Dennis and Sandra Hargreaves Luebking, eds. *The Source: A Guidebook of American Genealogy*. Revised ed. Salt Lake City, Utah: Ancestry, 1997.

Tepper, Michael. *American Passenger Arrival Records: A Guide to the Records of Immigrants Arriving at American Ports by Sail and Stream*. Updated and enlarged. Baltimore, Md.: Genealogical Publishing Company, 1993.

Thorndale, William, and William Dollarhide. *Map Guide to the U.S. Federal Censuses, 1790–1920*. Baltimore, Md.: Genealogical Publishing Co., Inc, 1987.

U.S. Census Bureau. *Measuring America: The Decennial Censuses from 1790–2000*. Washington, D.C. Also available at www.census.gov/prod/2002pubs/pol02marv-pt1.pdf.

White, Virgil D. *Genealogical Abstracts of Revolutionary War Pension Files*. 4 vols. Waynesboro, Tenn.: The National Historical Publishing Co., 1990.

## Computer Programs

AniMap www.goldbug.com

DeedMapper users.rcn.com/deeds

Clooz ancestordetective.com

Family Tree Maker www.familytreemaker.com

Personal Ancestral File (PAF) www.ldscatalog.com

Reunion Leister Productions www.leisterpro.com

RootsMagic www.rootsmagic.com

The Master Genealogist www.whollygenes.com

## Educational Opportunities

Brigham Young University Conferences and Workshops www.ce.byu.edu/cw/cwgeneal

Federation of Genealogical Societies www.fgs.org

Genealogical Institute of Mid-American www.rootsweb.com/~ilsgs

Institute of Genealogy and Historical Research www.samford.edu/schools/ighr

National Genealogical Society www.ngsgenealogy.org

National Institute on Genealogical Research www.rootsweb.com/~natgenin

Salt Lake Institute of Genealogy www.infouga.org

# Worksheets

The worksheets in this appendix are examples of forms used to organize your genealogy research. Use the research calendar and the correspondence log to keep a running summary of what you have accomplished. The research calendar shows you at a glance the records you have checked in reference to a particular surname and problem. Looking at the list, you can quickly determine whether or not you have searched a particular record and what the results were. The research calendar is meant to be an overview of your work, rather than the place for detailed notes. The correspondence log is a record of your letter writing. Scanning the list, you can quickly see to whom you've written and what the response was. For more on these two forms, see Chapter 3.

Use the pedigree chart as a sketch of your bloodline. Here is where you record the bare-bones statistics on your ancestors. Once you have filled in the chart with what you know, you can develop a research plan to find the missing information. The family group sheet is the form used to record more detailed information for the people on your pedigree chart. Family group sheets are the foundation for organizing the information you collect. Complete at least two family group sheets for each individual on your pedigree chart. On one family group sheet the individual appears as a child and on another as a mother or father. (An individual with more than one marriage should have a family group sheet for each marriage.) Pedigree charts and family group sheets are not the end products of your research. They are tools to help you organize your findings. See Chapter 4 for more on pedigree charts and family group sheets.

Also included is a checklist of questions for interviewing relatives. You'll think of others as you devise your own lists for each interview you conduct. See Chapters 2 and 19 for more on interview techniques.

**Surname**

### RESEARCH CALENDAR

| Search focus (brief statement of research problem) | | | |
|---|---|---|---|
| | | | |

| Date | Repository/call no. | Source | Findings |
|---|---|---|---|
| | | | |
| | | | |
| | | | |
| | | | |
| | | | |
| | | | |
| | | | |
| | | | |
| | | | |
| | | | |
| | | | |
| | | | |
| | | | |

## CORRESPONDENCE LOG

| Date Sent | To Whom | Request | Reply Date | Results (Positive, Negative, Burned) |
|---|---|---|---|---|
| | | | | |
| | | | | |
| | | | | |
| | | | | |
| | | | | |
| | | | | |
| | | | | |
| | | | | |
| | | | | |
| | | | | |
| | | | | |
| | | | | |
| | | | | |
| | | | | |
| | | | | |
| | | | | |
| | | | | |

## PEDIGREE CHART

CHART NO. _____

Prepared by _____
Address _____
City and State _____ Zip _____
Date Prepared _____

No. 1 on this Chart is # _____ on Chart # _____

**1.**
Born
Where
Married When
Died
Where

*Name of Husband or Wife*

**2.** [Father of No. 1]
Born
Where
Married When
Died
Where

**3.** [Mother of No. 1]
Born
Where
Died
Where

**4.** [Father of No.2]
Born
Where
Married When
Died
Where

**5.** [Mother of No. 2]
Born
Where
Died
Where

**6.** [Father of No. 3]
Born
Where
Married When
Died
Where

**7.** [Mother of No. 3]
Born
Where
Died
Where

**8.** [Father of No. 4]
Born
Where
Married When
Died
Where
Con't on Chart # _____

**9.** [Mother of No. 4]
Born
Where
Died
Where
Con't on Chart # _____

**10.** [Father of No. 5]
Born
Where
Married When
Died
Where
Con't on Chart # _____

**11.** [Mother of No. 5]
Born
Where
Died
Where
Con't on Chart # _____

**12.** [Father of No. 6]
Born
Where
Married When
Died
Where
Con't on Chart # _____

**13.** [Mother of No. 6]
Born
Where
Died
Where
Con't on Chart # _____

**14.** [Father of No. 7]
Born
Where
Married When
Died
Where
Con't on Chart # _____

**15.** [Mother of No. 7]
Born
Where
Died
Where
Con't on Chart # _____

# FAMILY GROUP SHEET

NO. _____

| HUSBAND [Full name] | | SOURCES: Brief listing. |
|---|---|---|
| BORN | AT | No. |
| CHR. | AT | No. |
| MAR. | AT | No. |
| DIED | AT | No. |
| BURIED AT | | (Complete source citations on reverse) |
| FATHER | MOTHER [Maiden Name] | |
| OTHER WIVES | | |
| RESIDENCES | RELIGION | |
| OCCUPATION | MILITARY | |

[Use separate forms for each marriage]

| WIFE [Full maiden name] | |
|---|---|
| BORN | AT |
| CHR. | AT |
| DIED | AT |
| BURIED AT | |
| FATHER | MOTHER [Maiden Name] |
| OTHER HUSBANDS | |

| Sex Children | | Day-Month-Year | | City/Town County State | REF. No. |
|---|---|---|---|---|---|
| 1. | b. | | at | | Ref. |
| Spouse: | m. | | at | | Ref. |
| | d. | | at | | Ref. |
| 2. | b. | | at | | Ref. |
| Spouse: | m. | | at | | Ref. |
| | d. | | at | | Ref. |
| 3. | b. | | at | | Ref. |
| Spouse: | m. | | at | | Ref. |
| | d. | | at | | Ref. |
| 4. | b. | | at | | Ref. |
| Spouse: | m . | | at | | Ref. |
| | d. | | at | | Ref. |
| 5. | b. | | at | | Ref. |
| Spouse: | m. | | at | | Ref. |
| | d. | | at | | Ref. |
| 6. | b. | | at | | Ref. |
| Spouse: | m. | | at | | Ref. |
| | d. | | at | | Ref. |
| 7. | b. | | at | | Ref. |
| Spouse: | m. | | at | | Ref. |
| | d. | | at | | Ref. |
| 8. | b. | | at | | Ref. |
| Spouse: | m. | | at | | Ref. |
| | d. | | at | | Ref. |
| 9. | b. | | at | | Ref. |
| Spouse: | m. | | at | | Ref. |
| | d. | | at | | Ref. |
| 10. | b. | | at | | Ref. |
| Spouse: | m. | | at | | Ref. |
| | d. | | at | | Ref. |

| PREPARED BY | OTHER MAR. OF CHILDREN |
|---|---|
| Address | Use reverse for additional marriages |
| City and State | Zip |
| Date Prepared: | |

b.=born   m.=married   d.=death   ch.=christening   List references at top and use ref. numbers on items. Use reverse if necessary.

# Interviewing Your Relatives

You need to know names, dates, and locations, but if you suddenly bombard your relatives with only those questions, they will become flustered. Or worse yet, they will lose interest. Try to fit those questions in among the ones that trigger the reminiscences. Much of the information you'll find in your search will pertain to your male ancestors. During interviews, make a special effort to elicit information about your female ancestors, too.

It is not likely that you will have time to ask all your questions, so decide which ones are most important to you. But don't be too rigid. Through the natural course of the conversation, you may get answers to questions you didn't think to ask or were hesitant to ask. And the answer to one question could lead to something you'll want to explore further. The following questions will get you started with your own list; you'll think of others. The list refers to males; adapt the same list for females.

- ☐ What was Grandpa's full name? Was he named for anyone else? What was he called? How did he get that nickname?

- ☐ When and where was he born? Was it a small town? A farming community? Do you know what took the family there?

- ☐ What was his father's name?

- ☐ What was his mother's maiden name?

- ☐ Did Grandpa have brothers and sisters? What were their names? When were they born; where were they born? Who did they marry?

- ☐ Where were the various towns in which the family lived? Did they like moving around? Were they following the available work? Just adventurous? Did other relatives move with them?

- ☐ What were the names of Grandpa's aunts and uncles? Did they live nearby? Were there often large family gatherings?

- ☐ What did Grandpa look like? Did he have a beard? Was he big-framed?

- ☐ Does anyone have any photos of him? Did he resemble anyone else in the family?

- ☐ What did Grandpa do to earn a living? Did he like it? Did any of the children follow in his footsteps?

- ☐ Where is he buried? Have you ever been there? Is there a tombstone?

☐ Did Grandpa ever serve in one of the wars? Does anyone have his uniform or other paraphernalia from the war?

☐ What church did he attend? Did he attend with Grandma? Was he active in the church?

☐ Did he have a trade? A hobby? Did he like gardening? Did he have any pets?

☐ Did he own land? Was it cultivated for crops? Did he like working on it himself?

☐ What was his nationality? Did he speak with an accent?

☐ Does anyone in the family have possessions that were handed down? Do you know the stories about the items?

☐ Tell me about your holiday dinners. Were birthdays celebrated? What kinds of gifts did you give and receive?

☐ What did the family do for recreation? Did anyone have a special hobby?

☐ How was the family's health? Robust or sickly? Allergies? Home remedies?

☐ Did they embrace newfangled ideas and technologies? When did they get their first automobile, electricity? Did they have indoor plumbing?

☐ What is the origin of the family expressions? Did the family have any traditions?

☐ Were they involved in politics, civics? Belong to any clubs?

☐ What were their attitudes toward religion, race, liquor?

☐ Did anyone play a musical instrument? Have artistic talent?

☐ Was anyone athletic?

☐ Is there some family trait that seems pervasive?

☐ What about you—how did you meet your spouse? How did you decide on a wedding date?

☐ What was your school like—one room in the country or a brick building in the city? Were you a good student?

☐ Who were your best friends, and what did you do together?

☐ What was your favorite age? Why?

☐ Did you get along well with your siblings? Your cousins?

# Appendix C

# Census Forms

The following pages contain forms for the 1800–1930 censuses. These forms can be photocopied and used to enter information you extract from microfilm.

| Page | Head of Family | Free White Males | | | | | Free White Females | | | | | All Others | Slaves | Remarks |
|---|---|---|---|---|---|---|---|---|---|---|---|---|---|---|
| | | Under 10 | 10–16 | 16–26 | 26–45 | 45 & Over | Under 10 | 10–16 | 16–26 | 26–45 | 45 & Over | | | |
| | | | | | | | | | | | | | | |

State _____ County _____

**1800–1810 CENSUS — UNITED STATES**

City _____ Call No. _____

1820 CENSUS — UNITED STATES

State _____ County _____ City _____ Call No. _____

| Page | Head of Family | Free White Males | | | | | | Free White Females | | | | | Foreigners not naturalized | Agriculture | Commerce | Manufactures | Free Colored | Slaves | Remarks |
|---|---|---|---|---|---|---|---|---|---|---|---|---|---|---|---|---|---|---|---|
| | | Under 10 | 10—16 | 16—18 | 16—26 | 26—45 | 45 and over | Under 10 | 10—16 | 16—26 | 26—45 | 45 and over | | | | | | | |

**1830-1840 CENSUS – UNITED STATES**

| STATE | COUNTY | CITY | CALL NUMBER |
|---|---|---|---|

| Page | HEAD OF FAMILY | FREE WHITE MALES | | | | | | | | | | | | | | | FREE WHITE FEMALES | | | | | | | | | | | | | | | Slaves | Free Colored | Foreigners Not Naturalized |
|---|---|---|---|---|---|---|---|---|---|---|---|---|---|---|---|---|---|---|---|---|---|---|---|---|---|---|---|---|---|---|---|---|---|---|

*(Free White Males and Free White Females columns each: Under 5, 5-10, 10-15, 15-20, 20-30, 30-40, 40-50, 50-60, 60-70, 70-80, 80-90, 90-100, Over 100)*

# 1850 CENSUS – UNITED STATES

STATE

COUNTY

TOWN/TOWNSHIP

CALL NUMBER

| Page | Dwelling Number | Family Number | NAMES | Age | Sex | Color | OCCUPATION, ETC. | Value— Real Estate | BIRTHPLACE | Married Within Year | School Within Year | Can't Read or Write | Enumeration Date | REMARKS |
|------|-----------------|---------------|-------|-----|-----|-------|------------------|--------------------|-----------|---------------------|--------------------|---------------------|------------------|---------|
| | | | | | | | | | | | | | | |
| | | | | | | | | | | | | | | |
| | | | | | | | | | | | | | | |
| | | | | | | | | | | | | | | |
| | | | | | | | | | | | | | | |
| | | | | | | | | | | | | | | |
| | | | | | | | | | | | | | | |
| | | | | | | | | | | | | | | |
| | | | | | | | | | | | | | | |
| | | | | | | | | | | | | | | |
| | | | | | | | | | | | | | | |
| | | | | | | | | | | | | | | |
| | | | | | | | | | | | | | | |
| | | | | | | | | | | | | | | |
| | | | | | | | | | | | | | | |
| | | | | | | | | | | | | | | |

## 1860 CENSUS – UNITED STATES

STATE _____ COUNTY _____ TOWN/TOWNSHIP _____ P.O. _____ CALL NUMBER _____

| Page | Dwelling No. | Family No. | NAMES | Age | Sex | Color | OCCUPATION, ETC. | Value–Real Estate | Value–Personal Property | BIRTHPLACE | Married in Year | School in Year | Can't Read or Write | Enumeration Date | REMARKS |
|------|--------------|------------|-------|-----|-----|-------|------------------|-------------------|-------------------------|------------|-----------------|----------------|---------------------|------------------|---------|
| | | | | | | | | | | | | | | | |
| | | | | | | | | | | | | | | | |
| | | | | | | | | | | | | | | | |
| | | | | | | | | | | | | | | | |
| | | | | | | | | | | | | | | | |
| | | | | | | | | | | | | | | | |
| | | | | | | | | | | | | | | | |
| | | | | | | | | | | | | | | | |
| | | | | | | | | | | | | | | | |
| | | | | | | | | | | | | | | | |
| | | | | | | | | | | | | | | | |
| | | | | | | | | | | | | | | | |
| | | | | | | | | | | | | | | | |
| | | | | | | | | | | | | | | | |
| | | | | | | | | | | | | | | | |

**1870 CENSUS – UNITED STATES**

STATE _____ COUNTY _____ TOWN/TOWNSHIP _____ P.O. _____ CALL NUMBER _____

| Page | Dwelling No. | Family No. | NAMES | Age | Sex | Color | OCCUPATION, ETC. | Value—Real Estate | Value—Personal Prop. | BIRTHPLACE | Father Foreign Born | Mother Foreign Born | Month Born In Year | Month Married In Year | School In Year | Can't Read or Write | Eligible To Vote | Date of Enumeration |
|---|---|---|---|---|---|---|---|---|---|---|---|---|---|---|---|---|---|---|
| | | | | | | | | | | | | | | | | | | |

## 1880 CENSUS – UNITED STATES

STATE · COUNTY · TOWN/TOWNSHIP · CALL NUMBER

Column headings:

- Page
- Dwelling Number
- Family Number
- NAMES
- Color
- Sex
- Age Prior to June 1st
- Month of Birth if Born in Census Year
- Relationship to Head of House
- Single
- Married
- Widowed
- Divorced
- Married in Census Year
- Occupation
- Miscellaneous Information
- Cannot Read or Write
- Place of Birth
- Place of Birth of Father
- Place of Birth of Mother
- Enumeration Date

# 1900 CENSUS — UNITED STATES

| | | | | | | | | | | | | | | | | | | | | | | | | | | | | | | | | | | | | | | | | | |
|---|---|---|---|---|---|---|---|---|---|---|---|---|---|---|---|---|---|---|---|---|---|---|---|---|---|---|---|---|---|---|---|---|---|---|---|---|---|---|---|---|---|

MICROFILM ROLL NUMBER

STATE

COUNTY

TOWN/TOWNSHIP

SUPV. DIST. NO.

ENUM. DIST. NO.

DATE

SHEET NUMBER

PAGE NUMBER

CALL NUMBER

**LOCATION**
- Street
- House Number
- Dwelling Number
- Family Number

**NAME** — of each person whose place of abode on June 1, 1900, was in this family

**PERSONAL DESCRIPTION**
- Relation to head of family
- Color
- Sex
- Month of birth
- Year of birth
- Age
- Single, married, widowed, divorced
- Number of years married
- Mother of how many children
- Number of these children living

**NATIVITY**
- Place of birth
- Place of birth of father
- Place of birth of mother

**CITIZENSHIP**
- Year of immigration to United States
- No. of years in U.S.
- Naturalization

**OCCUPATION**
- Type
- Number of months not employed

**EDUCATION**
- Attended school (months)
- Can read
- Can write
- Can speak English

- Home owned or rented
- Home owned free or mortgaged
- Farm or house

## 1910 CENSUS – UNITED STATES

STATE _____ COUNTY _____ TOWN/TOWNSHIP _____ ENUM. DIST. NO. _____ PAGE NO. _____

| LOCATION | | | | NAME | PERSONAL DESCRIPTION | | | | | | | NATIVITY | | |
|---|---|---|---|---|---|---|---|---|---|---|---|---|---|---|
| STREET NAME | HOUSE NUMBER | VISITATION NUMBER | FAMILY NUMBER | OF EACH PERSON WHOSE PLACE OF ABODE ON APRIL 15, 1910, WAS IN THIS FAMILY | RELATION TO HEAD OF HOUSE | SEX | RACE | AGE | SINGLE/MARRIED/ WIDOWED/DIVORCED | NUMBER OF YEARS PRESENT MARRIAGE | NO. OF CHILDREN BORN THIS MOTHER | NUMBER OF THESE CHILDREN LIVING | PLACE OF BIRTH OF THIS PERSON | PLACE OF BIRTH OF FATHER | PLACE OF BIRTH OF MOTHER |
| | | | | | | | | | | | | | | | |
| | | | | | | | | | | | | | | | |
| | | | | | | | | | | | | | | | |
| | | | | | | | | | | | | | | | |
| | | | | | | | | | | | | | | | |

## 1910 CENSUS – UNITED STATES (CONTINUED)

STATE | COUNTY | TOWN/TOWNSHIP | ENUM. DIST. NO. | PAGE NO.

| NAME | CITIZENSHIP | | | OCCUPATION | | | | | EDUCATION | | | HOME OWNERSHIP | | | | | | | |
|---|---|---|---|---|---|---|---|---|---|---|---|---|---|---|---|---|---|---|---|
| OF EACH PERSON WHOSE PLACE OF ABODE ON APRIL 15, 1910, WAS IN THIS FAMILY (FROM OTHER SIDE OF THIS FORM) | YEAR OF IMMIGRATION TO U.S. | NATURALIZED/ALIEN | NATIVE LANGUAGE | TRADE OR PROFESSION | NATURE OF BUSINESS | EMPLOYER/EMPLOYEE/ SELF-EMPLOYED | EMPLOYED/ UNEMPLOYED (IF EMPLOYEE) | WEEKS OUT OF WORK IN 1909 (IF EMPLOYEE) | ABLE TO READ | ABLE TO WRITE | ATTENDED SCHOOL SINCE SEPT 1, 1909 | OWNED/RENTED | OWNED FREE/ MORTGAGED | FARM/HOUSE | NO. OF FARM SCHEDULE | UNION/CONFEDERATE VETERAN | BLIND | DEAF AND DUMB | |

## 1920 CENSUS — UNITED STATES

STATE

COUNTY

TOWNSHIP OR OTHER COUNTY DIVISION

NAME OF INCORPORATED PLACE

NAME OF INSTITUTION

WARD OF CITY

SUPERVISOR'S DISTRICT #

ENUMERATION DISTRICT #

SHEET NO.

ENUMERATED BY ME ON THE _____ DAY OF _____, 1920. ENUMERATOR

| PLACE OF ABODE | | | | NAME | RELATION | TENURE | | PERSONAL DESCRIPTION | | | | CITIZENSHIP | | | EDUCATION | | |
|---|---|---|---|---|---|---|---|---|---|---|---|---|---|---|---|---|---|
| STREET, AVENUE, ETC. | HOUSE NUMBER OR FARM | NUMBER OF DWELLING HOUSE (VISITATION ORDER) | NUMBER OF FAMILY (VISITATION ORDER) | OF EACH PERSON WHOSE PLACE OF ABODE ON JANUARY 1, 1920, WAS IN THIS FAMILY | RELATIONSHIP TO HEAD OF HOUSEHOLD | HOME OWNED OR RENTED | IF OWNED, FREE OR MORTGAGED | SEX | COLOR OR RACE | AGE AT LAST BIRTHDAY | SINGLE, MARRIED WIDOWED, OR DIVORCED | YEAR OF IMMIGRATION TO U.S. | NATURALIZED OR ALIEN | IF NATURALIZED, YEAR OF NATURALIZATION | ATTENDED SCHOOL ANYTIME SINCE SEPT. 1, 1919 | ABLE TO READ | ABLE TO WRITE |
| 1 | 2 | 3 | 4 | 5 | 6 | 7 | 8 | 9 | 10 | 11 | 12 | 13 | 14 | 15 | 16 | 17 | 18 |
| | | | | | | | | | | | | | | | | | |
| | | | | | | | | | | | | | | | | | |
| | | | | | | | | | | | | | | | | | |
| | | | | | | | | | | | | | | | | | |
| | | | | | | | | | | | | | | | | | |
| | | | | | | | | | | | | | | | | | |
| | | | | | | | | | | | | | | | | | |
| | | | | | | | | | | | | | | | | | |
| | | | | | | | | | | | | | | | | | |
| | | | | | | | | | | | | | | | | | |
| | | | | | | | | | | | | | | | | | |
| | | | | | | | | | | | | | | | | | |
| | | | | | | | | | | | | | | | | | |

# 1920 CENSUS — UNITED STATES

STATE

COUNTY

TOWNSHIP OR OTHER COUNTY DIVISION

NAME OF INSTITUTION

NAME OF INCORPORATED PLACE

ENUMERATED BY ME ON THE _____ DAY OF _____, 1920

SUPERVISOR'S DISTRICT #

ENUMERATION DISTRICT #

SHEET NO.

WARD OF CITY

ENUMERATOR

## NAME

OF EACH PERSON WHOSE PLACE OF ABODE ON JANUARY 1, 1920, WAS IN THIS FAMILY
(from other side of form).

5

## NATIVITY AND MOTHER TONGUE

PLACE OF BIRTH OF EACH PERSON AND PARENTS OF EACH PERSON ENUMERATED. IF BORN IN U.S., GIVE STATE OR TERRITORY. IF FOREIGN BIRTH, GIVE THE PLACE OF BIRTH, AND, IN ADDITION, THE MOTHER TONGUE.

| PERSON | | FATHER | | MOTHER | | | OCCUPATION | | | | |
|---|---|---|---|---|---|---|---|---|---|---|---|
| PLACE OF BIRTH | MOTHER TONGUE | PLACE OF BIRTH | MOTHER TONGUE | PLACE OF BIRTH | MOTHER TONGUE | ABLE TO SPEAK ENGLISH | TRADE, PROFESSION, OR PARTICULAR KIND OF WORK DONE. | INDUSTRY, BUSINESS, OR ESTABLISHMENT IN WHICH AT WORK. | EMPLOYER, SALARY OR WAGE WORKER, OR WORKING ON OWN ACCOUNT. | NUMBER OF FARM SCHEDULE | |
| 19 | 20 | 21 | 22 | 23 | 24 | 25 | 26 | 27 | 28 | 29 | |

**1930 Census United States**

State _____ County _____ Township or Other County Division _____ Name of Institution _____

Name of Incorporated Place _____ Enumeration Date _____ 1930 Enumerator _____

Ward of City _____ Supervisor's District _____ Enumerator's District _____ Sheet No. _____

Line | House Number | Dwelling Number | Number of Family | Street, avenue, road, etc. | Name of each person whose place of abode on April 1, 1930 was in this family. Surname, given name and middle initial. Include every person living on April 1, 1930. Omit children born since April 1, 1930. | Relationship of this person to head of the family | Home owned or rented | Value of home, or monthly rent | Radio set (leave blank if no radio) | Does this family live on a farm? | Sex | Color or race | Age at last birthday | Marital condition (see codes) | Age at first marriage | Attended school any-time since Sept. 1, 1929 | Whether able to read and write

1
2
3
4
5
6
7
8

Line | PERSON | FATHER | MOTHER | Place of birth — If born in U.S., give state or territory. If foreign birth, give county where birthplace is now. | Language spoken before arrival in US | Year of immigration to U.S. | Naturalization (see codes) | Whether able to speak English | Occupation: Trade, profession or particular kind of work, as spinner, riveter, salesman, teacher, etc. | Industry or business, as dry-goods store, shipyard, school, etc. | Class of worker (see codes) | Whether worked last working day | Unemployment schedule line no. | Veteran of U.S. military or navy | What war/expe-dition (see codes) | No. of farm schedule

1
2
3
4
5
6
7
8

**Color or Race**
White — W
Negro — Neg
Mexican — Mex
Indian — In
Chinese — Chin
Japanese — JP
Filipino — Fil

**Marital Condition**
Single — S
Married — M
Widowed — Wd
Divorced — D

**Naturalization**
Naturalized — Na
First papers — Pa
Alien — Al

**Class of Worker**
Employer — E
Wage or salary — W
Working on own — O
Unpaid worker — NP

**Veteran of what war?**
World War — WW
Spanish-American — Sp
Civil War — Civ
Philippine Insur. — Phil
Boxer Rebellion — Box
Mexican Exped. — Mex

*1930 Census Form*

# Index

## U

## V